Ronnie Whelan made more than 350 appearances for Liverpool FC and was voted no.30 in a poll of the fans' favourite all-time players. He was capped for his country 53 times.

WALK ON

My Life in Red

RONNIE WHELAN

with Tommy Conlon

SIMON &
SCHUSTER

London · New York · Sydney · Toronto · New Delhi

A CBS COMPANY

First published in Great Britain by Simon & Schuster UK Ltd, 2011
A CBS COMPANY

1 3 5 7 9 10 8 6 4 2

Simon & Schuster UK Ltd
1st Floor
222 Gray's Inn Road
London
WC1X 8HB

www.simonandschuster.co.uk

Simon & Schuster Australia, Sydney
Simon & Schuster India, New Delhi

Pictures supplied courtesy of the author.

The publishers have made every effort to contact those holding rights
in the material reproduced in this book. Where this has not been possible,
the publishers will be glad to hear from those who recognise their material.

All pictures supplied courtesy of the author.

The publishers have made every effort to contact those holding rights
in the material reproduced in this book. Where this has not been possible,
the publishers will be glad to hear from those who recognise their material.

A CIP catalogue for this book is
available from the British Library.

ISBN: 978-0-85720-620-6 (Hardback)
ISBN: 978-0-85720-621-3 (Trade paperback)

Typeset by M Rules
Printed in the UK by CPI Mackays, Chatham ME5 8TD

I'd like to dedicate this book to my wife Elaine and daughters Elizabeth, Georgia and Amy, for their constant love and support during my life in football and beyond.

Acknowledgements

I have a lot of people to thank for my good fortune in life. But none of it would have been possible without the love and guidance that my parents gave me. I remain eternally grateful to them.

And I will always be grateful, too, for the unstinting support of my sisters and brother. Rosemarie, Ann, Janice and Paul: thanks for always being there for me, thanks for keeping me grounded when I needed it.

My life in football began at Home Farm FC. I am indebted to the people there who freely gave of their time to help me and thousands of other young players.

At Liverpool I learned how to become a professional footballer and I couldn't have done it without the brilliant staff there who made sure I never stopped learning. To the players at Liverpool who became my team-mates and then my friends: thanks lads, I'm still laughing.

Mike Jones drove this project from the beginning. I would like to thank Mike and his colleagues at Simon & Schuster for giving me the chance to tell my story.

This book involved a lot of research and no one was more generous with his time than Liverpool historian and lifelong Red,

Adrian Killen. I sincerely thank Adrian for sharing his fantastic archive with me. In Dublin, Sean Ryan was very helpful with his books and his football records – his contribution is very much appreciated.

Tommy Conlon didn't complain when I kept phoning him at all hours of the day and night. I didn't complain when he kept saying, 'Hold that thought'. I thank him for helping me find the words to match the memories.

There are numerous other people who helped me along the way, off the pitch and on it. I would like to express my lasting gratitude to them all.

Tommy Conlon gratefully acknowledges the help and support of Paul Kimmage, Kieran Shannon and Fergus Conlon.

Contents

Foreword

by Kenny Dalglish

It was a league game against Stoke at Anfield in April 1981 and Ronnie Whelan was a very nervous young man. He was about to make his Liverpool debut. Ronnie says he remembers me having a few words of advice for him in the dressing room that helped calm him down. But that was thirty years ago this year and it goes without saying that I don't remember a word I said. Anyway he apparently appreciated it at the time. But it should be said that I had plenty of advice for him in the years after too and I doubt very much if he appreciated everything I said – most of it wouldn't have been quite as polite!

What I do remember about his debut was the goal he scored to put us one up. We beat Stoke 3–0 that night and it was obvious to me that Liverpool had produced another player who was going to be with us for years to come. He had the ability, he had the right attitude and he took his goal with great composure for a lad making his debut. He made an instant impact with the supporters, which always helps, and he made an instant impact with us veterans too, which helps even more. Pretty soon he was part of the furniture. We gave him a nickname, slagged him about his Dublin accent and I moaned an awful lot when he didn't play the right ball. In other words, he was made to feel right at home.

Liverpool Football Club became his home for fifteen years. I shared ten of those years with him, as player and manager. For me there's no pecking order, there's no league table for the players who made big contributions to the club. But anybody who's educated in the story of that era knows how important Ronnie was to those Liverpool teams. And if someone plays nearly 500 games and wins as many medals as he did – those achievements speak for themselves. They are the testaments to a great career.

A lot of those games back then are a bit of a blur to me now. What I remember in general about Ronnie was his industry and movement, his tackling, passing and running. What I remember in particular are the big-game goals he scored. They are vivid memories for me, the goals against Tottenham and Man United at Wembley that swung those League Cup finals our way. He spent more of his time setting up goals for the likes of myself and Ian Rush but when the chances came along for himself, he could finish them off with a touch of class. Ronnie was a team player first and foremost but he had the temperament and the skills to score goals of that calibre too. In later years he made a huge contribution in a more defensive role, winning the ball back for us and getting attacks going with his trademark passes.

He had a reputation as one of the quieter lads in the Liverpool dressing room but I can tell you he had a fair bit to say, too, if he felt it was needed. He could look after himself in the verbal stakes, on and off the field. He matured as a player and as a person in the years after his debut and when I handed him the captaincy at the start of the '88/89 season, it was because he'd become a very influential figure in the dressing room. I felt he deserved to be recognised and I had no doubts he'd be able to show the right leadership. Alan Hansen was the senior pro at the time and it was his injury in pre-season that opened the door for Ronnie. Alan made it back for the FA Cup semi-final and final but Ronnie retained the captaincy. And I don't think Alan would have allowed me to give it back to him anyway because Ronnie had done it all season and Alan would've wanted him to have the honour of leading the team out at Wembley.

I think it was a reflection of how strong and united the dressing room was in those days – and of how popular Ronnie was, as a fella and as a player. Mind you, it wasn't all sweetness and light between us: I dropped him a couple of times when I was manager. I can't remember why but I can remember his reaction: he was mad as hell with me! I think he's just about forgiven me for leaving him out of the '88 Cup Final squad. But he had his moment of glory that day in '89 when he lifted the FA Cup and I was delighted for him because he had well and truly earned it.

Ronnie earned everything he won at Liverpool. We his team mates saw up close every week how good he was as a player and how important he was to all our success in those years. The fans saw it too and I think he will always be remembered as one of the club's greatest servants.

Kenny Dalglish
June 2011

Introduction

Two weeks after the European Championships in 1988 a letter arrived from a publishing house inviting me to write my autobiography. Shortly afterwards a second letter arrived and, within days of that, a third letter from a third company had landed on the hall floor.

I was a bit baffled by the offers. It had never even occurred to me to think about an autobiography. I thought the timing was strange too: I was twenty-six, I had years left in my career, it would be ridiculous to be bringing out a book at this stage. When I did finish playing I still wasn't keen on the idea – but for a different reason. I had this nagging doubt that anyone would be interested: who would want to read *my* story? Why would anybody care? So any time I thought about it – which wasn't very often – I knocked it on the head pretty quickly.

It was only in the last few years that I started thinking about it a bit more seriously. A big reason was the amount of feedback I was still getting from Liverpool and Ireland fans. I can't count the number of times that strangers have come up to me, in all sorts of places, wanting to share their memories of some goal I scored or some game I played in. It happens to this day. They can tell me where they were, who they were with, why that game stands out for them. It might've been twenty years earlier but they can still remember it. They usually remember these games better than I can. Like most players, I spent my career looking forward not back. You couldn't afford to look back. As soon as it was over, you forgot about it. Winning games, winning cups, scoring goals – it was all great but you didn't dwell on these moments. You didn't really think about them at all. You knew they made the fans happy but you had no idea that you were helping to create memories for them which one day, all these years later, they would want to relive with you.

It was these encounters that got me thinking: well, maybe I *did* do something that's worth talking about. Maybe I did get people off their seats at a football game, or off their settees watching the telly at home. Maybe I did help to spread a little joy around. It dawned on me, I suppose, that what you did for a living had an impact on people that went much deeper than you ever imagined. And if so many people wanted to share their memories with me, maybe I could share mine with them.

It was in 2010 that I decided it was time to write it down. I was going on forty-nine, I would be fifty in September 2011, and it just felt like the right time. I felt I was ready. I was a different person to the young lad who'd spent the 1980s tearing around football pitches. The distance between then and now has helped me look back and see things in a different light. I have a perspective on my career that I couldn't have had back then. It's a much more mature perspective, I hope, and I think it has made for a better book. This was important to me: I wanted it to be a good book – as good as I could make it. It needed to be honest; it had to reflect truthfully on all the ups and downs that came my way. What's in the book is what I felt at the time – and I know I felt it because I still feel it to this day. Going back over those times evoked a lot of memories but it also stirred a lot of feelings that surprised me, they were still so strong. It was a pleasure to revisit old games that made me happy and old incidents that made me laugh all over again. And when I turned over various episodes that were painful at the time, I realised I still felt a bit of hurt, even after all these years.

Setting out to write this book, I wanted to explain to people how I made my way from a childhood dreaming about professional football to playing in European Cup finals and all the rest of it. But I think I ended up explaining it to myself as well, and understanding it better too. And if some young lad out there with the same dream happens to read it, I would be pleased if it helps him understand how much commitment it really takes – and that it *can* become a reality if he wants it badly enough.

And I wanted to try and tell the story to my daughters too. They know bits and pieces of it but this was a chance to start at the beginning and take them right through the journey of my life in football. I wanted to give them a glimpse of the old days, before the Premier League, when there wasn't half the hype and the glamour but there were still good teams around and great times to be had. I wanted to put it down on paper so they could have it on their bookshelves and, who knows, maybe pass it on to their own kids in years to come. I suppose basically I wanted to leave a record of some sort.

And I also wanted to put on record my gratitude to all the people who helped me along the way. I'm glad I've been given this chance to do that.

When I started out on this project I still wasn't sure if I had a good story to tell. Now that I've finished it, I think I do. It's been a brilliant experience going back over it all. I hope you the reader will enjoy going back there too.

Ronnie Whelan

1

The Two Ronnies

We were watching *Match of the Day* one Saturday night. I can't remember who was playing, but the ball flashed across the box and it was just a matter of tapping it in the back of the net. But the player got his foot under it and somehow put it over the bar. So the next day me da decided to re-enact the incident in our back garden. Paul stood in goals because he was the younger brother and that's what younger brothers are for. Da got ready to cross the ball and I got ready to turn it past Paul.

I was a forward in those days and we spent a lot of time in the back garden, Da teaching and me learning: how to side-foot them in and volley them in and head them in. This one was a tap-in, or it would've been if I hadn't connected with fresh air when the ball came across. Missed it completely. Paul burst out laughing and Da was going, 'Stand back now and let a man at it, I'll show ye how it's done.' So this time I crossed the ball – and it's *Match of the Day* all over again. Da puts it ten feet over the fence and into the garden two doors down. And next thing all three of us are rolling around the ground in stitches, and Ma is watching from the kitchen window and she's doubled up with the laughing too.

That's forty years ago now. I hadn't been back much in recent years to the house where I grew up. My parents had both passed on and Paul and the girls had long since moved out to set up homes and families of their own. But in October 2010 the house was just about to be sold and I paid it a final visit. I stood in that garden and the memories came flooding back. Our home was at 48 Abbotstown Avenue, Finglas West, on Dublin's North side; and it was a really, really happy home.

Marie and Ronnie Snr were city Dubs. They both grew up in Cabra. After they got married they moved into the tenements in Gardiner Street in the heart of Dublin's inner city. The tenements were ancient, a lot of them were being torn down, but it was all they could afford at the time. I wasn't born there but we'd pass it on the bus from time to time as children. Ma would point it out to us and tell us about the time Rosemarie, the eldest, had a lucky escape when she was a child. She was playing out in the street one day when one of the balconies overhead started to fall down around her. The tenements were so dilapidated the walls were crumbling and part of the balcony just gave way. By a miracle Rosemarie escaped without a scratch.

In the late 1950s they moved to Abbotstown Avenue. It was one of the new housing estates that Dublin corporation had built on what was then the edge of the city. Finglas was still rural. Many more housing estates would be built there but for now it still had fields and hedges and country lanes. Years later, when the kids were reared and money was a bit more plentiful, my parents would buy their house from the corporation.

But in the meantime five children would have to be fed and clothed. We weren't poor but we weren't flush. Money was always tight, but there was always food on the table too. Da was a sheet-metal worker, he had a job at the Unidare factory on Jamestown Road. In later years he packed that in and worked for ALSAA, the Aer Lingus Social and Athletic Association, looking after the sports and leisure complex there. Ma always went out to work too: Cadburys, Gateaux, Cleeve's Toffees, Eason's book shop, she had loads of different jobs. She never didn't work and at home it was the same: making clothes, cooking meals, running the house and bringing up her children. Rosemarie arrived first, then Ann, myself, Paul and Janice. There were arguments, probably a lot of it down to money problems, but they did a remarkable job between them. We were brought up really well, we've all done well in life, and it's down to the loving childhood our parents gave us.

Ma was the disciplinarian, she was more likely to shout at you if you were out of order. Da was more laid-back, he loved a singsong and a few drinks and a laugh. But he brought in a bit of extra cash too from his second job, which he loved a lot more than his first one.

It might even have become his full-time job, had he stuck it out when Chelsea FC invited him to London for a couple of weeks in the early 1950s. He was by all accounts a very talented young prospect. But London was a big city and he was fifteen or sixteen and felt very alone. The homesickness got to him and he came back before he gave himself the chance to show what he could do. But he went on to have a long career in the League of Ireland and it was one of the first things I learned about me da: he was a footballer, he was well known in football circles, his name was in the papers. He won two international caps in 1963/64. He had a long spell with St Patrick's Athletic where he won two FAI Cups in 1959 and 1961 before eventually moving on to Drogheda FC towards the end of his career.

But he had to learn the game first and he learned it at the famous Home Farm football club where they produced some of the best schoolboy players in Ireland. He was taken to Home Farm on his first day by a young man who went on to play for Manchester United. Liam Whelan was one of the Busby Babes who lost his life in the Munich air disaster of 1958. We shared the same name although we weren't related. But our families were close, they both lived on Attracta Road, and I often heard Da talking about Liam Whelan: how good he was as a player, how proud they were of him in Cabra when he made it at United and how shocked the whole neighbourhood was to hear of his tragic death.

Ten years after Munich Manchester United came to Dublin and it is one of my favourite childhood memories. It was August 1968 and they were over to play an exhibition game at Dalymount Park. They were playing a League of Ireland XI, just ten weeks after their famous victory in the European Cup final at Wembley. The excitement was unbelievable; those United players were absolute stars. The crowd at Dalymount invaded the pitch at the final whistle. But I was just seven years old and it might all have gone over my head if I hadn't ended up in the United dressing room afterwards. Shay Brennan and Tony Dunne played for United that day. They were Irish internationals and Da knew them so he was able to sneak me into their dressing room. I stood in a corner, quiet as a mouse, and saw right in front of me George Best, Bobby Charlton, Denis Law, Paddy Crerand, Nobby Stiles and Matt Busby. They were shouting and laughing and talking. They were gods and I was dumbstruck.

Da had been bringing me to games since I was knee high. I can actually remember him playing for Drogheda. We were a bit older then, Paul and me, and we would sometimes travel on the team bus with him on a Sunday morning. They had a trainer/physio, Gerry Martina, a big man; Gerry had represented Ireland in the Olympic Games in wrestling. He used always to give us a bag of the glucose sweets he'd have for the players. In 1971 Drogheda got to the FAI Cup final having shocked everyone, including themselves I think, with a 5–2 drubbing of Shamrock Rovers in the quarter-final. Da was described in the *Irish Times* match report as 'the flying Ronnie Whelan'; he got the fifth goal with a powerful header but I have no memory of that at all. I do remember the buzz in the house for those few weeks of the cup run. They went on to beat Cork Hibs in the semi-final in a replay, after extra time, while the final also went to a replay. I think the Drogheda lads were shattered by then – Limerick beat them 3–0.

Two players from that team still stick out in my mind, Dave Shawcross and Dick Jacenuik. Shawcross was magnificent at taking penalties. A left-footer, if memory serves, he'd run up, feint to kick, the goalkeeper would go and he'd roll it and it'd just about trickle over the line. But the reason I remember them is because they had English accents. Mick Meagan, the Drogheda manager, had brought them over from Halifax Town and I remember that Mick had a bit of an English accent too from his time as a player there.

I was nine during that cup run and I guess I remember their accents because even by then I had this plan to go and play professional football in England. If you could call it a plan. I suppose a nine-year-old has dreams rather than plans. So it was my dream to go to England and be a footballer. I wanted to be part of that world. Something about it had clicked in my brain as a child and stayed there.

I'd been immersed in a football culture from the beginning. I'd see Da polishing his boots and preparing his kit for training and games, practically every day. I'd hear him talk about football all the time with his brother, my Uncle Christy. Christy went to loads of games that Da was playing in and when I started playing he started coming to my games too. I realise now that if you had potential as a footballer, this was the perfect hothouse environment. Even Nanny, my da's ma, she was really into football as well. She was great when I was growing up. Nanny lived on another road near ours and we used to visit her after games when I was a kid and gather round her bed; she'd been paralysed for years. And if I'd scored a goal that day she'd put a few coins in a jar and by the end of the season she'd have a jar full of money for me. We had our own little ritual, Nanny and me. After the last game of the season we'd all call round to her house but when it came to handing over the money, she'd shoo everyone else out of the room. Then she'd empty out the jar of coins and together we'd count it up; she'd put them in a little bag and hand it over to me.

The games I played, the games our da played, the constant talking about it, the travelling with him on the team bus and the getting into the dressing room afterwards. I was taking it all in, without knowing I was taking it all in.

But the England thing, that was my own little secret. I don't know when it clicked but it was there at the back of my mind all the time. We never talked about it, my parents and me, until I was in my teens and English clubs were starting to send them letters, inviting me over for trials. But it was in my head long before that.

I think television had something to do with it. The only thing I really liked on telly was *Match of the Day, The Big Match* and *Sportsnight with Coleman.* I loved *Sportsnight,* especially when they showed footage from the European Cup games. Those games were usually played at night and there always seemed to be fog and mist hanging in the air. To this day I still have an image in my head, in black-and-white, of the clouds of fog lit up by the floodlights. The games were played in strange cities by players with strange names a long way away from our little world in Dublin. The names were brilliant. Ajax of Amsterdam, Bayern Munich, Standard Liege, Red Star Belgrade, Borussia Monchengladbach, Real Madrid, Dynamo Dresden, Anderlecht, Saint Etienne. There was a magic about it that hooked me. I was twenty-three years old when the tragedy at Heysel happened. I never played another club game again in Europe and it is one of the biggest regrets of my career.

The only problem with *Sportsnight* was that it was screened on Wednesday nights, a school night. I shared a room with Paul and we had to be in bed by a certain time and if he was asleep by the time it came on, I was allowed down to watch it. But if he was still awake and saw me leaving, he'd be wanting to come down too. I'd be lying in bed, really quiet, getting all annoyed and frustrated if he was still awake. I'd wait to hear the theme music from the living room and then sneak out of the bedroom and down the stairs. My parents would let me because they knew how much it meant to me, even then.

I made my League of Ireland debut on my sixteenth

birthday. The day before the game, Da was quoted in the news-papers. 'From the time he was only three years old he started kicking a ball about with me in the garden. He was mad about soccer ever since he first kicked a ball and naturally when I saw there was a bit of ability there, I encouraged him in every way I could.'

And it was true; he did encourage me in every way he could. It was unbelievable what he did for me, the way he nurtured me along, not just in football but in life as well. But all the encouragement in the world wouldn't have worked if my heart wasn't in it. But it was – I was obsessed. With both parents out working I spent a lot of time on my own, kicking a ball against the wall at the front of our house. A lot of the time it was just me and the ball and the wall. Kicking it off the wall and trying to control it on the way back. Kicking it *hard* off the wall and trying to control it. Kicking it off the jagged parts to make it go different ways and trying to control it. Kicking it off the kerb and trying to control it. I was out there from early morn-ing till late at night, before school and after school, lost in my own little world. Once I had a ball I was content. I think it was a sort of comfort blanket for me. I'd bring it everywhere, down to the shops, over to Nanny's, round to Foxy's van where Foxy sold sweets and cigarettes and household items. There was always a ball in the house, any sort of ball. And if the ball was burst or lost, Da would bring a new one home on Friday after he got paid.

And if he was in from work and having his tea, he'd tell me to go out and keep it up on my right foot as many times as pos-sible. He'd set little goals for you. I'd come back in and tell him how much I'd got and he'd tell me, 'Do the same with your left foot. Keep it up twenty times with your left.' I would spend hours trying to do it twenty times in a row. If I got up to seventeen or eighteen and broke down, I'd start again. I suppose I could've come back in and told him I'd got twenty but it never occurred to me. England was planted in my head. And I was going to stay outside for as long as it took to do it twenty times because it would help me get to where I wanted to be.

It sounds a bit like Tiger Woods and his dad, that you have to be regimented and do this all the time, but it wasn't like that. If he hadn't said go out and practise, I'd have gone out anyway. He didn't get upset, he didn't go screaming and shouting at me, and he didn't complicate it. I was very lucky, I had a League of Ireland player teaching me the basics of the game, and he was a very good teacher. Left foot, right foot, how to head the ball, how to control the ball, how to pass it long and short. Many years later I scored a goal with my left for Liverpool. Jimmy Hill remarked about my 'natural left foot' that night on *Match of the Day* I had to tell Jimmy that actually the right was my natural kicking foot.

Recently I came across this idea of the 10,000 hours: that if you want to reach a high level in a chosen discipline, be it music or sport or science, you have to put in three hours of dedicated practice every day for ten years. I don't know how right or wrong this theory is but I do know that by the time I signed for Liverpool on my eighteenth birthday, I had without knowing clocked up the 10,000 hours – and an awful lot more.

My first competitive games were in the local road leagues. Abbotstown would play a team from Cardiff Bridge Road, and Cardiff would play a team from Mellowes Road, and so on. We'd play some of those games on the pitch belonging to Raven Athletic, a local junior football club; it's a halting site for travellers now. There were pitches on Cardiff as well and we once lost a road-league final there. I was in tears afterwards and Da carried me home 'cos I thought the world had ended. I was the ripe old age of six.

The next time I cried at a football game was the night of Heysel.

I was eight or nine when Da brought me to the Home Farm mini-leagues. The club had one of the best underage structures in Ireland at the time. It had a reputation as a sort of academy for young players. Parents from all over the city would bring their kids there. Players were graded according to their age and ability and we'd play against each other in the mini-leagues. Matt Butler says I 'stuck out like a sore thumb'. At nine I should've been playing for the under-10s but I was drafted into the under-11 and under-12 teams. I was small and skinny but I must've handled it OK because pretty soon I was playing against twelve-year-olds in the Dublin league, which was the biggest league in Ireland. It was a big step-up in standard, play-ing the likes of Stella Maris, St Kevins, Shelbourne, Belvedere and St Joseph's in Sallynoggin.

Matt was a great pal of Da's. He coached our teams right the way through from eleven to sixteen. We won loads of leagues and cups with him. They had strict standards at Home Farm and Matt was one of the people who drilled them into us. We were taught manners, we were taught how to behave off the pitch as well as on it. You had to be on time. You had to be neat and tidy. Your boots had to be polished and your kit had to be clean. You tucked your shirt inside your shorts. There was no bad language, no backchat to referees and no messing about in the clubhouse. It was a very, very good upbringing at Home Farm, and I thrived there.

Matt Butler: The first time I saw Ronnie it was in the mini-leagues and I recognised him straightaway from his da. The whole posture, very upright, chest out – the run of him was the exact same as his father's. Ronnie Senior was a lovely, easy-going man. But it used to amaze me the things he'd point out on a football pitch, the things he'd see in a player. He was my helper for many years and I can say without fear of contradiction that he was the most knowledgeable person that I've ever come across in schoolboys football.

Off the pitch young Ron was totally introverted, you hardly knew he was there in the dressing room. But the minute he went onto the pitch he started lording it, running around, bossing everyone. He was a natural on the pitch.

And any time I was stuck for a player I'd always go and get him, not because he was so good, but because I always knew where to find him. He'd be playing football down at Patrician College. A lot of other very talented lads fell by the wayside. The difference between Ron and them was that he was always, always playing football.

I can remember one time down on Mobhi Road, I happened to be standing behind the goal with nothing else to do but look down the pitch. And he was on the ball down the far end and I was giving out that he wasn't passing it out wide to a player who was unmarked. But he played it through to someone just in an inside-right position, threaded it along the ground, and the lad scored from it. Ron was thirteen at the time and he could see a better pass running with the ball than I could see doing nothing.

Da was there on the sideline for most of those games. Year in year out he was there. In the car home we'd talk about it: how did it go today, what did I do well, where could I have done something better? I remember only one time when he got really angry with me. It was a game at Home Farm, I must've been twelve or thirteen, and basically I was acting the eejit. I probably was thinking *I'm a bit ahead of these players*, or it was coming too easy to me or something. So I started being silly, doing daft things, trying to beat everybody and then giving the ball away and thinking it was funny. Da had been watching this from the sideline. Half-time came and he called me over, away from everybody else, and he was fuming. 'If you don't stop that nonsense I'm going to take you right off. Cut it out now or I'm gonna take you straight off this pitch.' I was shocked. It was a major kick up the backside. I went out for the second half stung and embarrassed, desperate to make amends. After the game it was just, 'That's how you should do it. Don't ever mess about like that again.'

And I never did mess about like that again. I don't know what came into me that day because I was never one for showboating, I was usually too nervous to be messing about. Far back as I can remember, I was always nervous going to play a match. I don't know whether it was a thing of trying to please people, but I was always afraid of playing bad. I didn't like playing bad, I didn't like letting the team down, I didn't like letting the manager down. And I brought that into Liverpool with me. There was no talking to me if I played bad. There was no talking to me on the bus, there was no talking to me at home – just thinking about it and turning it over in my head for days. And that went all the way back to the mini-leagues in Home Farm. I knew from an early age when

I played bad and I never liked that feeling and I never wanted to repeat it.

During Easter holidays the club would take a load of the underage teams to Blackpool. Home Farm stalwarts like Joe Fitzpatrick and Noel Griffin would organise the trips. We'd play a couple of friendlies against local teams but the highlight was going to a big first division game, usually in Manchester. I was eleven or twelve the first time I clapped eyes on Maine Road – or was it Old Trafford? Can't remember which. But we got there early, the stadium was empty and I remember walking up the steps and looking down at the pitch and around the terraces and stands. It was mind-blowing. And I can remember the thought that was going through my mind: this is where I want to be. *This is where I want to be.* It was another reinforcement for the dream I had. *England. I want to play there. I've got to go to England to play because that's what I see on TV.* I knew you could get paid to play but money didn't matter. I was too young to know about money. It was more a case of, this could be your job. And what a job to have!

Back at Home Farm, a few scouts were starting to turn up on the sideline. It wasn't that unusual – local scouts for the English clubs were frequent visitors anyway. Joe Corcoran was one of them. He was Man United's man in Dublin. He came to the house one day and asked Da if I'd go over. I was fourteen. A letter arrived a few weeks later inviting me over for a fortnight. Ma and Da came with me. I have a photo from my first day at Old Trafford on trial. I'm there in my new clothes, wearing a ridiculous pair of parallels, standing in the goalmouth at the Stretford End. What you don't see is the groundsman running over two seconds later: 'Get off the fucking pitch! You shouldn't be on the pitch!' Little did he, or I, know that I'd be scoring into that goal years later, and in fairly memorable circumstances too.

We trained at the Cliff. A fella called Frank Blunstone, a former Chelsea player and England international, supervised our training. I remember being intimidated by the whole surroundings but not by the other kids the same age as me. I wasn't worried that they'd be out of my league, I was more worried that my boots wouldn't be as good as theirs. The coaching was more structured than I was used to at home, they worked a lot on your passing, movement and control. In the canteen upstairs my eyes were popping out of my head: look, there's Jim Holton; over there, Martin Buchan and Sammy McIlroy. Stuart Pearson, Gerry Daly, Dave McCreery, Steve Coppell too.

You'd be told at the end of the two weeks if they wanted you back or not and I was told that they wanted me back the next school holiday. No one actually told you if they rated you or not. That's the way it was in general at the time. It was just, 'We'd like to see you back in the summer for another two weeks.' OK. Grand. That was enough for me. I didn't need anyone to tell me that I was good or bad. Same at Liverpool. All I needed was the manager to put me in the team every Saturday. And if you were playing every Saturday you were obviously doing something right and that was all you needed to know.

After that first visit, I went on my own to Manchester. If there was a home game at Old Trafford you'd be brought along to see the game. One time I was there and it coincided with the anniversary of the Munich air disaster. This was probably 1975 or '76. The bereaved families would usually have a representative there for the anniversary. The kids who'd signed apprentice forms with United would act as ball boys for the home games. I hadn't signed so I wasn't allowed. I was in and around the tunnel area this day when a man came up to me to shake my hand. He introduced himself: he was a brother of Liam Whelan. He'd heard that a son of Ronnie Whelan was over on trial; he made inquiries and sought me out and wished me well. It was a very nice gesture that I never forgot.

There was another very nice gentleman at the club by the name of Bob Bishop. He was United's scout in Northern Ireland and he was the man who discovered George Best. Bob would regale us with stories about finding George and how he told Matt Busby that he had to sign this kid from Belfast. Sammy McIlroy, Dave McCreery, and, later, Norman Whiteside, Bob discovered them all. This was music to our ears. We'd be devouring his every word because secretly you'd be thinking *That could be me. It happened to them, it could happen to me.*

The two players that I can remember from those days are Andy Ritchie and Scott McGarvey, who both went on to play for United. I was probably more pally with Scott than anybody else when I was there. The biggest eye-opener for me was what the apprentices had to do. They had to stay back and clean the showers and the baths, clean and polish the players' boots, sweep the changing rooms and get the kit sorted. I was offered apprentice forms at United but that was one of the reasons deep down why I didn't really want to sign. The biggest reason was that Da wouldn't let me sign. He wanted me to finish school and do my Leaving Cert. I wonder now if his real reason was to do with his own experience at Chelsea; that he was worried I'd be too young and too homesick to stick it out. He said United would come back for me anyway.

They didn't, as it happened, and at the time I was really worried that my chance had gone. But a part of me was secretly
relieved too, because I knew what the apprentices had to do
and I didn't fancy it.

More letters were starting to arrive in the post and Noel
Griffin remembers being in our house one night talking to Da
about it.

> **Noel Griffin:** I remember him showing me all these letters
> from clubs: Queens Park Rangers, Nottingham Forest,
> Chelsea, Manchester United, Aston Villa, Middlesbrough,
> all on headed paper, there was about twenty letters there.
> And they were very keen, all inviting him over for trials.
> Ronnie Senior was very knowledgeable about the situa-
> tion and, having been in England himself and seen the
> whole thing, he was certainly not going to take any
> chances with Ronnie. He told me that he wanted to do
> the right thing for him. He told me that himself. He was
> very, very conscious about making the right decision.

We didn't follow up too many of those invitations, for whatever reason. I did two weeks at Everton but I didn't enjoy it
there, just didn't feel comfortable. And they mustn't have
enjoyed me either because they never got back to me. Coventry
had me back a couple of times and asked me to sign as an
apprentice. I really liked the set-up there. Gordon Milne was
the manager. I was keen to make an impression my first time
there and one afternoon the lads a little bit older than me were
going to do a running session, up and down hills. I was told I
could stay with the younger group my own age or I could go
with the older ones. They would've been apprentices and

young pros doing a pre-season lung-burster. And I figured I'd show the staff a little bit more than whatever ball skills I had. I sort of knew I was OK on the football side; now, go and show them that you can do the hard stuff too. I'm thinking *I need to show them that I'm a grafter too.* So I went running with them and it was the hardest thing I'd ever done. I ended up spewing my guts up and the older lads laughing at me.

I was the same at United, naïve and mad to impress. I was over during the Christmas holidays one year, I think I was fifteen, and we were all told we could go home for the New Year. But me, in my stupid wisdom, decided to stay. I told them that I'd go training the next day. Bad call. The halls of residence were in a big old university building and the place was deserted. Everyone else had gone home. I could hear my voice echoing around the empty rooms. So there I was on New Year's Eve, feeling like an orphan and feeding money into a coin box in the corridor, crying down the phone to me ma and da in Dublin.

It's hard for a kid, when he's fifteen or sixteen, and all his mates are starting to discover pubs and clubs and girls, and your ambition is to play football and they're going, 'Yeah, but you're not *really* going to be a professional footballer, are you? I mean, realistically?' And you don't like to hear that, because secretly you believe that you have a chance, even if they don't. And they're saying to you, 'Sure, you might as well come out with us tonight.' And sometimes it's hard to say no, even if you know you have a game the next day. So one night I came down the stairs, all dressed up in my gear for the school disco, and Da took one look at me. I knew the look, and that was bad enough. There were words too. Then he said: 'Right so. If you feel it'll make you play better tomorrow, go ahead.' Then he stuck his head back in his newspaper. He didn't have to say any more. He'd tripped the guilty switch in me and he knew it. It was still my decision but I knew there was only one decision. I trooped back up the stairs, changed out of my disco duds and stayed in for the night.

It sounds a bit sad now, in hindsight, like I didn't have a life at all. But the truth is, I wasn't really interested in anything else at the time. School, beer, music – it more or less all passed me by. I just had this tunnel vision about England. But I liked being in that tunnel. I enjoyed it, it was where I wanted to be. Noel says he remembers me saying, years later when I was at Liverpool, that if you wanted to make it in England, you had to live like a monk growing up. I don't remember saying it, but I do remember living it.

It's why I avoided any trouble growing up in a place that had a rough reputation, although Finglas never seemed that rough to me. It was a proper working-class community where people were good neighbours and looked out for each other. There was always horses mooching about, mind you, and at Halloween there'd be massive bonfires on the estate. I remember one day I was standing on Foxy's corner with a girl and there'd been a bonfire on the green patch and a bunch of lads were hanging around it. Next thing this van pulled up and suddenly about ten coppers jumped out the back and waded into the lads with their batons. They battered the lads. I think that's what they called 'Getting them off the streets' in those days. But I saw very little of what they nowadays call antisocial behaviour. The only thing you didn't want to be doing was walking past the chipper late at night. You'd usually have some lads there passing around the flagons of cider. There were fights, all right, and various bits of vandalism, but this was still the innocent era, before drugs came on the scene, and I felt very secure growing up there.

And all this time I was progressing smoothly through the football grades. In my head I was climbing a ladder; as soon as I reached one rung I wanted to reach the next. In 1977 I hit a few big milestones, first of all getting capped for Ireland schoolboys. We beat Holland and Northern Ireland at home and in April we beat Wales 4–2. I scored from the penalty spot. My school, Patrician College, also achieved a major milestone that April. It was a small school, founded only ten years earlier, but it won its first Leinster Senior Cup and in May went on to claim the All-Ireland colleges title as well. It was a fantastic cup run.

Unfortunately, while I got to play for my country, I didn't get to play for my school. There'd been a clash of fixtures in an earlier round; I had a Home Farm game and the school had a game the same day. Everyone told me it was my decision. So I weighed it up and figured that I was only going to have another two years at school but I'd still be playing at Home Farm for the next few years if I didn't get a club in England. So I played for Home Farm. The Patrician coach, Kevin Fahy, who went on to rise through the ranks at the FAI, never picked me again. The prize for winning the national title was that Patrician would get to represent Ireland in a World Schools Tournament which was being held in Dublin that summer. It was a sixteen-nation tournament and it was very prestigious. I ended up going on the bus with the supporters to watch the team. Deep down I was gutted. I didn't show it but I was. And I resented the decision for a long time afterwards. I thought it was amazingly petty. *This big tournament is coming to Dublin and Whelan isn't going to play in it because*

I'm the boss around here. Maybe he was taking me down a peg
or two, knowing there was a lot of talk about United signing
me and all that. Anyway, so began my great run of luck at
World Cups!

But still, it was onwards and upwards on my imagined
journey to the big time. And, on 25 September that year, I
got birthday cards that said 'Sweet 16' – and a senior debut
with Home Farm that afternoon. It was against Drogheda
United and that's about all I can remember. It passed me by
completely. I didn't play a lot of first-team games that
season. But the word was out about me now and a few of the
resident hard men in the League of Ireland tried to do a bit
of chopping whenever they got the chance. I didn't mind
and it didn't bother me. I remember getting a good kicking
from a defender at Bohemians early on but when we played
them again later that season I was well able to handle it. I
was still skinny as a rake but I had quick feet – and two years
in the League of Ireland made them quicker. It made me
hardier too. It was a really good grounding in the world of
adult football and I think it was what Da had had in mind for
me all along: rather than being apprenticed at United, he figured I'd get a better apprenticeship this way. How right he
was.

Jim McLaughlin was manager of Dundalk FC at the time.
They were a top team and Jim would go on to be probably the
greatest League of Ireland manager ever. I'd heard rumours
that he'd put in a word for me but it was only when I was
doing research for this book that I found out his role in my
transfer to Liverpool. Jim had contacts at the club. I'd been
over for a two-week stint during the 1979 pre-season. I had
also been to Celtic that year and Celtic had made an offer to

Home Farm. Someone at Liverpool got in touch with Jim, wondering about the Celtic offer, wondering if they should make a move.

> **Jim McLaughlin:** And I said to them, 'It doesn't matter what Celtic are offering, just sign him. Sign him now and don't worry about the cost because you won't regret it.' I was fairly sure about it because Ronnie was head and shoulders above any other fella in Ireland at the time. I'd never seen a young fella who could look after himself on a pitch so well.

I could easily have signed for Celtic. My parents went over with me, the club looked after us really well and I loved it there. I played a reserve game alongside Willie McStay and Charlie Nicholas, who was already marked out for stardom. Bobby Lennox would pick me up every morning and bring me to training and didn't seem to mind when Da called him Billy, Celtic legend, European Cup winner, Bobby 'Billy' Lennox. I gave out stink to Da about that. He just laughed it off, and so did Bobby. It was a really friendly club and I was very tempted to sign. But I knew I was going over to Liverpool later that summer and if they didn't make me an offer, I was on my way to Glasgow.

I did my Leaving Cert in the summer of 1979 and in August had my two-week trial at Melwood. Things moved quickly after that. We got a phone call from Liverpool. They wanted to offer me a deal, when could I go over to sign? This was September, and I was about to turn eighteen.

We walked into the boardroom at Anfield and I was shaking with nerves and excitement. There was no agent or lawyer in those days, just me and me da. The chairman of Liverpool FC, John Smith, and the secretary, Peter Robinson, sat us down at this big fancy table in the boardroom and pushed a legal document across the table to us. They were offering me a three-year professional contract at £150 a week. They'd pay for four flights a year back to Dublin and they'd pay for my digs until I found a place to live.

And I'm thinking *That'll do me, let's sign this and get it over with.* But Da spoke up. 'OK, that sounds good, but we also want a £20,000 signing-on fee. Tax-free, paid into an account in Dublin.'

Messrs Smith and Robinson looked shocked. Or maybe pretended to look shocked. They said, 'Sorry, can't do that, couldn't possibly do that.' And Da said they could 'cos he'd spoken to people and this would be a legitimate payment for me giving up my amateur status to turn professional. The men in suits looked at each other. Then they asked us if we could step outside for a few minutes. We stepped outside and I was really agitated by now. I thought they were going to tell us to go home and never come back. Da was tense too but he was calm. He had spoken to Noel Griffin about this. Noel had sat in on the negotiations when another young Home Farm player, Martin Murray, signed for Everton a few years before.

Noel: Martin was a magnificent player. He was going to sign for Everton at the Shelbourne Hotel and his parents insisted on me being there. The amateur status thing was a genuine issue at the time. There was some sort of aura about being an amateur; players were very keen about keeping their amateur status; you weren't taking money for playing, you were playing for the love of the game. And before Ronnie signed for Liverpool his father had come and talked to me about it.

Mr Robinson brought us back into the boardroom. I was in a knot with the tension. We sat down. Then Mr Robinson turned to us and smiled and said, 'OK, that's fine, we can do it.' Just like that. And if I was ready to sign, here's the pen. I signed the contract there and then. Everything was in order, we shook hands and left the boardroom.

I was now, officially, a professional footballer. I was on my way to England.

We stayed in a Holiday Inn that night. Da had a couple of pints in the bar and I went to bed. I was a bit overwhelmed. I was relieved, I was happy, I was thrilled. The next morning Da told me he'd had one or two pints too many the night before. And then he said, and I never forgot it, he said: 'I was just sitting there and I was happy for you and next thing I realised I was singing on me own in the bar!' And he burst out laughing, and so did I. He'd been singing to himself in the bar and didn't even know it. He was just so happy for me. Both my parents were, because they *knew;* they knew that from a very young age this was all I'd ever wanted to do. And I'm sure they were gutted too, that their son was going away to England and wouldn't be around very much any more.

Rosemarie says I was Ma's 'blue-eyed boy'. Much as I'd like to, I don't think I can disagree.

Rosemarie: Oh he was! Ronald – she called him Ronald – could never do any wrong. Even though he was a prankster and a joker and got up to all sorts of tricks. But she was upset, she was brokenhearted, when he went away.

I suppose looking back, my parents did cosset me. Once they realised I had a talent, they looked out for it, they minded me carefully. Ma was very influential. She knew what Da was like, she knew what I was like, so most of my doings with him were football-orientated and she never interfered with that. She was always there for us, but in the background; never pushed herself forward on either myself or Da. And she was there loads of times watching the games as well.

Paul: Ah, he was wrapped in cotton wool! I remember we were on the road outside the house one day – this was, I suppose, when he was on the threshold of making it – and the next-door neighbour had a big Ford Cortina, one of the old Ford Cortinas, and it stalled on the hill up to the house. So our mother summons everybody: my dad, myself, even my sisters I think. And then she let a roar. 'Ronald! Ronald, don't you dare push that car up that hill!' And that was the day I knew there was something different about him. Ronnie wasn't allowed to push the car.

Da's cars needed a push every now and again too. But that changed after the twenty grand landed into my bank account in the AIB in Finglas. I went into the branch with Da one day to see if it had arrived. It had, and I told him to take out whatever he needed to buy a new car. I wanted them to have a good car.

Paul: Our da had the worst history of cars on the road. Not many people had cars them days but he used to get an awful slagging. This thing'd come round the corner, four wheels and a body on it and that was about it. They used to call it 'the skateboard' on the road. 'Stop the match, don't hit that car with the ball, it'll fall apart!' Then one day this black Mazda 323 arrives, brand spanking new.

Back at home the phone was ringing and neighbours were visiting. The word was out that I'd signed for Liverpool and people were calling to say congratulations and wish me luck. But my elation had disappeared within twenty-four hours of signing. I think the enormity of it all hit home. There was no turning back now. I'd signed. I was leaving home. *I've got to go and do it now. But what if I'm not good enough?* I was always a worrier, always nervous when it came to football. I never felt I was as good as people said. I was always frightened of not playing well. And I brought that fear with me to Liverpool. In hindsight I think it helped me, always having this bit of doubt about myself at the back of my mind. It never really left me, even after I was established in the first team. I never took it for granted, getting picked, not because I was trying to be a model pro, but because that bit of self-doubt never left me.

There was a big going-away party for me and everyone was celebrating – except me and Paul. Paul was upset that his big brother was leaving. At the party Da found him crying in the toilets. And he said to him, 'Don't be such an eejit, cop yourself on!' And Paul said back, between the sobs, 'But I'm his brother. You're only his da!' And I wasn't celebrating because this shadow was hanging over me: that I'd fail, that I'd miss my family too much, that I'd be back in Dublin pretty soon with my tail between my legs. A week later I started my new life at Anfield.

Writing this book has helped me reflect a lot on my upbringing. And it has made me appreciate how good it was, how loving it was. I always knew this, but I can see it clearer now, I understand it better now. My parents gave me everything they could. When I left home, I was prepared for life, not just for professional football. And as far as the football went, I couldn't have had a better teacher or better mentor than my own father.

At Home Farm too, I was surrounded by good people. They taught us how to play and they taught us the right values. I might've been a very worried young man at the time but, looking back, I realise that when I left for Liverpool, I couldn't have been better prepared. I couldn't have been more ready, they couldn't have done any more for me. Paul says that 'the stage was set'. And he's right. It was up to me to step onto it and perform.

I made my Liverpool debut some eighteen months after I left home. It was on a Friday night because the Grand National was on the next day. My parents were over to see it. The game was at Anfield and I scored a goal. Da rang Matt earlier that day to tell him I might be playing.

Matt: It was against Stoke and I drove up the Dublin mountains that evening because that was the only place I could hear the match on Radio Merseyside. I listened to it in the car and when I heard the Kop singing his name there was tears in my eyes. Because I could visualise him as a little tiddler in the corner of the dressing room, and suddenly there's the Kop singing his name. I felt real proud that night. Life doesn't get much better than that.

The people who gave me my education at Home Farm, I don't think I've thanked them enough for the help and support and good times I had there. But the older I get the more I appreciate it and the more grateful I am to them all.

I wish that we could've had more time with Ma and Da, for lots of reasons, but especially so I could tell them how much I appreciate what they did for me. If I didn't get the chance to thank them properly when they were alive, I hope it's still not too late to thank them now; I do so from the bottom of my heart.

2

School of Hard Knocks

It was my first day of training at Melwood as a professional footballer. I was keen to impress. We were playing a five-a-side, the apprentices and reserves, and the ball was played out to me. So I was on the ball and one of the coaches, this baldy ould fella, was coming in to tackle me. I was thinking *No problem, I've got a traffic cone in front of me here.*

So I went past him and was still on the ball about two seconds later. I quickly discovered that two seconds is about two seconds too long in a Liverpool five-a-side. Next thing, this leg came round the back of me, dragged the ball back, and the bloke pushed me over. It was none other than the bold Ronnie Moran, known affectionately as Bugsy, also known as Moransco. And he had a right go at me. 'Don't fuck'n run past me with the ball, young fella.' And he was serious. I got a fright.

It turned out Bugsy wasn't old at all, even if he was bald, and he was fit too. He wasn't happy with a young pup skipping past him with the ball. It wasn't the only time he upended me on the training ground. And I saw him do it several times over the years to young players who'd just arrived at the club. It was his way of saying, 'Don't think you can run past me son, just 'cos I look old.' Maybe it was hurting his pride but it was more to do with teaching you a lesson. They didn't like you running with the ball when you could pass it. They didn't really like you running with the ball, full stop. First lesson.

The second lesson I had to learn for myself. And I would like, if I may, to pass it on to any young lad starting out on the road to fame and fortune: never move into a digs that has a dog and a parrot. You won't get a wink of sleep. The club put me into digs on the Anfield Road, about 200 yards from the Shankly Gates. Mr and Mrs Pyke were very nice, they looked after me very well. But they had a German shepherd called Whisky and a talking parrot whose name I've managed to blank from my memory. In the afternoons, after training, I'd go to my room for a nap. But if anyone called to the door, Whisky would start barking and the bird would start squawking at the dog. I'd be in bed in the middle of a nice sleep when suddenly I'd hear a dog barking and a bird going, 'Sit down Whisky! Sit down Whisky! Sit down Whisky!' Bloody hell – not again! I was tempted more than once to storm down the stairs, take it out of its cage and drop-kick it over the Shankly Gates.

Something had to give. It was either me or the parrot. The parrot stayed. I moved round the corner to Elsie Road where Mrs Edwards had her digs. Alan Hansen had stayed there when he first moved down from Scotland and he recommended it. Kevin Sheedy was also starting out at Liverpool around the same time and he was there already. So I joined Sheeds for the company – and an uninterrupted afternoon nap. Mrs E was a great old lady. She was a smashing cook and she took good care of us.

From there we'd stroll down to Anfield every morning and get the team bus to Melwood. The team bus was part of your education. Everyone was on it, from fifteen-year-old apprentices to some of the most famous names in British football. Hansen was on it, Ray Clemence, Phil Neal, Phil Thompson, Kenny Dalglish, Graeme Souness. They were all there, sat down the back, gossiping and slagging and cracking jokes. It was good because it took away some of the mystique about top-flight football. These were ordinary blokes, really, who just happened to be very, very good at what they did. And being on the bus made you feel included, it was part of the process that bonded you to the club and made you feel you belonged there.

But in reality you only belonged if you were good enough. And I struggled a lot in that first season. First of all you had to learn how to be a professional footballer. I was coming from a background of training on a Tuesday and Thursday night with a game on Sunday. Now I was training for an hour and a half every day, more or less nonstop running. And I was knackered. I wasn't used to full-time training. I was going to bed at night tired and I was getting up in the morning tired, legs stiff and sore. It took a couple of months to reach the right fitness levels.

And on top of that I was homesick. I was living on my own in the first digs and ended up spending a lot of time on my own. Training was over at lunch time and you had the rest of the day to fill in, with not a lot to do. I'd train, go back to the digs, watch telly, eat dinner and go to bed. Next day, same again. Weekends were worse. You'd play a game Saturday morning, go to Anfield to see the first team play if they were at home and then go back to your digs. And Sundays were worst of all. There was nobody at the football club, you didn't have to go in, and there wasn't much happening on a Sunday afternoon in 1979 or '80. So you'd a lot of time on your hands to think and worry and think some more. I'd started off in the A team and was moved up to the reserves pretty quickly. I did OK for a while but my form started suffering and I was moved back down to the A team again.

There's nothing worse than when you're playing bad and you don't know the real reason why. I just thought it was because I hadn't done a pre-season and my fitness levels weren't up to the demands of the professional game. But actually it was the homesickness. I was spending a lot of time on the phone and my parents were spending a lot of time listening and trying to reassure me. Going back to Dublin didn't help, either. It only made me more homesick when I had to leave again. By Christmas I was talking about moving home altogether. I was thinking *I've a great family back home and they're not going to be hard on me if I go back*. Eventually Da dished out a spoonful of tough love. He told me to stop coming home. He told me to stay in Liverpool for the next six months, and stay there whether I liked it or not. 'This is part of the deal,' he said. 'You have to get on with it. You made your bed, you have to lie in it.'

It was the same at the club. There were very few shoulders to cry on in those days. Their attitude was, 'You've signed, we've put you in digs, now keep your nose clean and get on with it.'

So with no place to turn I had no choice but to knuckle down and get on with it. Eventually I started to settle. Thirty years later I'm still living in Liverpool.

*

We never really got much actual *coaching* at the football club. It wasn't what you'd see nowadays where it's like Dublin airport with all the bibs and cones. You'd do your warm-up and then you'd play a game, seven-a-side usually, two touches maximum, and it'd be bang bang bang. Machine-gun passing. You needed quick feet and a good first touch. And you never, ever stood still after making a pass. If you did, Roy Evans would be down on you like a ton of bricks. You passed it and you moved – somewhere, anywhere, just move. I didn't get it at first. Why are we doing this? Pass the ball and run forward and if you don't it's a free kick against you. Pass it and then get past the person you've passed it to. What are we doing that for? I didn't understand at the time why they were so obsessed with constant movement.

Roy was in charge of the reserves and he was great with us. He'd been through it himself as a young player at Liverpool and hadn't quite made the grade in the end but I think he related to us better for that reason. He was sympathetic to the young players who were there. He understood that we were immature, as footballers and as people, and he was fair and decent with us. It was his job to bring these players through to the first team so we had to learn their style of play and it was Evo who drilled it into us on the training ground every morning. And if you did get promoted it was just a progression of what you'd been doing in the reserves. Except now you'd have to pass and move even faster.

I spoke to Evo about this recently. He says I didn't stand out particularly in my first season. It was only players of the quality of Michael Owen who stood out a mile when they arrived. A lot of players came and went through the reserves and all Evo remembers about my early days was that I had 'great feet' and was homesick a lot. After that, I was 'a steady player' who listened and learned. I know that much is true. I was a shy lad who didn't say a lot and I suppose if you don't say a lot, you're bound to listen more. And the likes of Evo and Ronnie Moran were worth listening to.

So, you had a good teacher, you were surrounded by very good young players, and unbeknown to yourself you were getting better and better. I can remember distinctly one reserve game, we were playing Everton at Goodison Park, I got myself caught in the left-back position and hemmed in by an opponent. I had to hit it with my left and suddenly I pinged it forty yards down the line, over their full-back's head, without even really walloping it. And I was surprised I could do it. I couldn't have kicked it that far with my left before. It opened my eyes. I remember thinking *It's not a problem now to ping it forty yards with my left.* It was one of those moments where I realised I was doing things I couldn't do six months earlier. I was getting quicker and stronger.

But I was still naïve, I wasn't clued in to the rivalries and jealousies you get in professional football. In the Home Farm first team you'd been playing with amateurs, you weren't affecting anybody's livelihood. When I arrived at Melwood I was suddenly a threat to the other reserves and I didn't realise it. It took me a while to notice it. There'd be a few snotty remarks. I was eighteen when I arrived, I hadn't served my time as an apprentice and they knew I was on more money than they were. And I knew they were bitching about me behind my back because I'd hear them saying things about the other young Irish lads at the club. Brian Duff, Derek Carroll and Synan Braddish had signed for Liverpool the previous year or two years. Duffer was from Finglas and had gone to Patrician too, although we weren't mates there. He played on the Patrician team that had competed in the World Schools Tournament. It didn't work out for the lads at Liverpool but it was nice to have a few Dubs around the place. Derek and Duffer helped me settle down there in the early days, they were good company and I'd go out on the town with them from time to time. They put me straight too on some of the stuff being said by the other apprentices about us blow-ins.

There was a lot of, 'He's come over here, he's earning more than us, who does he think he is?' It was bad enough that you were earning more money, but when you took someone's place in the reserves they were doubly unhappy. 'Why is he in the team? He's only in the team 'cos they've brought him over from Ireland on a big wage.' Stuff like that. I'm sure it went on at every club and I'm sure it still goes on at every club to this day.

But it meant I had to wise up pretty quickly. I was probably too nice at the start. There's a saying in football that everyone takes to heart: always look after number one. Yeah, we're all team players but at the same time we all learn sooner or later that first and foremost you have to look after number one. Because it's your livelihood, and if you're getting into the team ahead of someone else, you're getting in the way of them making a better living. And I saw it at Liverpool, how ruthless it could be. You didn't really want anybody to get a major injury if you weren't in the team, but you wanted them to get a small injury so you could get back in the team. You learned to think like that. Because if you're in the team you're getting your win bonuses, but they're not getting their win bonuses. And I found out very early, people didn't like you taking their place in the team because basically you were taking their job.

It's probably why you don't get too close to too many people in football – because someone is always trying to force someone else out of the team.

But it's the only real way you can think about it as a footballer: if you're in the team ahead of me, I'm going to do everything possible to get you out of the team. So you're not exactly going to get along like a house on fire with that player, are you? When you're not in the team they're friendly with you because they're in the team! And when you're in the team and they're not, the vibes are different.

The competition for places at Liverpool was fierce – and that was just the reserves. I knew what some of the lads were saying and it made me change my mentality. I realised, hang on, I want to be in the first team too. I'm in a bit of a dogfight here and I'm going to have to start working harder at it. And that meant running harder, tackling harder, competing every day on the training ground.

So one day we were playing this game, a mixture of youth team and staff. Tommy Smith was the youth team manager, a Liverpool legend who had a well-earned reputation as one of the hardest men ever. He'd only hung up his boots two years before and he could still be an intimidating presence on the pitch. Roy and Ronnie Moran would also have been playing with the staff team that day. Anyway, a ball broke between me and Smithy and another lad whose name I forget. This lad, he pulled out at the last second and let the ball go and me, being a silly bugger, I went full in. The ball ricocheted between me and Smithy and it smashed him right in the face. Straightaway the red mist descended. People always talk about Tommy 'break your leg' Smith. But he didn't say that. He used to say, 'I'll break your back.' And he looked at me, his face was like thunder, and he uttered the immortal words: 'I'll break your fucking back if you do that again.'

I was a bit embarrassed, I didn't know how to react. But fair play to Bugsy, he stuck up for me that day. He said to Smithy, 'Oi! Wasn't his fault. The other lad pulled out of it, he went for it. Wasn't his fault it smashed you in the face.' And that sort of defused the situation. But I'll tell you one thing, my one-touch football improved that day! Any time I got on the ball I was laying it off as fast as I could for fear Smithy would put me in hospital.

I was rattled at the time but when I mulled it over that night I figured I hadn't done too badly out of that incident. Ronnie and Roy saw that I hadn't bottled it, I hadn't pulled out of it, which a lot of young lads might have done. And I figured they'd made a mental note: that lad doesn't pull out of tackles.

The following pre-season the reserves played the first team at Anfield. They always played each other the week before the first game of the season. We were four or five up after forty-five minutes and they stopped the game. The first team were told to get togged in. We were called into the middle of the pitch and we were all made up because we'd battered them. But Bugsy was part of the first-team coaching staff and he wasn't one bit happy. 'Bet you wouldn't be able to do it on a Saturday when the chips are down.' And that was it! Talk about bursting your bubble. The point is, though, that that was a very good reserve team: Steve Ogrizovic in goal, Richard Money, Avi Cohen – who sadly died long before his time in 2010 – Colin Irwin, Alan Harper, Kevin Sheedy, Howard Gayle, Sammy Lee, myself, Ian Rush and Colin Russell. Mick Halsall was sub. There was an awful lot of quality in that team; most of us went on to have good careers in the game. Even at the time you had a lot of people around town talking about that team. There was a bit of a buzz about Sheedy, Gayle, Rush, Lee and a few more of us. It meant you'd get a couple of thousand people coming to the reserve games.

We won a lot of those games but only one stands out in my memory. We played Aston Villa away in November 1980. We beat them 3–0, and I got two. They were good goals, one curled into the top corner from the edge of the box, the other after I broke with the ball from midfield and chipped the keeper from outside the box. That was four goals in four games I'd scored now and I was thinking *This is going OK, I might be getting the hang of this.* I'd never felt stronger, the confidence was flowing, and I sensed – I could feel it – that Joe Fagan and Bob Paisley were marking my card.

3

Breaking the Ice

Liverpool were at home to Stoke on the Friday night.

Me and Kevin Sheedy went to Aintree on the Thursday and when we got back the landlady was waiting with a message. Someone from the office had called: I had to report for training the next morning and I had to bring my suit because I'd be going to the team hotel. I was in the first-team squad.

It was 3 April 1981. I was nineteen and a half. Ray Kennedy was injured but he played on the left and I was sure they'd have gone for a natural left-footer like Sheeds ahead of me. Then I was sure I'd be no more than a sub for the night. But an hour before kick-off Bob told me I was playing. I was scared to death, in and out of the toilet several times, surrounded by household names who didn't really know me at all. Kenny Dalglish was thoughtful enough to come over and have a few words. 'You've obviously been doing something right so just do what you've been doing and you'll be fine.' And it was great advice because it settled me down and got me thinking straight.

Don't try to do too much, just do what you've been doing all along.

Then, on twenty-seven minutes, I was one-on-one with the Stoke keeper Peter Fox. A through ball from Sammy, I'd broken the offside trap and was running for twenty yards with the ball at my feet. *Jesus, don't bottle it now.* And I suppose this is where your years of training take over. *Just concentrate on your touch, not too far ahead of you, don't get it caught under your feet either. Another touch, now a quick look-up, the keeper is coming out, just roll it past him.*

The keeper dived but the ball was on its way. I watched it cross the line and then wheeled away. There was a crescendo of noise and I was surrounded by famous players happy to hug me though they hardly knew my name. The game restarted and my body was electric with adrenaline but I needed to calm down and concentrate. I was following the play but somewhere in my head I could hear the crowd singing. They were singing, 'Ronnnnie Wheeeelan, Ronnnnie Wheeeelan, Ronnnnie Wheeeelan.'

Somewhere in the Dublin mountains Matt Butler was sitting in his car listening to the same chant. Ma and Da were hearing it too because they were in the stadium. They'd come over for the National, not expecting to see me make my debut, and they were somewhere up there in the stand, bursting with pride. And I was down on the pitch, my heart pounding out of my chest.

We won 3–0. I was interviewed by a reporter after the game. I said I didn't know if I'd ever get another game but at least I'd done it: I'd played and I'd scored for Liverpool at Anfield. So if they never saw fit to pick me again, at least I'd done it one time. And it was all over the sports pages the next day, in

Ireland as well as England, and my friends and neighbours were reading about it.

I was hoping in particular that my career guidance teacher would be reading about it, maybe telling the other teachers about it in the staff room at Patrician. Because in my Leaving Cert year I'd gone to his office for the big conversation about what I was going to do with my life. He asked the usual questions: what subjects are you doing, where do you think it'll take you, what options have you lined up? Finally, 'What do you want to do?' 'I want to be a professional footballer.' 'Right. OK.' It was obvious he was sceptical. 'But you'll have to have something to fall back on if that doesn't work out.' 'Well, I don't. There's a lot of clubs interested . . .'

To be fair, he knew there were a lot of hard-luck stories around Dublin of young lads who'd dreamed about making it in England. So he gave me the spiel: it's very risky, very few people make it, one bad injury and it's all over. But I was adamant about it. I was clear in my mind. 'I want to be a professional footballer, and that's it.' He told me I still needed to have other plans, just in case. He was right and he was wrong. If I was talking to talented young prospects now, I'd be saying the same thing. But when he said it to me, I didn't listen. I had no other plans because I *was* going to make it. So I had this picture in my head of my career guidance teacher back in Dublin picking up the papers the next day and going, 'Well, he did make it after all.' Except I hadn't made it. I'd played one game.

Ray Kennedy came back in for the next game, as I knew he would, and I was back in the reserves playing Newcastle, as I knew I would be. But I wasn't complaining, not at all. I knew I'd pulled ahead of the pack. I'd broken the ice and the big step-up didn't hold any great fears for me now. They put me on the bench for the last two games of the season, they even took me to Paris for the European Cup final, though I didn't make the squad.

All of a sudden I was a young man in a hurry. I played six of the first sixteen league games the following season, including my first Merseyside derby that November at Anfield. I still have a nice souvenir from that game on my shin, a scar from the five stitches I needed after Eamonn O'Keefe chopped me in a tackle. It was a sort of rite of passage, your first Merseyside derby. I had no idea how big it was or how much it meant in the city. It started with the build-up that week. Everywhere you went, people wanted to talk about it. They left you in no doubt that you had to win it. They told you that they couldn't face work on Monday morning if you didn't win it. You just could not escape the pressure or the excitement. Nothing prepared me for that.

Nothing prepared me either for the blast of noise that hit you as you came up the tunnel. And nothing could prepare you for the speed and intensity of the action. The sheer speed of the play, you didn't have a second on the ball. But once I got into the thick of it I loved it. It was a right royal battle and I was loving it. Nearly scored, too. A corner from the right at the Kop end, I caught it with a volley just inside the box; the keeper couldn't hold it and Kenny lashed it in. We won 3–1 and up in the players' lounge everyone was on a high, grabbing one another and hugging and celebrating. A magic atmosphere. I woke up the next morning, body hurting and aching all over, thinking *I would love to do that again. What a buzz! What a brilliant buzz.*

It didn't last long. I was still in and out of the team and

coming up to Christmas I was running out of patience. So I decided to visit the manager's office. That would've been a bit of an ordeal for me but the Merseyside derby had given me just about enough confidence to go through with it.

Deep breath, nervous as a kitten, I knocked on the door. 'Come in.' Bob was sat at his desk with a newspaper in front of him, probably opened at the racing page. I asked him why he wasn't giving me more starts. I told him I thought I'd done well in every game I'd played. So what was the story? And Bob's reply totally caught me on the hop. 'Why didn't you come to see me before this, then?' I'd thought he was going to run me, get rid of me pronto. I was stumped for an answer. Bob just muttered something and that was it, conversation over. I realise now that Bob was probably waiting to find out, from me, if I really *believed* I was ready for the first team. He knew I was a shy lad, he probably knew I wasn't the type to go banging on a manager's door, and the fact that I did go to him maybe convinced him that I was ready.

Anyway he put me into the team for the very next game, Manchester City at Anfield on Boxing Day. We lost 1–3, and I scored with only five minutes left in the game. It was Liverpool's fifth home defeat of the calendar year, having been unbeaten at Anfield for the previous three years. We'd finished fifth in 1980/81, nine points behind champions Aston Villa, and now we were twelfth at Christmas 1981/82. It was the first time City had won at Anfield since 1953.

On *Match of the Day* that night the BBC's Alan Parry asked Kevin Bond, the City defender, for his impressions of Liverpool. 'What's gone wrong, they used to be impregnable here?' Kevin Bond's analysis wasn't far off the mark. He said City were used to coming to Anfield and getting 'hammered' every time. 'The only thing I can think of is they've got a lot of youngsters playing. And although they play really well for them, when I think of the Liverpool teams I used to play against and used to watch, they never really had hardly any youngsters. And if they did it'd be only one. So I think maybe that might have something to do with it, they've got so many youngsters in the side.'

The team that day was: Grobbelaar, Neal, Lawrenson, Thompson, Hansen, Johnston, Souness, Lee, Whelan, Dalglish, Rush. I'd made my debut in April; Bruce, Lawro and Craig Johnston had made their debuts together in August, on the opening day of the season; Sammy Lee was twenty-two. Ian Rush had made his debut a year earlier but he was struggling for form and was in and out of the team. I'd imagine Bob Paisley was a very worried man by Christmas 1981. There was a huge transition under way and it wasn't working for him. Those new players would remain part of the Liverpool set-up for practically the rest of the decade but he wasn't to know that at the time. After the City game he took the captaincy off Phil Thompson and gave it to Graeme Souness. He would not have done that lightly but he was searching for solutions to a worrying run of form.

In hindsight we can see that the new generation was basically going through its growing pains in the first half of that season. In the second half, we clicked. Everything fell into place. The 2–1 win against Wolves on 16 January was probably a turning point. They'd taken an early lead and held out until the 75th minute when I managed to equalise; with six minutes left Kenny hit the winner. We won six of our next seven, and the goals were raining in.

Then it was down to Stamford Bridge for the fifth round of

the FA Cup. It was the first time I ever felt physically intimidated by a match crowd. The streets around the stadium were packed as the team bus crawled along. Chelsea supporters were out of the pubs with pint glasses in their hands and looking like they were going to throw them at us. There were no police escorts then and they were banging on the bus and rocking it. I'd never experienced this before at a football game. We were beaten 2–0, we didn't play that day; I'd been a bit unnerved and I think a few others had been too.

We lost 2–0 against Swansea next game in the league and lost again to Brighton at Anfield in early March. There were sixteen games left in the league after that; we won thirteen and drew three. Halfway through that unbeaten run we played Manchester City in the return game at Maine Road. It was just over a hundred days since the 1–3 defeat but we were a transformed team. We'd played twenty-five games in the meantime; we were no longer spare parts trying to fit in; we were now operating as cogs in a well-oiled machine. A week earlier we'd beaten Notts County, a result that took Liverpool back to the top of the table for the first time in fifteen months. City were taken apart, 5–0.

John Bond, Kevin's father, was City manager at the time. This time he was interviewed afterwards on *Match of the Day*. He looked a bit shell-shocked. 'They were so superior to us in every way,' he said. 'In their will to win, their determination, their skill, their habits, their methods, the way they knocked the ball about, everything they did. It looks very much in many ways as if they just do what they want to do, when they want to do it, and that's sickening really. And I'd just remind you that there was nine of those (City players) played at Anfield on Boxing Day when we won three-one.'

We coasted that game but we were digging out results too and we came out the right side of a five-goal humdinger down at the Dell later that April. That was a huge result for us. Southampton had a really good team at the time with the likes of Kevin Keegan and Alan Ball and Mick Channon. They scored a brilliant goal to leave it 1–1 at the break, a fantastic passing move that Channon finished off. My confidence was sky-high by then and when I got behind their defence in the 57th minute I spotted their keeper off his line and chipped him from the edge of the box. Keegan equalised two minutes later but with two minutes to go I came up with the winner.

It was turning into a dream first season. In March we'd played Tottenham in the League Cup final and, to be honest, I still get a bit of a tingle when I watch the footage. Spurs had one hand on the cup when I popped up with the equaliser three minutes from time. It was my Wembley debut and I'd barely slept the night before. Wembley! When I equalised I went skipping behind the goals and when I scored again in extra time I did the same. Couldn't contain myself. It was literally a boyhood dream come true. Some things stick out in your mind and of all the things I remember it's Phil Thompson coming up to me in the celebrations on the pitch afterwards and shouting into my ear, 'You were absolutely fucking magnificent.'

That was important to me because I felt I was being accepted now by the senior men in the dressing room, players who had won everything and done it all. You always had a feeling that they were waiting for you to really prove yourself. They never said it but it was kind of, 'We don't just let anyone into this dressing room, you know, we're choosy about who we let into this team.' After a few games they'll accept certain things: OK, he can play; he can pass it, he can head it, he can score. But can he win? Has he got the attitude? After Wembley I felt I'd answered those questions. I felt I'd earned the right to be in that dressing room.

It was also against Tottenham that we wrapped up the title with a game to spare. It was at Anfield, we beat them 3–1 and the fans were already celebrating another triumphant season when I finished off the scoring with three minutes to go. Icing on the cake. In the dressing room afterwards I was looking forward to a big party. A night out with fanfares and speeches and medal ceremonies and all that. Then I saw Bob walking around with this cardboard box that looked like a shoe box. And he's shaking hands with each player and handing him a little red box with a medal in it and moving on to the next fella. It was like he was handing us a glucose sweet or something. No one made any fuss at all.

I played forty-seven games in all competitions that season and scored fourteen goals from left midfield. I hadn't gone to Liverpool as a left-sided midfielder, nor had I a natural left foot. But I knew for sure that all the years I'd spent working on it with my da back home had paid off in a big way. I was still better with the ball on my right but by now I was nearly as good on my left. I wasn't whipping crosses in with it but I was comfortable controlling the ball and passing it. And I believe that it made the difference. They were looking for someone who could take over from Ray Kennedy down the left and Sheeds had such a cultured left foot I was sure they would go with him. In fact he got his debut first, in February 1981, but when I got mine in April I scored and my performance that night might have swayed it a little bit in my favour. It was a bit awkward for us at times because we were in digs together, we were good mates, and we both knew we were fighting for the same position. It could have gone either way but I was determined that it didn't. I wanted it to go my way.

Sheeds moved to Everton at the end of the season and went on to have a great career. Ray played his last game for Liverpool in December 1981, just weeks before the City game on Boxing Day. He was sold to Swansea in January. I'd seen off a fair bit of the competition, my place in the team was mine to lose. I knew they'd be signing new players and I knew that others were capable of stepping in and taking over. But I'd worry about that the following season – and every season thereafter.

But for now, happy days. We'd won the league, we'd won the League Cup and I went back down to Wembley for the FA Cup final because Ron Greenwood, the England manager, would be on hand to present me with the Robinsons Barley Water Young Player of the Year award, live on television. My first ever car was the Rover 2000 that Robinsons donated as part of the prize.

It was the cherry on top of a season that had actually changed my life. I'd been blooded and tested and accepted. I was a Liverpool player now. I was there to stay. I was a made man.

4

Model Athletes

It's no state secret that we liked a drink in those days. But we didn't like it as much as winning trophies. And it was very seldom that we put the cart before the horse. You had to get the points on the board before you put the pints on the table. And that's how we did it. We were self-motivated when it came to winning things, we self-managed our way through games, and we self-policed ourselves when it came to the socialising.

I don't mean that someone was counting the units of alcohol every time we went on a session. I mean that we didn't do it at the wrong time. Bruce Grobbelaar used to call it 'a full dog day'. It would usually be on a Monday with no game until the following Saturday. With the decks clear, you could go full steam ahead without worrying about an upcoming game.

The other thing was, we got on well together in those teams in the 1980s. We enjoyed each other's company and there was nobody in that dressing room I wouldn't have turned to and said, 'Fancy a pint later?' There were a few dressing rooms, maybe from 1990 on, where I would've been thinking *I'm not going for a pint with him*, or *I wouldn't fancy being in his company for a couple of hours*. Then again, I was getting older as well and probably the younger lads wouldn't have wanted to go for a drink with me either. But right through the 80s you were surrounded by great characters and good lads who enjoyed plenty of crack along the way. And I'll tell you, when the crack was good, it was very good. You'd have lads taking the mickey all day. It'd be one round of laughs after another. One round of drinks after another too. Kenny didn't drink much, Peter Beardsley didn't drink at all. But there weren't many who didn't get stuck in.

A full dog day usually started after training in Melwood. We'd go to a pub across from the back of the training ground, the Derby Arms, and anybody who was slow to the bar didn't escape because you'd have a whip-round; everybody would lash the money in and that'd be it for the day. Next thing the bullets would be flying. If you said anything at all you were liable to get shot down with a retort. Our lads were very quick on the draw. Steve Nicol was one who took the brunt of it, especially from his fellow Jocks, Hansen and Souness and Dalglish. In the early days Nico was the new Jock on the block and he wanted to be part of their gang. But these lads were a little bit older and smarter and they wound him up without mercy.

Someone was always liable to do something stupid before the night was out. Bruce would try one of his acrobatic stunts, standing on his hands on the bar or something silly like that. There was one night out in Liverpool and there was this big fella, a judo expert or something, and he could stand up straight, hands behind his back, and fall towards the floor. And just as he was about to hit the floor he'd get his hands out and break the fall. So Bruce said, 'I can do that. Watch this!' So we all watched as Bruce assumed the position. You can guess what happened next. He left it a bit late to get his hands out. He had amazing reflexes on a football field but they were probably a bit impaired this night. He smacked himself full frontal on the floor, split his chin right down the middle and had to get about six stitches in it.

Bruce was one of the most popular characters in the squad. He was just a naturally funny man. As for the match-fixing allegations, I find it very difficult to accept that he would ever have done anything illegal. I wouldn't like to think that within a game situation he did anything wrong against the lads because he was one of us; we all liked him and we still do. We didn't give him flak over the mistakes he made because we'd remember all the brilliant saves he pulled off. Bruce was a unique character in the game at the time. We got used to his antics, we enjoyed them, it was just a case of, 'That's Bruce!' He was an entertainer and there weren't many of them around in football, then or now. He had a famous line in the papers one day, to the effect that he was going straight, he was finished with the comedy. The headline was something like, 'That's it, my clowning days are over!' It wasn't long before he was on the back page of the papers with coins in his eyes or a funny hat on his head with flapping hands. Another case of 'That's Bruce!'

As the full dog day wore on into a full dog night, things would only get funnier. It would always reach the stage where someone would try to have the dreaded serious conversation. You know the way it is with some fellas: they start getting deep and meaningful when they start getting drunk. Naturally, we'd take the mick out of them even more. There were a lot of intelligent lads in that team (believe it or not), and a few dozy ones too, but when someone started trying to talk in a sensible, serious way, it usually didn't come out right.

Mind you, this happened when lads were sober too. One day Kenny was trying to explain something in a team meeting and Steve McMahon decided to offer his tuppence worth. Macca jumped up off his chair and gave this long rigmarole about how we'd solve this particular problem. He was being very serious, very analytical about his great idea. Then he finished off by saying, 'So, why don't we do it that way? That way we can kill two birds with two stones.' He looked around the room. There was a pause, then the whole dressing room exploded.

The Christmas party, you had to be in the whole of your health for the Christmas party. It was no place for amateurs. You might end up facing the dawn over Merseyside. Again, it was well timed to coincide with a long lead-in to the next game. It had its own rituals. It was usually a fancy-dress job and I have some great photos of some famous footballers looking very silly in their costumes. The tradition was that any pro new to the club would have to sing a song at the Christmas party. I had to go through it too. I knew the lads would be throwing sandwiches and sausages and drinks at me so I decided to be clever. I buttonholed Jimmy Case and I said to him, 'Jimbo, you know when I start, just throw something at me and that'll get it over with.' He said fair enough. So I'm launching into 'When Irish Eyes Are Smiling' – well, the first verse of it anyway – when Jimbo appears from behind my back and smashes me in the face with a big potato pie. It's dripping off me face and of course the lads are falling off their chairs at the sight. Another lesson. If I'd said nothing I might have gotten away with a few flying sausages and triangular ham sandwiches.

We were young, we were fit, and if you had ten pints, sure you might as well have fifteen. But the real test wasn't how many pints you could drink that night, it was how many laps you could do the next morning at Melwood. There was always training the morning after the Christmas party or, to be more precise, a few hours after the party had ended. Some lads would turn up still in fancy dress. The coaching staff would bring us in for an hour or so, make us run around, do a few shuttles, just to sweat some of the beer out of us.

Some fellas had unbelievable powers of recovery. The best I ever saw was Terry McDermott. I had many a good night out with him. A real larger-than-life personality was Terry Mac, liked by everyone at the football club, always laughing and joking. He took a lot of money off me on nights out, usually in the wee small hours. I was young and foolish and Terry would persuade me to go playing snooker with him at three in the morning when I couldn't see a ball let alone pot one. There'd be a few quid riding on the first frame, which he'd always win. Then it'd be double or quits and of course I'd go again, thinking I'd get my money back.

Terry Mac was skin and bone. But he was a tremendous footballer and an incredible athlete. He could drink all night and be first in running the next morning. John Wark was the same. Those lads had serious engines. I'd be in the middle of the pack somewhere, hiding myself away, trying to survive, cutting inside the cones to save a few yards. To be fair, you always had a chance of not being the one bringing up the rear if John Aldridge was around. Poor old Aldo struggled the morning after a night out. There was one Christmas party, Aldo had a good skinful like the rest of us, and the next morning was torture for him. I never saw anything as funny at training in my life. With every lap we did, Aldo was falling further behind. Eventually he was about a hundred yards behind the rest of us and we just couldn't stop the laughing. Aldo's head was hurting so badly that he was trying to keep it still while running at the same time. So he was just shuffling along taking these baby steps because he didn't want to move his head. It was the funniest way of running I ever saw and the look of pure misery on his face was absolutely priceless.

I suppose nowadays they'd call what went on at Liverpool a 'drinking culture'. I don't like that phrase because it suggests that the socialising was a bigger factor than it actually was. There was one dominant culture at Liverpool and that was its football culture. That's what everyone strove for at the club. Playing the game the right way and playing it consistently. Nothing came in the way of that; it was too serious not to take seriously. Out of that culture came the winning culture. The drinking, if it was anything, was a subculture, and nothing more than that. If it was it wouldn't have been tolerated, not in the boardroom, not in the manager's office, not in the boot room. But they were quite relaxed about it because they trusted us to do it at the right time and because they believed it did us no harm to let off a bit of steam every now and again. And anyway, players were allowed to enjoy their pints because it was accepted more in those days, not just at Liverpool but throughout the game.

There's a different attitude to alcohol now in the game and that's fair enough, times change. But I believe those drinking sessions were great bonding sessions too. We were a very united team on the pitch and that unity took us through some hostile situations, especially in Europe. It's hard to quantify these things, I know, but when your back is to the wall in some high-pressure game, that's when a strong team spirit will pull you through. Did those nights out help us on the pitch? They didn't make us better individual footballers, obviously, but I would argue that they contributed to making us a better team.

Modern-day fitness methods are a lot more scientific than they were back then. They are able to monitor energy levels, calculate the amount of running every player does and guard against fatigue. Proper nutrition is considered essential and alcohol is almost taboo now. Personally I'd be curious to know how much better I'd have been if I never drank. It probably would have helped my rehabilitation from injuries if I'd been teetotal. Almost certainly I'd have been a better athlete. But I don't believe I'd have been a better footballer, a better ball player. The emphasis nowadays seems to be as much on athletic ability as on ball skills. But I'd rather have a very good footballer who is less of an athlete than a very good athlete with a poor first touch. It's not about being six foot three and fourteen stone of muscle. You look at Barcelona, they're midgets compared to a lot of teams, especially in the Premier League, and they're the best team in the world. Who knows, maybe they like their beer too.

But every team has its own time and era. I have nothing but fond memories of those nights out and the thousand laughs we had. I wouldn't swap them for the world.

5

The Master

Bob Paisley spent forty-four years at Liverpool in one capacity or another. He was manager for the last nine of those years. He won six league titles, three European Cups, one UEFA Cup and three League Cups in those nine years.

And yet if you asked any of his players how he did it, they'd probably say, 'You know, I'm not really sure.' None of us can put a finger on what, exactly, made him a great manager. He didn't say a lot, he didn't seem to do a lot, he was just always there, pulling the strings in the background.

He didn't have the charisma of a Clough or a Shankly. In fact he was the dead opposite. Some quiet people have an aura about them but he wasn't one of those either. You see certain people walk into a room and they have this vibe about them. Heads turn, everybody's looking at them. Not Bob. You'd never know he was the manager of the best team in Europe. It's been said before and it's true: Bob *was* the archetypal old grandfather in his flat cap and his slippers and cardigan.

He wasn't a motivator either. He rarely raised his voice and never sent us out of the dressing room pumped up for the battle. He didn't say a lot in team meetings, or before a game or at half-time. There was no sermon, no spiel, no thumping the table. He managed his teams with a very light touch. It just proves there's no manual for the successful manager. Each one does it his own way.

You look at managers like Bill Shankly and Brian Clough: they were always on the TV talking about how good their teams were, what they were going to do; always making wise-cracks and generally loving the limelight. Bob, if he was on the telly once or twice a season, all he'd say in his little Geordie accent was, 'Yeah, yeah, doing OK, yeah, yeah, no problems.' He was a very modest man and that's how he wanted us to be as well. He'd say to us, 'Let your talking be done on the foot-ball pitch, don't go shouting in the papers if you've won something.' And we didn't go shouting if we won something. We went, 'Well, it's a job, it's what we do.' And you learned that off Bob and Ronnie and Joe.

And any analysis of Bob's success has to include Joe Fagan and Ronnie Moran. It was a partnership between them, it really was. Between them they got the word across to us. Bob was the manager but Joe and Ronnie played huge roles within that structure. Ronnie and Joe were the ones on the training ground day in day out, motivating you all the time for another performance and another performance and another performance. Bob would be watching and taking it all in. He'd sit in his little office at Melwood, usually with his radiator on, and that was his vantage point. Or he'd come out and stand on the sideline and walk around and stand again and then shuffle back into his office. If the mood was low, Moransco would start shouting and cajoling to get us going again. If the mood was high, Moransco would start shouting and cajoling us anyway. He is seen, I suppose, as the sergeant-major figure in that set-up but, as Roy Evans rightly points out, Ronnie had a good eye for things and gave plenty of solid advice too.

Joe, we all liked and trusted Joe, because he was honest and straightforward. It wasn't often he'd fly off the handle, it might be twice in a season, but when it happened you remembered it. And if he gave you a bollocking you had to take it because you knew deep down that you deserved it. Evo then was a bit more arm-around-the-shoulder in style, a sympathetic ear if you wanted to get something off your chest. Between them they covered all the bases.

There was a lot of double psychology with them. Whether they had little meetings about it or not I don't know, but we could win a match 5–1 and get stick for giving the goal away, or for some mistake you made in the game. We could lose 2–0 and they'd come in and go, 'Ah, you battered them, how did you manage to lose that one?' When you expected a bollocking sometimes they'd turn it completely around and tell you how well you played. Likewise, when we played really well, they'd turn that around too. Mind you, when you expected a bollocking you often got one. And if you played really well they seldom said, 'Lads, you were really good today.' It was just on to the next game straightaway.

One of Bob's strengths was his insight, the way he could read games and opponents. He was very good at giving you nuggets of practical information that you could take into a game. 'This team comes in too narrow.' 'The right-back doesn't like you taking him on on the outside.' 'Their keeper comes off his line.' That's all he'd say but it'd be enough. Kenny or Rushie would know to keep an eye out for that keeper and, if the chance came, go for the chip. If it didn't come off, you wouldn't be lectured for trying it. But that was more or less the extent of his team talks. I had to laugh when I came across a quote from Bugsy in an old newspaper cutting. It goes back to 1983, when Joe was appointed manager after Bob retired. Ronnie is trying to explain the way things work at Liverpool. 'The secret is brevity,' he says. 'You could talk for half an hour on how to fry an egg. But at Anfield we'd just tell someone to heat some fat in a pan, crack in the egg and start cooking. That simple approach is very much Joe's style. When he was in charge of the reserves he would use a box of matches to illustrate his tactical talks. There are no airs and graces about him.' I must remember Bugsy's instructions the next time I'm frying eggs for breakfast. Beats Delia Smith any day.

Every Friday morning we'd have the team meeting at Melwood: cup of tea, chocolate biscuits and a talk from Bob. It was always short and sweet. Sometimes it was so short there was no meeting at all. We'd all be sitting there waiting for his words of wisdom and Bob would come in, 'Same team, same sub, let's go.' Job done, everyone out the door.

At half-time in a game Ronnie and Joe would do the talking but if Bob spotted something he'd pass it on. He was very shrewd at making the right switch. 'Take him off, get him on.' And it worked too often to be a coincidence. In those days only one substitution was allowed so he had one chance to get it right. Sometimes it'd just be a tactical adjustment. The day we wrapped up the title at Anfield in 1982, Tottenham were one up at the break. We'd been all over them but Glenn Hoddle had scored a spectacular goal out of the blue. At half-time Bob told Mark Lawrenson that he was playing too close

to Souey in centre midfield; he was getting in his way. He told
Lawro to move further over to the left. Lawro did what he was
told and it worked like a magic wand. He scored the equaliser
six minutes into the second half and only four minutes later set
up Kenny for our second.

But it goes without saying that Bob was a hard man too. The
club came first and if a player had to suffer the consequences,
so be it. He wouldn't play power games with players, he was
much too principled to do that, and he would think long and
hard before making a decision that was going to hurt somebody. But once the decision was taken, he'd implement it.
When a player's time was up he was shipped out and the show
moved on. He knew Phil Thompson would be very upset over
the captaincy issue in that 1981/82 season but he decided it
had to be done – and he did it. Souness went on to be one of
the great Liverpool captains. The day we lost to Chelsea in the
FA Cup that February, Bob told us not to carry the ball. The
pitch was rough, so we should keep the ball moving. Terry Mac
got caught on the ball at one stage and Chelsea went straight
down the field and scored. Next thing he was taken off. Bob
could show who was boss when he needed to. If he told you to
do something you'd better well do it. Apart from anything else,
he was usually right.

But maybe Bob didn't need to say a whole lot during the
season because he had the main part of his job done by then.
Bill Shankly once said that the number one talent in any successful manager is 'the natural ability to pick a player'. Bob
was a brilliant judge of a player. He bought high-quality players and found a role for them in the team. Usually they were
good enough to fill a few different roles. But it wasn't enough
that they were talented, they would have to fit into the system

too. And Bob always seemed to buy players who fitted in
socially as well. Joe Fagan and Kenny Dalglish were the same,
they wanted very good footballers who had a team mentality.
I think they looked deeper into players' psyches, trying to find
out how they behaved as people: are they good lads, do they
mix well? Or are they standoffish, are they difficult to handle?
If a player was good in all these areas too, then OK, let's bring
him in and put him into the group of winners that we've
already got.

However he did it, Bob usually managed to get players with
the right chemistry on and off the field. You just have to look at
some of the talent he brought in: Hansen, Souness, Dalglish,
Lawrenson, Rush. They are among the greatest players Liverpool
have ever had. And then, if there were young players at
Anfield with the right stuff, they were blended slowly and carefully into the side too. Time and again he found the right
formula. And once he had the right players in the right forma-
tion, it was a case of 'get them fit and then get the results' week
in week out.

So if a manager is assessed on his ability to build teams, then
Bob for me was the best. He was a master builder of teams.
Bob had built the team of 1978/79 that is considered by many
to be the best team Liverpool have ever had. They won thirty
out of forty-two league games, drew eight and lost four. They
scored eighty-five league goals and conceded just sixteen. Just
eighteen months later he dismantled that team and by the end
of that 1981/82 season five rookies had been bedded in – and
we'd won the title too. And those five players would still be
winning titles long after Bob had gone.

This is where I believe Bob's class as a manager stands apart.
It's not an exact science, and it can never be, because you're

dealing with human beings after all. It's very hard to pinpoint exactly when a player who has given good service is in decline, and when a young player is ready to step up – or if he's good enough to step up. I'd imagine that at the start of 1981/82 Bob wasn't sure either. But he would have managed the process very carefully. He'd have monitored us closely. He'd have been scrutinising the veterans for signs of age catching up on them, and he'd have been learning as much as possible about us reserves. Not just about your football ability but your temperament and attitude as well. And he'd have been picking up clues, because Bob knew players inside out. I'm sure there would've been long conversations about it all with Joe and Ronnie and Roy in the boot room too.

The 1981/82 title was Bob's fifth. The day after the Tottenham game he was quoted in the newspapers. 'I'm proudest of this one,' he said, 'because there was so much more to do.' And he talked about the dilemmas he'd been faced with that season. 'Our most difficult job is to decide when to introduce new players. Any clown can bring in youngsters but if you do it at the wrong time you can crucify them. When we were struggling earlier on, people were shouting for us to get rid of this player and bring in that one. But you can't do it like that. You don't throw out a man who has served you loyally. There has to be some sentiment. Then when you think the time has come, you go to a youngster and you say, "Right, you've finished your education, now go and do the job".'

He also acknowledged, and I was chuffed to read it after all these years, the part some of us played in that campaign. 'The lads we have brought in this season, Whelan and Rush, have given the older players an extra yard to work in and they have revelled in it. Earlier the older players were controlling games for us without punishing opponents. The youngsters have had the extra pace to run the opposition back to their own goal.'

To be fair, Bob wouldn't have said something like that to your face. It wasn't the done thing. In fact, for the four years I was there when he was in charge, Bob never said anything much to me at all. I think the longest conversation I ever had with him was when he hauled me into his office one day. He'd got a letter from some busybody saying I was seen out drinking somewhere. Bob got these letters from time to time, usually if we'd lost a few games. So Bob called me in and showed me the letter but he was just going through the motions. Far as I could see, he didn't give a damn. All he said was, 'If you're going to go out and have a drink, do it bloody some place where you won't get caught.' OK, gaffer, sorry about that.

He liked a laugh and he loved the gee-gees. There was a television in the players' lounge and on a Saturday Bob would be watching the two-thirty from wherever before he'd come in to start getting us ready for the game. At the team meeting the day before he'd have had us sniggering away at one of his lines. 'Keep your high balls low.' 'He's not quick but he's nippy.' Who are you talking about, gaffer? 'Yeah, you know, Duggie Doings.' Every player who didn't play for Liverpool was Duggie Doings. And the way Bob would say his name, you got the distinct impression that whoever Duggie Doings was, he was no Pele.

Bob retired at the end of the 1982/83 season. The lads ordered him up the steps to collect the League Cup in March, knowing it would be his last big day at Wembley. It was a nice touch for a lovely man. A few weeks later he delivered the sixth league title of his career. And come the summer, he just slipped out the door and he was gone. There was no big hullabaloo, I can't even remember if we organised a whip-round.

Looking back, I realise now that I was very lucky in the people who helped me along the way. From Home Farm to Anfield I had good people around me who made good decisions on my behalf and who cared about my development. Bob and me never had long conversations but he'd ask me from time to time about how my life was going: are you looking after yourself, is everything going OK? He nurtured me along as a professional footballer, brought me through some difficult times when I was at the club. And he saw something in me on the left side of midfield that I don't think anybody else did.

You don't forget the man who gave you your debut and I feel really proud that it was Bob Paisley who signed me and Bob Paisley who put me in the team. I feel privileged to have played for one of the greatest managers who ever lived.

6

The Iron Curtain

The thing about making your way in this game, there is always another level to reach. The Home Farm mini-leagues, the Dublin schoolboys league, youth international, the Irish senior league. No sooner do you put your foot on one rung but there's another rung above it. The Liverpool reserves, the Liverpool first team, Irish international, English champions. Next step, Europe.

The cliché has it that if you're good enough you're old enough. It's not always true. Sometimes you're good enough but you're just not old enough. We were too young for Europe, the five rookies who broke into the team that 1981/82 season. This was another apprenticeship you would have to serve, another ladder you'd have to climb.

In March 1982 I scored my first goal in Europe. It was at Anfield against CSKA Sofia in the third round first leg of the European Cup. Ten days later I was high as a kite after the League Cup final at Wembley. Four days after that, it was on to Bulgaria for the second leg. For a lot of us it was our first trip to one of the old communist countries. The Berlin Wall was still standing at the time. These were what the old football writers used to call 'difficult trips behind the Iron Curtain'.

When you landed in one of those places, you knew you were in for a strange experience. It'd start at the airport. They'd leave you waiting in customs for hours. There'd be no one around. Blokes in uniforms would come and go, pretending you weren't there. When they finally got down to business they'd check your passport over and over again, staring at you, staring at your passport, muttering stuff you couldn't understand to another bloke in a uniform. None of them ever looked happy. Then they'd grunt and hand it back to you and let you through. It was all to intimidate you and annoy you and upset you.

The Levski Stadium in Sofia that night, I think we knew what the gladiators felt like in the Colosseum when the crowd turned on them. The noise and chaos came raining down on top of us from 75,000 fans. It was dark and hundreds of them had set newspapers on fire and held them up like torches. It had snowed that day and the pitch was a bog. The snow was heaped up around the perimeter of the pitch. The referee, an Austrian, was totally intimidated.

But we made a balls of it too. We were far better than them, missed several chances, and I was guilty for two of them. I was clean through in the opening minutes, and then hit the bar later on. Rushie scored a goal, the ball was about a yard over the line when their keeper stopped it. The goal wasn't given. It was 1–1 on aggregate at full time and in extra time they got the winner. Mark Lawrenson got sent off late in the game. It was totally unlike him but we were at the end of our tether with their antics. We were totally unused to that kind of behaviour. Part of the learning curve in Europe was dealing with teams who would try everything to get you sent off. They'd spit at you, say stuff, catch you with sly digs. If you reacted at all they'd throw themselves on the ground, rolling around and holding their faces. Shameless stuff. It wasn't just CSKA but, on the night, Lawro reacted and the crowd went apeshit and the ref sent him off. This wasn't a lesson in football skills you were learning here, it was a lesson in temperament and discipline. You had to learn to be very cautious and very clever in the way you played teams like this.

The other lesson for me was that you got fewer chances in European football. When they came you *had* to take them, especially away from home. The *Liverpool Echo* the next day said I'd seen both sides of the game in the space of four days. 'Whelan,' it said, 'must put it down to experience along the tough road to the top in soccer.'

A year later we were back in eastern Europe and getting turned over again, this time by the Polish champions, Widzew Lodz. Again, we were naïve and made silly mistakes. We lost 2–0 when we could've held out for a 1–0. But we went looking for an equaliser when we didn't need to and got caught. Now we needed to score three at home, which we did, but they scored two and again we were knocked out in the third round. The issue was concentration as much as anything. We were finding out that the margin for error is smaller against top European teams. We were getting parts of the job right but still hadn't learned how to get it done right to the bitter end.

The margins were very skinny after our 0–0 with Athletic Bilbao at Anfield in the second round in October 1983. For the second leg we had to face 47,000 passionate fans in the

Basque region and we knew it was going to be hostile. This was a game where we needed to be very tight and conservative; so much so that Joe Fagan decided to go with Steve Nicol in midfield instead of me. I wasn't happy about it but a year earlier I'd have been very aggrieved. But I was learning the ropes about Europe and I understood his reasoning: Nico had a more defensive mind-set than me and that's what we'd need on the night. It was going to be a containing job.

And even if you're not playing, you can still learn a lot by listening to the people who've been through it before, and by watching from the sideline as the game unfolds. Joe and the veteran players kept emphasising in the dressing room that we needed to quieten the crowd through the first twenty-five minutes. Above all else, just hold out. They'll be gung ho, they'll be coming at us in waves; just hold out and hold out and hold out. Physically it was a matter of nonstop running and covering and tackling. That's OK, you're supposed to do that in every game anyway. Mentally it's draining because the concentration has to be intense, just pure tunnel vision for the ninety minutes.

Joe said afterwards that you could see the Bilbao flags gradually being lowered as the first half wore on. And you could also hear the crowd getting quieter and quieter. Then midway through the second half Alan Kennedy – aka Belly – got a cross in and Rushie made the header look simple. Now they had to get two but our lads had contained Bilbao when they were full of fire early doors and it was a matter now of maximum concentration and no silly mistakes. As they came on to us we got chances to counterattack but didn't pile forward in numbers. This is where I might have been tempted to break upfield, hoping to get on the end of a ball in the box. But what works in England mightn't necessarily be a good thing here. I noticed that our lads stayed sitting in midfield and just saw the game out. It was a tremendous performance.

And then it dawns on you afterwards: ah, so that's how it's done! Right, I've got it now, I'm starting to understand how this thing works. It was one of those games where you felt you'd learned some important lessons. A lot of games in England, you were winning easily and learning nothing. In this ninety minutes my education took a big leap forward and I hadn't kicked a ball. It's the sort of experience that goes straight into the bank in your head. We'd won 1–0 away from home against a quality team in a hostile environment and we felt we were on the right track at last.

Four and a half months later it was Benfica in the third round and again the margin for error was tight after a 1–0 win at Anfield in the first leg. Benfica were one of the top names in Europe at the time and the Stadium of Light was vast. The place was rocking with 70,000 fans all booing and whistling and barracking – and we stuffed them 4–1. This time I played and this time I took my chances, the first and fourth goals, with Rushie and Craig Johnston getting the two in between. I'd learned the lesson from CSKA two years earlier. I got a chance in the ninth minute and I took it because you have to take it. Craig's goal just after half an hour was brilliant and we polished them off in the second half.

Three weeks later we played Dinamo Bucharest in the semi-final first leg at Anfield. The gulf in standard between England and Europe was there for all to see. Four days before Dinamo we thrashed West Ham 6–0 at home. Now we managed just a 1–0 win against the Romanian champions. Coming off the pitch we already knew the second leg was going to be horrible.

There was bad blood brewing because Graeme Souness had taken out one of their players, Movila, breaking his jaw. At the final whistle they were pointing and gesticulating and threatening what they'd do to us in two weeks' time. They were going to get us in Bucharest.

At the airport the place was coming down with cops and soldiers. They were supposed to be there to give us an escort and protect us from any crazy Dinamo fans but of course they'd been briefed to start the softening-up process long before we even set foot in the stadium. If looks could kill we'd have all been dead. They were all doing the slit-your-throat sign and generally treating us with as much contempt as they could muster.

And on the night, the atmosphere in the stadium was pure poison. It was the most intimidating crowd I ever faced in my career. The pitch was a mess too. It had been raining all day and the surface was just muck and water. Every time Souey touched the ball the booing started. But Souey was loving it, he was in his element. And we knew that we were the better team: if we didn't bottle it we had the ability to beat them. Then Rushie got an early goal and that really settled us. Suddenly the noise around the ground turned to dead silence. But there was a long way to go and the crowd found their voice again. On the field the tackles were flying in, along with the usual provocations and play-acting. But we knew what they were trying to do and we rode it out. We held our discipline and went about our work. They pulled one back and the crowd went hysterical again. We kept our shape and kept going. Then, with less than ten minutes to go, we nailed the tie. I nutmegged the full-back just inside the box and crossed it, a crap cross that the defender should have cleared but didn't; Rushie tucked it home. We were through, we were sorted. After the match it was a case of, let's get the hell out of here as fast as we can.

I believe myself that I personally came of age that night. There was nothing ever really going to frighten you after an experience like that. You could go anywhere after that and face up to anyone. It was one of the most satisfying games of my career because of the circumstances and the way we came through it. Many a team would have folded completely. Each and every man on the pitch that night stood up and accepted responsibility. Dinamo Bucharest in the 23 August Stadium was for me – for all of us, probably – a special night.

For the new generation in that Liverpool team, Bilbao, Benfica and Bucharest had put a bit of iron into us. From the outside you wouldn't have been able to detect much of a difference in the players who'd struggled in Sofia two years earlier. But inside there was no comparison; mentally we were tougher, and a lot less innocent. As it turned out, we were lucky to get the draw we did that season. Those three away games were all potentially treacherous but, having weathered them, they did us a huge amount of good. To face the Italian champions in a European Cup final, in their own backyard, you needed to be seriously battle-hardened – and we were.

Maybe it's because we won it in a penalty shootout, but I don't think we've ever been given the credit for winning the 1984 European Cup. I just think the scale of the achievement was never fully understood. I mean, to beat Roma in the Olympic Stadium in Rome – it would've been hard enough doing it at a neutral venue. They had two members of the Italy team that had won the 1982 World Cup in Conti and Graziani. They had Falcao who was part of that fantastic Brazilian midfield in the same World Cup. They had Cerezo who had over fifty caps for Brazil and had also played in Spain 1982. They had five others – Nela, Bonetti, Righetti, Pruzzo, Tancredi – who had played for Italy or would soon play for Italy. And to repeat the point: they were at home. They would parade out in front of more than 60,000 of their own fans. It was totally wrong. Imagine if they'd had to come to Anfield for the final? I don't think UEFA would have allowed that to happen.

We went for a walk on the pitch before the game. The Liverpool fans who'd made the trip gave us a brilliant reception. But they were drowned out by the boos and jeers coming from the other three-quarters of the ground. When the Roma players walked out to that reception it must have lifted them. But maybe it was a double-edged thing too; maybe they thought there was no way they could lose this now. I firmly believe Roma thought they would easily beat us. No problem. I got that vibe from their attitude on the night. Maybe they thought the job was half-done just by playing at home; that the crowd would do their job for them by intimidating us.

Now, you don't want to ruin a good story, but a lot has been made of us singing a song in the tunnel before we went on to the pitch. Someone had a Chris Rea tape in the dressing room and decided it'd be a bit of a brainwave to sing 'I Don't Know What It Is But I Love It' while we were lining up against the Italians in the tunnel. A lot of us weren't sure about this idea. But then a few of them started it up, I think it was Craig Johnston and David Hodgson, and next thing it was karaoke night in the Olympic Stadium.

The song was getting a lot of airplay at the time so we were all belting it out, even though none of us knew the words. I think we must've sung the same line over and over. 'I don't know what it is but I love it. I don't know what it is but I love it.' Er, em, 'I don't know what it is but I love it.' In fairness, it wasn't exactly a song to get you pumped up for the battle, but some of the lads reckon that it rattled the Roma players. I don't think it intimidated them the least little bit. When the ref blew his whistle to start the game, I don't think our opponents were still unnerved because we had sung a pop song in the tunnel. It might have helped us more than it hindered them. It was a quirky thing to do and I'd say it relaxed us a little and brought us all a bit closer together before we entered the lions' den.

Once the game started the priority again was to take the heat out of the crowd. It probably helped that there was a running track around the pitch to put a bit of distance between us and their supporters. But there's no better way of silencing them than with a goal. When Craig delivered a long ball to the far post I knew I had a chance of getting something on it. But you knew too that the ref was going to give a free kick for the slightest contact with the goalkeeper and I was conscious of not giving him an excuse to blow his whistle. Tancredi went up for it but I had a good spring in those days and managed to head it out of his hands without fouling him. A bit of pinball in the box followed, they should've cleared it, but Nealy slotted it home.

A while later I got done by Falcao. It was a bad tackle and he knew what he was doing. I slid in to win a ball in the centre of midfield and he waited for me. He just put his foot right in and got me good and proper down the shin. I actually thought he'd broken my leg at first. I was down for a few minutes after it. Then around the half-hour mark I saw my chance for a bit of revenge. Roma had upped the tempo by now, they were chasing an equaliser. Their midfielder Di Bartolomei had dropped way back onto his centre-backs; he was taking the ball off them and spraying a lot of passes, long diagonals, especially out to Conti on the left. Anyway, they were forcing us back and this time Falcao picked up the ball outside the box. And I just ploughed into him. For all the experience gained in Europe that season, I was still a bit raw because it was a stupid thing to do. I got up from the challenge really worried because they had a free kick on the edge of the box and Falcao had a great reputation for planting them in the net from this position. I was thinking *If this goes in the top corner I am going to get slaughtered by everybody.* To make matters worse, I hadn't even hurt him. He saw me coming a mile away and evaded it easily, like the seasoned pro that he was. To my great relief he blazed the free kick miles over the bar.

Then Pruzzo levelled it just before half-time. It was a brilliant header, he managed to twist and improvise and nod it into the net. The crowd had gone quiet but now there was an unbelievable racket around the stadium. Roma then really came for us in the third quarter. This is where you're back into hold-out mode. If you can at all, just survive without conceding. Mark Lawrenson was magnificent in this period. Lawro had a tremendous game on the night. At one stage a Liverpool move broke down in midfield and suddenly there were four or five of them pouring through on the counterattack. It was a really dangerous situation and Lawro got across to make this huge tackle, sliding in from way back and deflecting the ball out for a corner. It was a perfectly timed tackle and it needed to be because it was inside the penalty area.

Our backs were to the wall for a good twenty minutes after half-time. But we kept them out and when the goal didn't come the pressure eventually subsided. It's funny the way games ebb and flow like that. Sometimes it seems as if someone has just flicked a switch somewhere and one side starts playing at a higher tempo while the other team goes into its shell. Then the reverse happens and the other side takes over. In this case, once we survived the storm, both teams became very cagey again. It was a chess match for the last quarter. No one wanted to make a mistake or really take a chance. We started getting on the ball again and playing it around without really going all out for a second goal.

Of course, Bruce was the only one not too bothered about being cautious. In the first half of extra time he came dashing out to the edge of the box to win a tackle. Then he decided to take it around Graziani, which he did, and pinged a pass to Nico in midfield! Unbelievable. He liked to play a bit, did Bruce. We were playing Sheffield Wednesday once at Anfield. Bruce had a rush of blood and came running right out of his area and over to the left-back position. There was a lad called Imre Varadi facing him and Bruce tried to dribble the ball around him. But Varadi took it off him and knocked it into the empty net at the Kop end. And Bruce came in after the game and said, 'Why didn't somebody cover for me?' Eh, because we weren't expecting you to play left-back at the time, Bruce.

But he was so agile and so athletic you'd sometimes end up standing there with your mouth open, watching him make these acrobatic saves. You really had to see him in training to see some of the leaps and saves he could pull off. And I remember a reserves game, I think it was against Leeds, and there was a shot from twenty yards that was heading straight for the top corner. Bruce just flew up and across and any keeper in the world would've been proud just to get his fingertips to the ball. The amazing thing was that he caught it and held on to it and came down with it. And the lad who had the shot was running back out to midfield and he turned to me shaking his head: 'Where'd you sign the monkey from?!' I don't know any other keeper who could've pulled off a save like that.

But it was his downfall as well from time to time because he'd be wanting to come over loads of bodies to make the catch and it just wasn't always possible. He'd drop it or miss it or something. He copped a lot of flak for his mistakes over the years, especially the early years, and he did very well to come through that period. But he had broad shoulders and a big personality; he took it on the chin and kept going.

The upside of Bruce's fearless attitude was that he was great at cutting out through balls on the edge of the box. And because he attacked crosses and high balls all the time, it took a lot of pressure off everyone too. You'd be jumping for a ball in your penalty area and next thing Bruce would be clobbering you in the head with his knees as he came to make the catch. Bruce was his own man and sometimes it got us into trouble, but it got us out of trouble a lot more often. And, as we all know, it was exactly this unorthodox mentality that made him a Liverpool legend that night in Rome.

It was hot and balmy and I don't know if we were actually fitter than Roma in extra time but we looked to have more running in our legs. But I don't really think it's got much to do with energy levels when a game reaches that stage. It's just about willpower. It's about heart taking over when the legs start struggling. Everybody's fatigued from ninety minutes of hard running, and from the nervous tension that goes with an occasion like this. Eight of our lads had played over sixty games that season. I don't think this team had the class of the team of 1987–90 but for work rate and spirit and mental toughness we were hard to beat. It was a total team performance that got us through on the night. Nothing else would've got us through it except a massive collective effort. When we were under the cosh in the third quarter it was that willpower and unity that kept Roma at bay.

In extra time Cerezo tried a shot from outside the box that Hansen got his head to. Straight afterwards Cerezo went down with cramp. Both his legs had seized up. In contrast, Lawro went flying up the middle with the ball, and they had to hack him down to stop him. You could tell that Roma were playing for penalties in extra time. The ball went behind their goal after a Liverpool attack and the ball boy was about to throw it back to the goalkeeper but Tancredi signalled to him to put it down. The boy dropped the ball and Tancredi slowly walked the fifteen, twenty yards to pick it up himself and walk back with it. They were counting down the clock.

Penalties? I'd have taken a penalty, but only if Ronnie Moran had taken out a shotgun and marched me down to the penalty spot. I'd never practised penalties and I don't think many of the other lads had either. But as far as I'm concerned you could practise penalties every day at Melwood, or indeed wherever the Roma lads trained, and it wouldn't have made any difference on the night. This wasn't about technique; it was about nerve. It's a simple thing to do, to kick a ball at a goal, but the circumstances here transformed it into a frightening task. A European Cup was at stake. Millions of people were watching around the world. The crowd in the stadium was frozen with tension; so what was it like for the players? You needed to train your brain, if you could, for a situation like this, just to stop it from turning to mush. Just to keep the negative thoughts at bay. Will I place it or hammer it? Will I hit it to his left or his right? What if he reads me, what if he guesses the right way? It takes a very clear-headed, tough-minded man to take that lonely walk, put the ball on the spot, walk back, wait for the whistle and beat the keeper. If he misses and you don't win the European Cup he'll be remembered for ever. It's an awful thing to ask of a player.

If you were to compare their technical abilities, Alan Kennedy wouldn't have been in the same league as Bruno Conti and Francesco Graziani. These were brilliant players, World Cup winners. And yet Alan scored and they missed. To be fair, Alan wasn't facing an eccentric goalkeeper from Zimbabwe who decided to unnerve the penalty-takers by chewing the net and wobbling his legs like they'd turned to jelly. It looked nuts, it *was* nuts, but it had some effect on the Italians. It must have had. Because they would have been right on the limit of their nerves already. And they were looking at something they'd never seen before; a goalkeeper behaving like that? In a penalty shootout in a European Cup final? We'll never know for sure, but it might just have tipped them over the edge. Again, no amount of practice could have prepared them for something like that.

I stood in the centre circle with the rest of the lads and watched the drama. Nico was first and that one was in the lap of the gods. But at least if he missed – which he did – we'd still have a small chance of recovering. Di Bartolomei scored Roma's first. Phil Neal was next. We expected Nealy to score because he had proven bottle and class in these situations. Then Conti missed Roma's second and we were all square. Then Souey stepped up – we just knew he'd score. Souey wouldn't crack. We knew that if he didn't score, it wouldn't be the end of his world. Which is why we knew he would score, if you know what I mean. Righetti made it 2–2 and now it was Ian Rush's turn. Rushie had scored forty-seven goals that season, we figured Rushie would get the job done. When Graziani missed we were 3–2 up with one penalty each left. Alan was up next and if he scored, we were champions.

As Belly walked up to the spot, most of us were very dubious – to say the least. We told him afterwards too, and we tell him to this day: 'I just didn't fancy ya! Don't know how you did it!' At this stage Nealy couldn't look any more. He turned his back and stared at the empty goal down at the other end. I was standing beside him and started doing a running commentary for his benefit. 'Belly's walking up with the ball now. He's putting the ball down. He's getting ready for the run-up. Here he goes an . . .' And I was gone. Soon as the ball hit the net I was gone, leaving Nealy with his back to goal waiting to hear the news. The Italians were on the other side of the centre circle. I never thought about them, never looked over. That's the game we were in, everything riding on one kick of the ball. Heads or tails, the toss of a coin, heroes for life or hurting for life. It was as cruel as that.

Once we calmed down, I was hit by a wave of exhaustion. Completely shattered. Bob Bolder, our reserve keeper, came over to me on the pitch to shake hands and I could just about raise my arm. Although I know I managed to raise it a few more times that night as the beer and champagne flowed.

Alan Kennedy deserves his place in history for hitting the penalty that made us champions of Europe. They all do. We all do, I suppose. It takes a long time for an achievement like that to sink in. Because, as ever, no sooner have you won it than you're told to forget about it and move on. So you just bury all your memories of a night like that at the back of your mind.

And actually I think you only start to put it all into perspective many years later, when you've retired and you can finally look back instead of having to look forward all the time. It's a long time ago now, twenty-seven years and counting; I don't think about it very often. But when I do, I still get a sense of deep fulfilment from it. The players who have won European Cups, it's a small, exclusive club of people. It's a good feeling to know you're one of them. And given the circumstances, I don't think there were many teams could have done it. Really, not many teams could have done it.

7

Inner Sanctum

We might have sung a song that night in Rome but I absolutely hated music in the dressing room. On match days I wanted peace and quiet. Some players liked to get pumped up but I was the other way. I wanted to be left to my own thoughts in a nice, serene atmosphere.

And usually that's what you'd get before games. Half-time, though, was a different story. This was a dressing room packed with strong characters, big egos and natural leaders. These were great players with a fierce will to win. So with that sort of personal chemistry packed into a small room, you were bound to get bust-ups. I don't mean fights. It's all gone wrong when fellas start fighting. But if things had gone wrong in the first half there'd be lots of screaming and shouting. Even if things had gone well there'd be words, strong words, not many of them polite. And Bob and Ronnie and Joe and Roy would just hang back and let us at it. Everybody could have their say. You could have the whole eleven having a go, and manager and staff would wait until we'd cleared the air before taking over.

Typical: I'm holding onto the ball while the girls are left holding the baby. Rosemarie (left) and Ann with little Janice and Paul and me in our back garden at Abbotstown Avenue.

Senior and Junior. I suppose it's true: the apple doesn't fall far from the tree.

Check out the strides! My first day at Old Trafford. I'm about to be ordered off the pitch by an angry groundsman. Shortly afterwards, the fashion police were called.

The Home Farm first team squad. Martin Murray is 3rd from left, back row; I'm 2nd from left, front row, still glued to a ball.

April '81: first game, first goal – saluting the Anfield Road End.
Peter Fox is the Stoke goalkeeper, Brendan O'Callaghan the Stoke defender.

October '81: Lansdowne Road – the famous 3–2 against the famous Platini & Co.
One of the great Irish performances.

Two elder statesmen: the great Joe Mercer and Bob Paisley present me with my Young Player of the Year award for 1981/82.

Wembley ecstasy: scoring the equaliser in the '82 League Cup final. Ray Clemence and Steve Perryman aren't sharing the joy.

April '82, Southampton at The Dell: I've just scored and the ref has just given them
a penalty to make it 2–2. I calmed down enough to hit a late winner.
If the ref didn't book me here, he should have.

May '82: we've beaten Tottenham 3–1 at Anfield and Lawro and me have
won our first championship. We both scored that day, as did Kenny.

Bob making a fuss – not! He hands me my first championship medal
and says he'll see me for pre-season in July.

September '82: many happy returns. I score twice against Southampton
at Anfield on my 21st birthday. Mark Wright is their number six.

Rome '84: Phil Neal has silenced the crowd with his early goal on an epic night.

Rome '84: the Liverpool Jocks always got a photo taken together with the latest trophy, so the Paddys decided we'd do the same. Just Lawro, me and Michael Robinson. Kenny, of course, had to ruin it.

August '85: Kenny's first league game as manager, against Arsenal at Anfield, ends with a 2–0 win. Jim Beglin's (out of picture) cross is inch perfect and I get my head on it to put us one up.

May '86, Stamford Bridge: Dalglish the player has scored the winner at Chelsea to clinch the title and launch our celebrations. A week later Dalglish the manager completes the double in his first season.

Souness and Dalglish were the worst. They were many a time nose-to-nose, screaming blue murder at each other. Phil Thompson, Phil Neal, Alan Hansen, they were very vocal too. But there was nothing personal in it. At least I don't think there was. Fellas didn't fall out after a bust-up. Souness and Dalglish were good mates, they roomed together. That was the thing I loved about Liverpool in the '80s: you could have these brutal arguments with people and then go for a pint with them afterwards. Especially if we'd won. And that's what it came down to: those rows were always about us not doing the right things, and how we could do them better in the second half, or in the next game. They were mainly about the *mechanics* of the performance.

Say we're down a goal at half-time. We have ten minutes now to sort it out so there isn't any time for pleasantries. Who's not performing? What's your problem? Where are we struggling, what can we do to sort it out? Well, I'm getting overrun here, somebody needs to double up and get round behind me. OK, I'll stand closer to you second half, I'll make sure you're covered. Or, you need to pass it to me quicker, you're always having another touch, why aren't you passing it quicker? Or, I've gone forward and you haven't dropped back, why haven't you dropped back? Those arguments were the way we managed ourselves and managed our way through games.

Footballers are great for excuses. If there's an excuse somewhere to be found, they'll find it. The weather's too cold, the ball's too hard, the pitch is too soft. It's not my fault, it's his fault. We didn't have that mentality, by and large. If someone was giving you stick, you wouldn't get away with pointing the finger at someone else: 'Well, he's not doing it either, what are you looking at me for?'

The older lads set the standard here. They didn't too often look for excuses. They were strong enough characters to know themselves when they were playing badly and to take responsibility for it. We as the novices had to take our cue from that: if we weren't doing it we weren't doing it. Fair enough. Let's try and change it. It was all about getting the result that afternoon. And that winning mentality was ingrained into our psyches as soon as we started sharing the dressing room with them. It was there already from our days in the reserves but it was hammered home here.

You didn't always need eleven players playing well every game. If you had eight, you could carry three. And there were days when it just wouldn't go well for you no matter what you tried. The ball's not coming off your foot properly, your legs are heavy, your head's not right for some reason. You didn't know when you were going to have an off day but everybody was going to have one. And for all the recriminations, if you had a bad performance there was sympathy for you too. Joe or Ronnie used to try and protect a player who hadn't done well. They'd say, 'If he has a bad day, get round him and help him 'cos you might have your bad day next week and you'll be looking at him to help you.' And Liverpool players were great at that. If somebody was going through a bad time, say if a player was getting ripped by a winger, other lads would get round and make sure he was OK and got through the bad spell and came out the other side.

You couldn't but thrive in an atmosphere like that. These lads had vast knowledge of how to win games and they were passing it on to us. But essentially, what you were being exposed to in that dressing room was peer pressure. Good peer pressure. Pressure from your peers to perform. To do the right things, make the right decisions, play honestly and own up to it if you played bad. The initial buzz you got from playing with these great players disappeared very quickly. You saw how serious they were about it, how much it meant to them, and you understood that this was business now. Points were at stake, money was at stake and there were trophies to be won.

In the three seasons between autumn 1981 and spring 1984 we were more or less untouchable. You would never have said it at the time, and I hope it's not being big-headed to say it now, but that was a Rolls-Royce team – smooth and strong and high-powered. We finished the 1982/83 season eleven points clear at the top. It would've been nearer thirty points if we hadn't mentally gone on our holidays with seven games still to play. We lost five of the last seven and drew the other two. I suppose once the job was done we switched off the engine. In 1983/84 we finished thirteen points clear to win our third successive league title and we completed a club four-in-a-row in the League Cup too.

The 1983 League Cup final against Manchester United meant a lot to me personally, having been to Manchester United all those times as a teenager. I got the winner and it was probably one of the most important goals I ever scored for Liverpool.

It was one apiece after ninety minutes. Kevin Moran had gone off injured by then, Gordon McQueen was still on the field but injured, and Frank Stapleton was operating as an emergency centre-half. In the 98th minute I was on the ball, about to thread it through to Alan Kennedy, who'd gone racing into the box. I tried to nutmeg Frank and it just bobbled back to me at a nice pace. In the corner of my eye I noticed Gary

Bailey had come too close to his near post. The ball was waiting to be hit and so I hit it, a twenty-yard curler into the top corner, far post.

It's an amazing thing to experience the effect a goal can have on a crowd. The more important the game, or the more crucial the timing, the greater the reaction. Outright euphoria and downright agony, all in a second. It's a strange kind of power that footballers can have, or sports people in general. Maybe it's like a singer singing a song and holding thousands of people in the palm of his or her hand for that moment. In the case of football, it's not just in the stadium but back home where thousands more are watching. Nowadays it's millions of people watching all over the world.

I scored seventy-three times for Liverpool and my League Cup goals in 1982 and '83 are special memories. But my all-time favourite came against United in April 1985. It was an FA Cup semi-final at Goodison Park. It didn't win us the match, and we lost the replay, but it's my favourite because I think it's the best one I ever scored for the club. It was also the 87th minute of the game, so there was a bit of drama about it too.

As soon as Sammy rolled it to me, I had it all mapped out in my head. Phil Neal was on the edge of the box with his back to the United goal. The wind was blowing into that goal and I knew that if Nealy just cushioned the ball for me I was set up to have a crack. I didn't want him to play it back to me, I just wanted him to stop it dead. I rolled it to his feet, Nealy read my intentions; he just took the pace off the ball and left it there for the strike. That's one of the pleasures of playing with great players: they know exactly what you want them to do. Everyone is on the same wavelength. I came on to the ball and bent it right-footed into the top corner at the Gwladys Street

End. It's not often you have a picture in your head of a goal and then the picture becomes a reality. That's what was so nice about it.

Three league titles, three League Cups, one European Cup in the three seasons since I'd established myself in the side. The team of this era wasn't as flamboyant as the side of 1987–90 but I think it was a harder team to beat. You had five of Liverpool's all-time great defenders in Hansen, Lawrenson, Neal, Thompson and Kennedy.

Phil Neal was just an amazing athlete. Physically and mentally he was phenomenally consistent. Nealy is so highly regarded by all the players he played with at Liverpool. We knew what he did for us: he could tackle, he could pass, he could read a game and he could score goals. A top defender and a good bloke as well.

Phil Thompson was nearing the end of a great career when I broke into the team. Tommo was obviously another big personality and a leader at the back but I remember him as much for the way he looked after young lads coming into the team. Tommo was captain at the time and he made us feel welcome. He was friendly, he'd talk to us, and he'd get you involved in things. If the lads were organising a night out, he'd make sure you were included. Not just me, he tried to look out for all the young lads coming through. I was very lucky to come to a club where there were a lot of good people around and Tommo was another of the good ones.

We weren't just hard to beat because of our defence. Up front you had Dalglish and Rush, the best striking partnership Liverpool have ever had. And in midfield you had Graeme Souness, in my opinion the greatest Liverpool player ever. A lot of people go for Kenny when this debate comes up, and Kenny had unbelievable skill and class. But I always go with Souness because of his all-round influence and leadership on the field. He was the ultimate midfield general: the best I played with, the best I've seen. He could control the flow of a game with his vision and his range of passing, which was magnificent.

But against good teams you had to win the ball before you could start playing with it. And of course this was where Souey came into his own. He could blow fellas off the ball in a tackle, and frequently did. If you wanted to play football, that was fine; if you wanted a scrap, that was fine too. Whatever way it was going to be played, Souey wanted to dominate. He wanted to be the top dog, he wanted to be the alpha male. He had a high opinion of himself and he liked being the centre of attention. He had the designer gear, the hairdryer in the dressing room and the fancy bottles of cologne. The 'tache was always nicely groomed too.

But we were never going to be bullied when he was playing – if anything, Souey was the bully. He would bully people into submission, he would stand up to anyone. And if any of the rest of us was getting a bit of treatment from an opponent, he'd be in like a shot to sort it out. In September 1982 we played Southampton at Anfield. They had a big centre-back, Chris Nicholl, and I went in pretty high on him in a tackle. Nicholl wasn't happy, he grabbed me round the neck and pushed me away. It must've been pretty close to half-time because as I was heading into the tunnel I heard these running footsteps behind me; I turned around and there was Chris Nicholl coming for me. I kind of set myself for a confrontation but then Souey arrived on the scene and grabbed me and pushed me down the tunnel and into the dressing room. He watched your back like that, did Souey, and it was another reason why we looked up to him. In May 1982 we were 2–0 down at half-time away to Tottenham. We were edging ahead in the title race but a defeat here would have put serious pressure on us with just four games remaining. Souness came off the bench in the 46th minute and changed the match. Four minutes later Dalglish scored our first goal and, eleven minutes after that, got the equaliser. It was Souness who dragged us back into that game.

Bob had made him captain the previous Christmas but I think Souey was captain in his own head long before that anyway. He relished the responsibility but I don't think it changed the way he played. When he left in the summer of 1984 he left a void that we didn't fill the following season. We won nothing that year and it spoke volumes for his influence on the team.

Souness, Dalglish and Hansen were three very proud Jocks. They thought the Scots were the master race when it came to football and they weren't shy about reminding us, especially the England internationals in the dressing room. I had a broad Dublin accent on me and if I said anything that sounded remotely funny to their ears, they'd be straight in with the jokes and the piss-takes. You were always wary about what you said in case you left yourself open. Tommo, Terry Mac, the Jocks, it was a competition between them. And in the early days, if you tried to have a go back, it'd be 'Show us your medals son' – 'Have you won anything yet?' – 'Come back to me when you've won something'. For me it was mostly in one ear and out the other, which is why I can't remember any of the quips and comebacks that were fired around in those days. But even if I could, I probably wouldn't be able to repeat any of them here anyway. Some of it was fairly raw and ruthless.

In hindsight I can see that some of the banter could be cruel and hurtful. But we didn't realise it at the time, I suppose, and it wasn't meant to put people down or damage their confidence. It was just the dressing room culture back then. And you had to suck it up. It was a case of sink or swim. If you couldn't take the banter and give it back, you were going to struggle in that environment. You just had to get used to it and get yourself a thick skin as quickly as possible.

The other thing was, you also realised that for the established players it was their way of bringing you into the fold. It was kind of a sign that they thought you were good enough to be part of the pack. The lads who weren't really going to make it, they were usually left out of the slagging matches.

And once you had a few medals won yourself, you started throwing it down to the next fresh-faced young fella coming in the door. It was always the stand-by comment when it came to opponents too. If any lad started giving you lip on the field it was 'Put your medals on the table' or 'What have you ever won?' Not very mature, I know, but it usually shut people up. I remember once Jan Molby and me were playing in an A game – we must've been coming back from injuries or something – and this lad was through on goal and managed to pull his shot wide. He came running back out and one of his team-mates said, 'Jeez, I'd have put me mortgage on you to score that one.' And Jan looked at your man and went, 'What? The full tenner?' English wasn't his first language but Jan was a fast learner. We were playing Crystal Palace one time and Ian Wright and Mark Bright were having a go at him over something. And Jan went, 'Whoa, whoa, hang on a second. Youse have a bit of a head start on me here. Youse know my name, I haven't got a fucking clue who you two are.'

These days I doubt if there's as many barbs flying around dressing rooms. First of all there's the language barrier, with all the various nationalities at English clubs now. I presume it's harder to take the mickey out of someone if they don't know what you're saying. And maybe lads today are a bit more fragile when it comes to being insulted high up and low down. When you think about it, why wouldn't they be?

But we didn't think about it as much back then. In fact we didn't think about it at all. Nothing was sacred and no one was spared. If you got hurt on the pitch you weren't supposed to show it in front of your opponents. And if you were hurt by a comment in the dressing room, you definitely didn't show it in front of your friends.

8

The Dark of Night

It's only in the years after that you get a broader perspective on things. When you're a professional footballer the last thing you have is any sort of perspective on anything. It's been drilled into you for so long that it's all about competing and winning, you end up with tunnel vision. You see nothing else but the ball, the game and the rectangle of grass.

So when I cried that night in the Heysel Stadium, I was crying for myself.

We didn't know that thirty-nine people had died. Rumours were floating around before the game that something bad was happening up above us but we were stuck in our bunker below. Some lads might have asked questions about what was going on but we were spared any of the terrible details and I just assumed it was a worse than usual case of crowd trouble. What really got me agitated was the delay and the not knowing if there was going to be a game or not. We were just left there stewing in the dressing room. It felt like an eternity to me. Standing up, sitting down, walking round in circles, getting eaten by your nerves for over two and a half hours.

Eventually the word came through that the game was going ahead and, like soldiers following orders, we didn't question it, we just got ready. It was late at night now and nothing felt right about the occasion any more. You could sense the bad vibes in the air. And when we walked on to the pitch the atmosphere was horrible. When we lined up before the game started I could feel the animosity, the hatred even, coming from the Juventus end. And then in other parts of the stadium there seemed to be no atmosphere at all. There was a really strange and unpleasant mood around the ground. It didn't feel like a European Cup final atmosphere; it didn't feel anything like the Roma game the year before. That was normal, this was different. And the only way to handle it was to do what you were trained to do: forget about the crowd, concentrate on the game. You got your professional footballer's head on and you tried to win the match.

I've never watched it on video since. Maybe one day I'll get around to looking at it but it's become the forgotten game, almost as if it never happened. Because it was Heysel, it became irrelevant as soon as it was over. And that is right and proper. It's just a footnote to the tragedy and that's where it should remain.

I think it became irrelevant for millions of people before it even started. They knew what had happened. But on the night, for those ninety minutes, it was the centre of my universe. I don't think anyone else on the pitch felt any differently either. We badly wanted to win it and so did they. I felt we were ready for Juventus having played them at their place in January in the European Super Cup. They'd beaten us 2–0 but we'd gotten a valuable insight into how they operated. They had two of the biggest stars in European football at the time in Platini and

Boniek. They had four of the Italian team that had won the World Cup in 1982: Cabrini, Scirea, Tardelli and Rossi. But we were the reigning European champions and we weren't going to take a backwards step.

It was only when you shared a pitch with him that you realised the pace of Zbigniew Boniek. The amazing thing was that he could run as fast with the ball as without it. And that's how he got the penalty. Everybody knows now it was never a penalty, Gary Gillespie brought him down at least a yard outside the box. Platini stepped up to take it and I for one never doubted that he'd score. I was equally sure that I was going to get a penalty when Bonini brought me down inside the box with about fifteen minutes left in the game. It was a nailed-on penalty. I instantly looked at the ref and I could see the panic in his face. He hesitated, looked at the linesman, and then waved play on. I was shocked he didn't give it.

If he had and we'd equalised, the game would probably have gone to extra time. But of course the last thing the authorities wanted was this game to go to extra time. We'd have still been playing at midnight if it had, and they just wanted it out of the way. I'm sorry, but I wanted it to go to extra time if that's what it took. But almost everyone was beyond caring at that stage, except me.

The Juventus players got a lot of stick afterwards for celebrating on the pitch but they could've been in the same boat as us. Maybe their dressing room had been sealed off from the tragedy the way ours was. Personally I can't condemn them for it because we probably would've celebrated as well, not knowing enough about it not to celebrate.

When I got back into our dressing room the whole emotion of the night just got to me. The long delay beforehand, the penalty that was, the penalty that wasn't; the fatigue and disappointment. I was crushed. The whole thing got on top of me in the end. While the other lads were milling about, I just disappeared into one of the cubicles in the toilet area on my own and sat down and cried. I still had my blinkers on. I was still thinking like a selfish footballer. And I cried that night because I believed I'd been hard done by: I should have had a penalty; they shouldn't have had a penalty; I could have won another European Cup.

And if someone had told me that I'd never play in Europe again I'm sure I'd have cried some more. Because playing in Europe was a magnificent experience. It was everything I thought it would be when I watched it on *Sportsnight* as a kid in Finglas and dreamed about being out there in those faraway cities, playing in the floodlights and the fog. I was twenty-three at the time of Heysel and maybe it was just as well I didn't know that my European career had ended that night.

It was only in the small hours of the morning that the scale of the tragedy finally started to dawn on us. More and more information started filtering through. Back in the hotel room you were flicking the TV channels and watching the news and the story was everywhere. I didn't understand the language of the news reports but the awful pictures told the story anyway. I was stunned at the loss of life. Governments were now involved, politicians were talking, it was an international story.

The team bus was a sombre place the next morning. People were banging on it before we left the hotel. They were angry and they were taking it out on anyone associated with Liverpool. I remember one lad banging on the window next to Roy Evans. We got a police escort to the airport and it took us straight on to the tarmac, right up to the door of the plane.

There was no passport control, no security checks, they wanted us out of Brussels as quickly as possible.

Poor old Joe Fagan was shattered by it all. It was so sad to see him hunched over and crying as we landed at Liverpool airport. That memory has never left me. He had announced his intention to retire before the final. He loved Liverpool Football Club, he had served it magnificently, and this was how it was going to end. It was all wrong. It was a terrible burden to have to take into retirement after a lifetime's service. Joe Fagan was a gentleman, he'd always been good to me, and the way his great career at Liverpool ended was just too sad for words.

9

The Green Mile

It was the greatest era in the history of Irish football and I was there. But I wasn't always involved. Some of the best highs and worst lows of my career came in a green jersey. There were times when the country was partying and I was partying with them. There were times when the country was partying and I was alone in a hotel room, miserable and frustrated.

The day before we played Egypt at Italia 90, Jack Charlton called a team meeting on the pitch in the stadium. It was 16 June. On 18 April I'd gone into a tackle with Arsenal's Paul Davis at Highbury and wound up with a hairline crack on the bone of the instep. I would miss Liverpool's last four league games but the title was more or less in the bag anyway and I set my sights on being back in time for Ireland's first ever World Cup. I'd played in six of the eight qualifiers and was captain when we beat Malta in November 1989 to qualify. I'd scored the breakthrough goal against a dogged Northern Ireland team in Dublin a month before the Malta game. I'd been in the form of my life during that campaign. Missing out now was unthinkable.

The bone healed after about four weeks and I was back running. Then I strained a thigh muscle. It often happens: coming back from one injury, you pick up another. I ran out of time for the big one, England in Cagliari, but I was on course for the match against Egypt in Palermo six days later. By the time we played a training game in Palermo I was running freely. In fact I felt great. We played twenty, twenty-five minutes and I was flying. Jack had gone with Paul McGrath and Andy Townsend in centre midfield for the England game but I figured I'd make the bench against Egypt at least.

So the day before the game Jack called the players into a circle and made his announcement. 'Same team, same subs.' I couldn't believe it. I was shocked. I'm thinking *Has he forgotten about me here or what?* There was a loose ball beside me on the grass. I picked it up and booted it as hard as I could into the top tier of the stand. Pretty stupid when you look back on it, but I did it to say, 'Look, I'm OK! My leg's all right!' And Jack turned round and said in one of his gruff angry voices, 'Who did that?' And I turned round in my gruff angry voice and said, 'I did.' And he totally dismissed me. 'Aw, just go and train or something.' And then, me being stupid, I just turned my back and started walking around the pitch on my own. And Maurice Setters, Jack's assistant, came over and said, 'Come on, do some running.' And I said, 'How can I? I'm not fit.' 'You said you were fit.' And I nodded over at Jack. 'He said I'm not fit, so I'm not fit. Right?' Maurice walked off. I assume he reported it all back to Jack.

And then Noel King came over. Kinger was brought along as part of the coaching staff and he said, 'Come on, you have to do something.' I said the same thing to Kinger. 'He said I'm not fit so I can't.' So like a big kid I just walked around the pitch on my own while the others were training. The World Cup was slipping away from me and emotions were taking over.

Later that day a bunch of reporters told me Jack had told them I was out of the squad because I wasn't fit. I told them that was his opinion. I told them that I *was* fit and able to play. That night all the lads were in their rooms at the team hotel. I was rooming with Steve Staunton but I was in no humour for sleeping. I didn't want to keep Stan awake either so I went moping around the hotel for a while. But the situation was wrecking my head and eventually I said to myself, I'm gonna have to go and see him. I went down to the restaurant and there was Jack with Maurice Setters, Mick Byrne the physio, Charlie O'Leary the kit man and Maurice Price, an FAI coach. The place was almost empty apart from them.

I went up to Jack. 'Can I have a word with you?' He grunted and nodded. But I wanted this conversation in private. 'On our own?' 'No. If you've something to say, say it here. We're all in this together.' 'I'd just like to talk to you.' He glared at me. 'If you've something to say, say it here.' It was obvious he wasn't going to budge. I turned and walked away, really boiling now. Jack was playing power games with me and I knew it. He was basically saying, 'I'm the manager, I'm in control here, and if you don't like it, that's your problem.'

I didn't like it and I did have a problem with it. Yes, we were all in it together but this was between manager and player. A kit man and a physio listening in? It was none of their business what I had to say to Jack. I'd wanted to clear the air with him, I thought it would've been the easiest thing in the world. I'd say my piece, he'd say his, then we'd move on. But Jack wanted to put me in my place.

The irony is that he put me on the bench for the Holland game four days later. Then he put me on the pitch with a half-hour to go. But I think my World Cup must've been jinxed from the start because Niall Quinn equalised nine minutes after I came on and the rest of the game was a bit of a non-event. Word leaked on to the field that England were leading Egypt 1–0. If England won that game, a draw would suffice for Holland and Ireland to both go through to the last sixteen as well. So the two sets of players just looked at each other. No one needed to say anything, it was just body language, winks and hand signals. *Let's take it easy here.* Basically both sides downed tools. It was the only time I've ever seen it happen in a game I played in. At the same time there was a bit of a culture gap between the Dutch and the Irish. I think we were just a little bit *too* shameless for their liking. Because we'd pass the ball across the back four and back to Packie Bonner – the keeper could pick up back-passes in those days – throw it out, pass it across, back to Packie. And they're not comfortable with this at all. They're like, 'But you have to try and *look* as if you're competing. You have to make *some* effort!' They were getting the ball and pinging it around everywhere but they were only trying to look respectable. We were being dishonest in a more honest sort of a way, if you like.

That was my only appearance at Italia 90. Jack had his mind made up already. I heard afterwards that I wasn't two minutes on the pitch when he turned round and said, 'Look. I told you he's not fit.' I was sub for the Romania and Italy games but I think that was just to keep me placid, and maybe keep the press off his back. I'd say that was his thinking: 'If I leave him on the bench at least he's not going to come shouting and moaning to me.'

Jack wasn't finished with his fun and games either. Every afternoon I would go for extra fitness work, doing what exercises I could in this crappy little hotel gym which kids wouldn't have used, it was that bad. One night the lads were allowed out after dinner. It was a free night and we could relax and have a few beers. As I was leaving the table Jack said to me, 'Maurice will see you in the gym in half an hour.' I'm thinking to myself *He wants me in the gym at this hour?* But I wasn't in any position to question him so I said OK. I went up to the room, got my gear together and was ready to leave when Stan arrived back. He told me to put the bag down. 'They're winding you up. You don't have to go to the gym. Jack was taking the piss.' Apparently he and his mates had a good old laugh after I left the dining room.

The tournament rolled on and I watched from the dugout while the lads performed their heroics. A part of me was jealous. I wanted to be out on that football pitch with them, not sitting on a bench and then running out and trying to share in all the joy that they were feeling. After the penalty shootout against Romania I came charging out of the dugout like everybody else and jumped on top of everyone and cheered and celebrated. But you don't feel much joy when you go back to your room that night. You've had your few pints and you're thinking *This is desperate, this. Hang around now for another game and not be picked and not be involved.* Horrible. You don't want the lads to lose, you really don't, but there's something inside you that's saying, 'You know, maybe if they draw I might get in the next game. Or someone might pick up a knock. Something might happen and we'll kick on from there.' I know it's selfish but I was twenty-eight pushing twenty-nine and this might have been my only chance of playing in a World Cup.

What made it worse was that you knew nobody else cared, apart from family and friends. Nobody was listening because everybody was on the bandwagon. 'We're on a roll here, we're having a brilliant time!' It was like being at a great party but you're only drinking water while everyone else is having a ball. Because deep down I knew that the lads were getting on fine without me. The fact was, Andy had come into the team and was doing a good job, he was doing the job that Jack wanted. Getting around the pitch, getting his tackles in, him and Paul were doing a great job. And Jack was thinking, 'Why should I break this up? There's no point in breaking it up.' That's how the game works and there was no getting around that either. The show was moving on. The lads were doing well. They reached the quarter-finals of the World Cup and my problems didn't amount to a hill of beans.

I felt they were robbed against Italy in the quarter-final. I thought the referee was a disgrace. I don't know if it passed people by or what, but I thought he absolutely robbed us on the night. I was livid at the final whistle. I went on to the pitch and started shouting at him and giving him the money sign – rubbing my thumb and fingertips together. He gestured back that he was going to book me if I didn't clear off. But I suppose, playing Italy in Rome, there was no way we were ever going to come out the right side of that result.

And then it was over. One day you're playing a game, you go in for a tackle, you come out of it limping, and the consequences are massive. Some players go in for a tackle and never play another game. The consequences of that innocuous tackle with Paul Davis weren't as serious as that. But Italia 90 was the worst moment of my professional football career and, to be honest, it hurts me still whenever I think about it.

Mind you, no matter how low you're feeling, you're never too far away from a laugh in football. And one of the funniest things I ever saw happened in that same crappy gym in Palermo. Me and Mick Byrne were doing weights one day and Mick was pumping iron as if he was Arnold Schwarzenegger. He was sitting at this chest-exercise machine where you grip the handles far apart and pull them in until your arms are in front of your face. And Mick was working his arms in and out, giving it socks, when the nail holding up the weight plates fell out of the hole. Suddenly Mick was pumping air instead of iron. There was no pressure on his arms at all but it was too late to stop and he smashed himself on both sides of the head with the handles. It just went boinnngggg! Next thing he'd split both his eyebrows, matching cuts on both sides. And the blood started to trickle out and he was effing and blinding and his head was in his hands. It was killing him but I couldn't stop laughing. I was on the ground laughing, practically thumping my fist off the floor. He rushed off to the doctor and I couldn't go with him I was laughing so much. Poor old Mick had to get stitches, matching stitches on both eyebrows. But seeing it happen was pure comedy. Yeah, I know, we're easily amused, us footballers. But I have to say, even to this day I still have a chuckle when I think of Mick sitting at that weights machine and nearly knocking himself out.

I won my 39th cap that night against Holland in Palermo. I had five more years ahead of me in international football and in that time I picked up just fourteen more caps. The wear and tear of ten seasons started to take its toll. I had numerous injuries. I played just four out of the twelve qualifying games for USA '94. But after three years of physio, x-rays, doctors and rehab, I finally turned a corner in the second half of the 1993/94 season. I featured in fifteen of Liverpool's last sixteen games and played in international friendlies against Russia, Holland and Germany in the spring/summer of 1994.

But I knew before the World Cup that I was now well down the pecking order. Andy and Roy Keane had developed a strong partnership in centre midfield and I was going to struggle to fit in anywhere else either. So I went to America with a different mind-set to Italia 90. I knew I wasn't going to be in the first team anyway so I just decided to go and enjoy it as much as I could. I was on the bench for all four games and saw sixteen minutes of action against Norway in the third group game. I would've loved to have played more, if only because the pitches were magnificent. They were perfect. You didn't have to even *think* about passing a ball on those carpets.

But good and all as they were, we still didn't pass it enough. We should have passed it a lot more right throughout Jack's reign – but especially in the heat of an American summer. We should have kept the ball more, played it around more and let our opponents do a bit of chasing for a change. But, constantly kicking it back to them in that heat, it was just impossible. For the likes of Stan and a few more of the Irish lads it was almost a form of cruelty out there, having them running around in that heat, giving the ball away and then chasing after it.

But we were all too set in our ways. Jack was well over eight years in the job by then and we all knew the drill. When you got the chance, put the ball in behind their full-backs and then push up on them. Put 'em under pressure. Because Jack felt that all international full-backs thought they could play and would try and play their way out of there. And if you put them under pressure further up the pitch then you could get on the ball and try and do something from there. But it wasted an awful lot of energy. Your front men are putting them under pressure and you're following up behind to put them under pressure in midfield. As a midfielder, you weren't told to come and look for the ball from your full-backs. Our full-backs would play those balls down the line behind their full-backs and you as a midfielder would push up and try and win it when it came back out of there.

So: put it in there, everybody push up, block them in, keep them in the corners; run the channels, run the lines, run till you drop.

But that wasn't how I wanted to play football and it certainly wasn't how we played it at Liverpool. At Liverpool we wanted to keep possession of the ball at all times. Jack's argument was that we were giving it back to them in an area where they might give it back to us if we harried them enough. But we already had the ball – why do you want to give it back?! I always had reservations about that style and sometimes I wonder if Jack picked up on it from my body language or whatever. I mean, he knew that the way I played at Liverpool was the direct opposite of his style. And I'm not sure if he ever really trusted me to carry out his orders. But I think *he* could have trusted *us* a bit more. Because we had players who could play proper football. And I just wonder if we'd been trusted a little bit more with the ball, when to pass, what ball to pick out, would it have made it easier to play and easier to watch. You know, give us a little bit of credit here, Jack.

It wasn't even a case of trusting us that we could pass the ball; just trust us that we will not pass the ball in bad areas. That's what Jack hated, losing a ball across midfield. Playing a crossfield ball, rolling it say to Ray Houghton's feet and a fella comes in and steals it and everybody is taken out of the game. Jack hated that and he was right. But trust me that I wouldn't do that! I'm not going to put a ball at risk if I think a fella's going to intercept it. Give me a bit of credit. I didn't do that at my football club, I'm not going to do it at international level. At the same time I shouldn't have to put it in the corner all the time for people to chase it down there.

But if you wanted to play for Ireland, that's what you had to do. And again, not many people cared one way or another. Jack's way was working. We started winning loads of games when he took over. We started picking up confidence and momentum and soon the whole thing took on a life of its own. At Lansdowne Road you'd have a full house behind you roaring their heads off. We were hitting long balls, Packie was pushing everybody up and booming it down and everybody was excited and we were getting results.

And despite my reservations, I was happy to go along for the ride too. I knew, we all knew, that something special was happening. We didn't know where it would take us but you definitely didn't want to miss out on it. In the end it was the trip of a lifetime. Jack brought us to the highest level in the game, he opened up a whole new world for us of big-time international football. A lot of the lads, he transformed their careers and improved their lives. The success, the fame, the glamour, the extra money – it all happened under him. We were on a roll those years and we had a ball.

For those of us who'd known the lean years, it was even more enjoyable. I made my senior international debut in a friendly against Czechoslovakia in April 1981. I'd made my first-team debut for Liverpool less than a month earlier. A crowd of about

8,000 turned up at Lansdowne that day. I came on after sixty-three minutes for Gerry Daly. Da was bursting with pride that day. All the family were. For anyone brought up in Dublin's traditional football heartlands, getting capped for your country was the ultimate honour. Ireland was one of the minnows in world football at the time but that didn't matter. Playing for the senior international team brought its own status and prestige. It was a landmark for me and my folks were proud people that night.

But I was nineteen, it was all new to me, Ireland had an established core of players and socially I felt like a bit of a stranger. On the pitch it was different. I made my first start in October 1981 in that famous 3–2 win over France at Lansdowne and the atmosphere was fantastic. All of a sudden you were facing stars of the European game. Michel Platini and Maxime Bossis played that day for France and I got the great Bossis' jersey afterwards. A month earlier we'd drawn 2–2 in Rotterdam against a Dutch side that contained the likes of Arnold Muhren, Frans Thijssen, Johnny Rep, Ruud Krol and Rene van der Kerkhof. I came on midway through the second half for Mick Martin. Those were the last games in the qualifying campaign for the 1982 World Cup and we came agonisingly close to making it. It would've been brilliant to get there but I don't remember brooding over it for too long. It must have hurt the veterans of that Irish team but I hadn't put in the hard years of disappointment like they had.

And anyway, I was still trying to make my way at Liverpool. I still hadn't nailed down a place in the first team by then and once I did, I was swept along in the chase for the title that 1981/82 season. This is what happened at Liverpool. Points were precious, they wanted you fit and they wanted you playing every game. They had first call on your services. After the Czechoslovakia game I could've picked up a few more caps in friendlies that May but Liverpool still had the small matter of a European Cup final. I was on the bench for the last two league games of the season and was brought to Paris for the showdown with Real Madrid. I missed those summer games with Ireland, and this became something of a pattern.

My international career lasted fourteen years. The Republic of Ireland played something like 120 games over that period. I played 53 of those games; I started just 40. That's a poor return, all told. Trying to make sense of those stats, I went back and checked on a lot of the games I missed. Sometimes, as in the World Cups, I just wasn't selected. In the vast majority of cases I was injured. If I didn't play in a midweek international, the records show I didn't play for Liverpool the previous Saturday either. I could've picked up more caps in end-of-season friendlies but Liverpool were usually involved in competitions right through to May. And if we'd wrapped up the title with a few league games to spare, I often didn't play in those games because I needed to fix something – a bad ankle, groin strain, Achilles, whatever. A lot of the time you were playing with some injury or another and this was a chance to recuperate.

Liverpool had a reputation for pulling out players on an international week but all I can say in my case is that it only happened in friendlies – and very seldom even on these occasions. One such occasion would have been a friendly against Algeria on Wednesday, 28 April 1982. I played the previous Saturday against Southampton and the following Saturday against Nottingham Forest. So did Mark Lawrenson. There was no way in hell we were going to be allowed to travel to

Algiers, even if we wanted to, which we didn't. We had six games left in the league, four away from home, and were dead set on winning it. I can't remember if Liverpool even bothered to give us phantom injuries, or just said straight out that they weren't releasing us – in those days the rules on releasing players for international friendlies weren't as strict as they are now.

We wrapped up the title with one game to spare. That was against Middlesbrough on 18 May and I didn't play because the job was done, we'd won the title, and I needed to rest an injury of some sort. I rested it up by going on the piss with the Liverpool lads in Middlesbrough. Roughly about the same time, the Ireland squad was en route to South America for that infamous tour that took in Chile, Brazil and Trinidad & Tobago. Where would I rather have been? What do you think? I'd have three more caps to my name now, but every season at Liverpool was long and hard and I needed every day of the summer to rest, heal, and get ready for the following season.

Later that year, in November 1982, Liverpool played Shamrock Rovers in a friendly at Glenmalure Park. I was back in my home town but it didn't feel like it. I'd missed an important European Championship qualifier against Spain a week before the Rovers game, and another against Holland in September. In both cases I didn't play for Liverpool the previous Saturday, nor was I a sub either. I'd picked up a knock on the knee a week or so before the Spain game and I missed the Holland game because of a freak accident on the night of the Charity Shield a month earlier.

We beat Tottenham 1–0 at Wembley that day, got the train back to Liverpool and went out celebrating. A few hours later – a good few hours later – I went home in a taxi with a few friends. I got out and said my goodbyes and my friend slammed the door shut. Unfortunately my hand hadn't cleared the door. My ring finger got jammed in it. Instinctively I yanked it away, howling with pain, and the top of it, the part around the nail, came clean off in a lump. My friend picked it up off the taxi floor and we went straight to hospital, where the doctors sewed it back on. I had to wait a few weeks to see if it would join back with the finger. But it never took. The top went black and then dead. So I had to go back in to have it amputated. They managed to save a bit of the nail but to this day, once the weather turns cold I can feel it in that fingertip, or what's left of it. I had to miss a few games after the operation, the doctors didn't want the risk of me falling on it or catching it in anything. So, I missed Swansea at the Vetch Field and Ireland *vs* Holland in Rotterdam.

Anyway, the Shamrock Rovers fans weren't impressed with my recent no-shows. Every time I touched the ball in the first half I was booed and barracked. Pretty soon the chant went up from the crowd. 'Why don't you play for Ireland? Why don't you play for Ireland?' I could hear it loud and clear. Around the half-hour mark I had a shot on goal; it was blocked, the rebound fell to Rushie and he tucked it home. On our way back out to the centre circle I gave the fans the finger – maybe two fingers, I can't remember. But I am fairly certain that I didn't use the finger that caused all the problems in the first place. Maybe I should have – I'm sure the Rovers lads would've understood then. It was the only time in my career that I ever gave any fans a bit of stick back.

'Ronnie! Don't be backheeling the ball! You can't backheel the ball on a pitch like this!' Our manager Eoin Hand was going mad at me. It was March 1983, and we were playing Malta in

Valetta in a European Championship qualifier on a pitch that was actually dangerous. It was unplayable, holes and ruts and divots everywhere. The stadium was a building site and the day before there was rubble and bricks and all sorts of building material still on the field. They cleared most of it away but you could've done your ankle or knee on it at any stage. You had to play on it to realise how bad it was. Then there was a gale blowing which whipped up a bit of a sandstorm, the Malta players were getting stuck into us, and in the middle of it all I was trying some sort of fancy backheel. It's no wonder Eoin flipped. This was a horrible match and we were in real danger of being embarrassed by a useless team. Frank Stapleton's winner in the 89th minute is still remembered, if only because of the sheer relief it brought. And how did he score it? With a backheel.

It was two years since I'd made my debut but Malta was only my fifth cap. I picked up my sixth a month later against Spain in Zaragoza and it would be another full year before I picked up my seventh. Most of the rest of 1983 was lost to the pelvic injury that seriously threatened my career. Spain beat us 2–0, Holland beat us 3–2 in Dublin in October and the lights went out on another qualifying campaign.

I wasn't at Dalymount Park that day and, to be honest, I probably didn't care. I wanted my career back, I wanted my injury to go away. But even if I had been fit, I think emotionally I was still a semi-detached international player in those years. All the fun was at Liverpool. I was loving it there. I was with a brilliant team at a famous club; we were playing scintillating football and we were winning trophies every season. Playing for Ireland was a good learning experience. You were playing against the best players of every country now. Club teams in England, they usually had a few weak players, the standard wasn't as high. International players were better, they had more knowledge and experience and their teams were harder to break down. So it was a step up in class and I learned from it. But it wasn't very enjoyable. I never seemed to fully settle into the Irish scene in those early years. I wasn't enjoying the training, I wasn't enjoying being a sub and I wasn't enjoying the general atmosphere around the set-up.

And maybe it showed because I was in and out of the team for the 1986 World Cup qualifying campaign. We finished second bottom of the group and Eoin's time in charge ended with the 4–1 home defeat to Denmark in November 1985. The three most-capped players in the Irish team that day, apart from Tony Grealish, were Liam Brady, Frank Stapleton and Dave O'Leary. We had a decent team in those years and there's been plenty of speculation that the problem at the time was in the dressing room. That the senior players were too strong and the manager was too weak. I've never seen it that way. I always thought that Eoin had fair enough control over the players he had there. The lads seemed to like him and get on well with him. Eoin was the manager and he picked the team as he saw fit. I didn't see while I was there that they were running the show. The problem basically was that we weren't good enough. If you keep falling short, you can't just be unlucky all the time, although they *were* unlucky a couple of times. But if you didn't get the amount of points you needed to go through, maybe you just weren't good enough in the end. We had top players, like Liam and Frank and Dave and Lawro, but there were a lot of good teams in Europe at the time who were better. I think if you're good enough you'll get there and we just came up a bit short in terms of overall quality.

The other issue we possibly had in those years was self-belief. I think there was a bit of a defeatist attitude with Ireland. We never really *felt* we belonged in the big league. Because it was a small country with no tradition of making it to major championships, deep down we didn't really feel that we belonged in a big tournament with the likes of Germany or Brazil or Italy or Argentina. It was probably a subconscious thing: Ireland are not really supposed to be in these big tournaments because we're only a small country and no one has ever done it before. Deep down I think the main consensus was, 'We'll give it a go. Probably won't get there but we'll give it a go.'

Then along came Jack. Now Jack had won a World Cup. And Jack felt he was entitled to be at every major tournament. Eoin wasn't like that, loud and brash and full of his own importance. Jack walked into our dressing room like he owned it. And players pick up on that sort of attitude. They feed off it. And Jack was always right. Even when he was wrong he was right. And he was big enough and stubborn enough to say, 'This is how I'm gonna do it. If you don't wanna do it, I'm not gonna play you.' He believed it would work. He believed it in his bones. And he passed that belief on to us.

The friction between me and Jack didn't begin at Italia 90. We didn't get off to a great start in his first year because again I was missing games due to injury and club commitments. Our first competitive game was away to Belgium in September 1986. I replaced Tony Galvin on the left side of midfield with ten minutes to go. It was the first qualifier on the road to Euro '88 and it was the day Liam converted a penalty in the 89th minute to earn us a 2–2 draw. In February '87 we notched our first big victory under Jack, beating Scotland at Hampden Park. In my opinion that was one of the best Irish teams ever fielded. If you look at the names that played that day, our team was packed with quality and we delivered one of the best ever away performances by an Irish team: Bonner, McGrath, McCarthy, Moran, Whelan, Houghton, Lawrenson, Brady, Galvin, Stapleton, Aldridge.

I played left-back that day because Chris Hughton was injured and when we played Bulgaria in Sofia that April, I started right midfield because Ray Houghton was injured. I was at left-back again for the return game with Belgium in Dublin four weeks later.

By now it was becoming clear to me that if Jack had everyone available, I wouldn't be in his first eleven. Next up was a friendly against Brazil in May and I wanted to play in it because any player in his right mind would want to play against Brazil. But Jack came up to me in the airport hotel that morning and said he was putting me on the bench. Dave Langan would start instead. 'Langy's fit, I'm thinking of playing him left-back and I'll put you sub.' And he gave me all this shite about how this was a brilliant idea. 'I can have you on the bench and bring you on in any position, it'll be great.' I was pissed off listening to this. I heard him out and then I said, 'Jack, listen to me, if that's your decision, that's your decision. But I've played left-back, wide right, wide left, centre midfield. I've played everywhere that you've asked me to play and I've not let you down. And now Langy's fit, you want to put him straight back in the team! I don't think you're right, I think you're giving me a load of crap here.'

It's fair to say he was taken aback. I said, 'Why can't *I* start off left-back, I can still go to any position anywhere else on the pitch if you want me to? It's your decision, it's up to you.' Then I walked off. That was before lunch. I was still fuming during lunch because I felt he was trying to fob me off with this nonsense. I think I was more annoyed about that, Jack thinking that I was going to fall for this crap that putting me on the bench was a great idea. I should be delighted! It was a load of garbage and I told him so.

The big surprise was that Jack backed down. After lunch I was told by Mick Byrne that Jack wanted to see me. So I went to him and he said, 'Look, I've listened to you and I've thought about it and you're right. You haven't let me down, you've played wherever I've asked, so you're gonna start.' And that's the only reason I played that day. If I'd said nothing to him I wouldn't have played. But that's how far back the friction went between me and Jack. And the next time I challenged him, three years later in Italy, he didn't back down.

But I was still depending on injuries to get into the team. I played left-back when Chris Hughton was out, and in centre midfield it would've been two from Paul McGrath, Liam Brady and Lawro if everyone was available. I don't think I'd have started any game in Euro '88 had Liam and Lawro not missed out. In January of that year Mark sadly played his last game for Liverpool because of a ruptured Achilles that more or less ended his career. Injury and suspension would also rule Liam out of the tournament. They were two of the best players in England at the time and I don't think people ever fully appreciated how big a loss they were to the team. But it left the door open for me and in the last two friendlies before the tournament Jack put me centre midfield. I was in. And I was determined to stay there. I had a point to prove, not just to Jack but to Kenny, who'd left me out of the Liverpool side for the FA Cup final with Wimbledon.

*

By now the country was going crazy. Ireland had reached its first major tournament, the people were on a high and the atmosphere was something else. In the squad we soaked it all up. You could feel we were on the brink of something special. You had strong characters in that squad, the likes of Mick McCarthy and Kevin Moran at the heart of the defence who you knew would put their heads on the line to keep a ball out of the net. And having strong people like that playing behind you, it gave you confidence in midfield to go and play as much as you could. Kevin had a Dublin accent, Mick had a Yorkshire accent, but it didn't matter what accent you had. You are what you are as a player and pulling on a different jersey won't change that. If you're flaky in one jersey you'll be flaky in another; if you've got guts and heart it'll shine through no matter who you're playing for. In that team we had strong characters who wanted to win.

The game against England in Stuttgart was one of the great days and nights. But we were lucky. In the end we got away with it. Me and Paul were up against Bryan Robson and Neil Webb in midfield. It was always going to be a hell of a battle with Robbo on the other side but I fancied it. Me and Paul against anybody! You wouldn't have been fazed coming up against anybody with Paul in midfield beside you; the man had such power and class.

We were staying in Finnstown House hotel near Dublin once, the Ireland squad. It was a lovely country house that was built originally a few hundred years earlier. The word going around the squad was that the house was haunted. One day a few lads were joking that they'd heard strange sounds in the middle of the night. And then Jack piped up: 'It's not haunted. That's just Paul sneaking back in at four in the morning.' We all laughed because none of us had any idea at the time what Paul was going through. The full extent of his problems with alcohol only came out years later. We had many a good chat, the two of us, but he kept to himself too and spent a lot of time in his room. He used to even eat his meals alone in his room sometimes. You look back now and you understand why; a lot of it makes sense now. He was having his struggles and it must have been desperately tough for him.

In theory it should be one rule for all in any team squad. But no one ever questioned why special allowances were being made for Paul McGrath. If it had been almost any other player, people would probably have been grumbling about it. But he was a great lad and he was a special player and it was never an issue. We knew he needed an extra bit of looking after and it wasn't even up for discussion. If he went missing you'd have a bit of gossip going round the squad the next day. 'Did you hear about Paul last night?!' And we'd have a bit of a chuckle about it. Then it'd be, 'Will he be OK for Wednesday?' We always wanted him in the team. The man was world class. And to think he was this good with all his problems, not to mention the knees that seemed to be tormenting him for as long as I knew him. You felt sad when you found out afterwards how much he'd been suffering through the glory years. But I can't think of another player who is loved as much in Ireland as he is. And it was an absolute privilege to play alongside him.

Not a lot was said in the dressing room before the England game. Not a lot needed to be said. It was one of those steely atmospheres you get occasionally in a dressing room where the silence tells you all you need to know about the mood: this was a major game, and we were ready for it. I remember feeling the same atmosphere among the Liverpool players that night in

Rome in 1984. But for an Ireland team to play England in a major tournament with the world watching, this was as big as it gets. We knew the whole country back home was coming to a standstill for the game. This was bigger than football, bigger than sport. It was a national event; there was history in the making.

We all had our own private agendas too: none of us wanted to be going back to our clubs for pre-season having to face the England internationals if they'd turned us over in a game of this magnitude. That was an awful thought. The banter would be unbearable. They'd be ripping us to shreds and we'd have to grin and bear it. There was plenty of motivation on that front.

And of course the English press helped us as well. They were talking about England winning the European Championships outright. Ireland were the plucky underdogs, they'd go and enjoy themselves, they'd bring a bit of colour, etc. etc. The thing was, we didn't feel like underdogs at all. We had players from Liverpool, Manchester United, Celtic, Spurs, Arsenal and Everton in our team. It wasn't pie in the sky, thinking we could beat them, it was a very realistic possibility for us. And it would be one of the biggest games in any of our careers, for club or country.

I didn't know leaving the dressing room that day that we were going to win the game; I knew for sure we were going to give an almighty performance. We all knew too that the commitment and effort would have to be immense. They would have a slight edge on us in terms of creativity with Barnes and Beardsley, Waddle and Lineker, in their team. We'd have to make up for that gap by running ourselves into the ground; we'd have to tackle anything that moved; we'd have to get our bodies in the way of shots. And Ray Houghton's early goal gave us even more incentive to do that. We had something to hold on to.

It took its toll, all that effort, and when Glenn Hoddle came on for England after an hour they started to turn the screw. Jack's golden rule was not to give any team room to play and as we tired, Hoddle started getting on the ball and picking passes. We couldn't get close enough to him and England created a lot of chances in the last half-hour. But that was the day Packie Bonner had one of his great games. When they broke through our lines, Packie stood up and kept them at bay. We held out, we just about survived. We shaded it, I believe, because we had a bit more passion and desire. We wanted it that little bit more. In a 1–0 game, that was the difference.

England in Stuttgart is the number one game of my international career. Most games when they're over go into the record books and are forgotten. This one will always be remembered. It had such an impact. It's not just part of sporting history but probably part of Irish history. If it had ended in a draw, if Gary Lineker had taken one of his chances, it would have faded away by now. The difference in winning it is that twenty years later people still come up to you and talk about it.

The team hotel that night was packed. And all the lads were joining in with the fans and having a drink and a singsong. You wouldn't see it now. You wouldn't see the players in among all the fans, just mingling with them and chatting and joking and signing a thousand autographs. It was just a brilliant night. Jack had a curfew for us, around midnight I think, and eventually we started peeling away from the party and heading to our rooms. The one standout memory I have is getting the lift up and stepping out on to the landing, only to be confronted by a very bizarre sight. This figure was running down the corridor with a black blanket round his shoulders and trailing behind him like a cape. It was Tony Galvin. And he was there on his own. And he was running up and down singing, 'I'm a bat! I'm a bat! I'm a bat!' And I was looking at him, totally puzzled at first, before I cracked up. And he went by me again. 'I'm a bat! I'm a bat!' And then he disappeared round the corner. It was hilarious. It was mad. But on the night, it all seemed to make sense. Tony had a really good tournament. There weren't many players who could get crosses in the way he did. He did a great job for us in those years.

Three days later we faced the USSR in Hanover. It's twenty-three years and counting since I scored *that* goal. If I had a pound for every time someone asked me about that moment . . . And that's all it was, a moment. But on a football field a lot can happen in a moment. Footballers have to process in their brains a lot of information in milliseconds. You're always computing angles and space and movement and weight of pass.

I was standing on the edge of the box. I was watching Mick wind himself up for a long throw from the left. And I was being tracked by Mikhailichenko, a big blond fella who later went to Rangers. And I was darting here and there, trying to shake him off. I shot out in front of him, he followed and then I dropped in behind him. Mick launched the ball and at that point you don't know where it's going to land. You're just wondering, will I have to fight him for it, will I head it, where's it going to drop? And then I saw that the ball was arriving in exactly my little pocket of space and that Mikhailichenko was going to be caught out. And it was only then that the idea flashed up: maybe I can hit this. I was never afraid to try things. If you make an eejit of yourself, you make an eejit of yourself, but people soon forget it. So in that split second I made my mind up and got my body in position. People say it was a classic overhead kick but it wasn't. My back wasn't to the goal. I was side-on; it was a side-on bicycle kick. And I didn't catch it clean. I caught it high on the foot, where the ankle meets the shin, and it might have caught a little bit of the shin guard too. But that's what made it float beyond the reach of Rinat Dasaev, the great Russian goalkeeper. I had a volley in the second half which I caught much cleaner but it more or less flew straight at him and he was able to turn it over. But the first one: the ball flew into the net and that moment became for me a moment in time. I feel blessed to have scored it and I feel privileged that people remember it to this day.

The only downside was that they equalised. Other than that it would have been a perfect day. Because that was one of the greatest ever football displays by an Irish team. We played much better than we did against England. I don't think I've seen many Irish performances that come anywhere near it. The long ball went out the window that day. Kevin Sheedy was in centre midfield with me, you had Ray Houghton and Tony Galvin on the wings, and we just passed the ball. Frank Stapleton and John Aldridge were up front and they could hold it up and bring people into play. Everything just clicked. We created chance after chance and then we just slipped up defensively one time and they scored. That's what happens at international level. One mistake and you're punished. But we controlled that game for long periods and it was a huge disappointment only to come out of it with a draw.

Everyone was buzzing about the performance afterwards, but continuing with that style of play was never on the cards. We all loved the way we played that day but we never sat down and said, 'Let's just pass it more, let's not listen to Jack.' It wasn't on the agenda for the Holland game. And anyway, I'm sure there were times against Russia when the full-backs put it into the corners and the rest of us pushed up. We wouldn't just have abandoned it completely. It would've been a more modified version with more emphasis on playing our way through midfield. And that's how football should be played: if there are times to hit long balls in behind, hit them long in behind. If there's time and space to pass it, pass it.

I think the tank was running low by the time we faced the Dutch. We'd played England on 12 June, USSR on 15 June and now it was Holland on 18 June. You chase hard for an hour and a half against England, you do it again for an hour and a half against Russia, how long can you keep doing it? It was a really hot day and my legs weren't feeling the same as they had against England. I was feeling very leggy in fact, the zip was gone out of them.

And Holland were a class above us. Half the time you couldn't get the ball off them. We were rocked back on our heels, we couldn't get out, they just kept coming at us. And they were still fresh, they'd been keeping the ball for two games while we'd been chasing, chasing, chasing. We just didn't have it to give any more. And people forget that, physically, Holland were a big, powerful team. Gullit was huge, Rijkaard, Koeman and van Basten too. I've got a photo of me and Gullit going for a header. My feet are two foot off the ground and yet Gullit is so far above me his feet are up by my chest. That was an outstanding Dutch team. Jan Wouters did a great job as the defensive midfielder and they had class all over the field. But it still took a late goal for them to beat us 1–0 and knock us out of the tournament. They beat Russia in the final so we were in top company in that group and I think we did ourselves proud.

Euro '88 was one of the best times of my life. It was just magnificent, by far and away the best experience of my international career. It's right up there with anything I did in club football. You had your country behind you, you had a brilliant bunch of team-mates, off the pitch and on, and it was one fantastic week. The homecoming crowned it. A million people on the streets of Dublin. We were utterly amazed by the scenes. You felt on top of the world.

I suppose the few sherbets we'd consumed that day added to the good vibrations. As it happened, myself, Aldo and Ray Houghton were booked on a late flight to Liverpool that night. We made it back out to Dublin airport and it wasn't long after take-off that Rayzor decided that a visit to the toilet was in order. So he climbed across me and Aldo and just as he got to the front of the plane he turned around and started singing at the top of his voice. 'Who put the ball in the England net? I did, I did.' There was a load of Scousers on the plane and they all started joining in. Rayzor was up the top conducting the choir. There were a fair few encores. So by the time we landed, everyone was still flying, in their own way.

Our wives were there to pick us up in Liverpool. I was first through customs, well oiled but holding it together. Rayzor came through next, not totally steady on his feet, shirt and tie a bit scattered. We waited for Aldo in arrivals. Five minutes later we heard this commotion, fellas shouting and singing, and next thing we saw a bunch of the same Scousers pushing Aldo through on a trolley with his legs up in the air laughing his head off. That just about put the tin hat on it. Aldo off his trolley on a trolley.

It was the end of one adventure but it was really only the beginning. As a team we were bursting with ambition and confidence now. We were also seen in a different light by other teams after Euro '88. Ireland were a threat now in international football. We were in the big league, we were rated, and we were respected. And now we wanted more of the same. If the European Championships were this big, then what would a World Cup be like? I couldn't wait to find out. I suppose that's why Italia '90 hurt so much. I knew what I was missing.

The bandwagon rolled on to USA 94 but my career was running out of road. I played just twice more for Ireland after that and by then it was all going downhill. Jack recalled me to the squad in June 1995 for the European qualifiers against Liechtenstein and Austria. Several players were out injured and I was awarded the captain's armband. But I'd spent the season at Southend and I was a long way away from the glory days.

Still, Liechtenstein was bound to be a comfortable return to the international arena. They were amateurs, they were terrible, they weren't even big enough to be minnows. But I'd imagine that the Liechtenstein players who played us that night in Eschen are still talking about it. They might even be regretting that they didn't win. They had a couple of chances to score, completely against the run of play, while we bombarded them. We had twenty corners, we had sixteen attempts on target, it was a siege. But we couldn't get the early breakthrough and the longer they survived, the more they started putting their bodies on the line. Their keeper was inspired, he pulled off save after save. And with every chance we missed, the more anxious we became. We just kept lobbing the ball up to Niall Quinn for knockdowns and they kept scrambling it away. We kept trying to put it in behind their full-backs but the whole team was camped on the edge of the box and it was nigh-on impossible to get it in behind them.

I remember at one point screaming at Stan Staunton and Gary Kelly to stop knocking in long balls. We couldn't keep doing it. All we had to do was pass it around, play a bit of football and lure them into tackles further up the pitch. But we couldn't change. Everyone was programmed to play only one way. It was embarrassing that we couldn't change our style of play against a team like Liechtenstein. But not half as embarrassing as the final result: 0–0. It was their first ever draw in a competitive international. At half-time Jack had come in and he had no answers either. All he said was, 'You've got yourselves into this mess, now get yourselves out of it.' And that was more or less it. It was a strange thing to say and a strange attitude to have. To me, that was the beginning of the end. Jack was running out of steam too.

We had a week to get over Liechtenstein and prepare for Austria at Lansdowne Road. The day before the game Jack was quoted in the papers. He said it had been 'a very pleasant week for everybody'. It had been a very pleasant week, all right, because we'd gone on the lash in Limerick for three days while Jack was away. Then we got stuffed by Austria. Maybe Harry Ramsden's extra portions of fish and chips were still in our system. The build-up that week had been a shambles and it resulted in a shambolic performance. The wheels were coming off, the era was coming to an end. I was booked against Liechtenstein, booked for dissent against Austria, and never played for Ireland again. Jack stepped down after we lost the play-off to Holland that December at Anfield.

*

Looking back now on my international career, there's a lot of mixed emotions. The good times you'll always remember. The bad times – you remember them too. When a manager is putting you in the team, you're happy with him. When he's not, it's a different story. To this day I still have my doubts that Jack ever really trusted me as a player to do the job he wanted. And I've often wondered if it was a coincidence that the lads he fell out with were all Irish-born: Dave O'Leary, Frank Stapleton, Liam Brady, myself. Or maybe it was that we played with big clubs and in our day had big reputations. As a manager he was very touchy about being questioned or challenged. And maybe he sometimes saw us as a threat. But I don't know, I can't say that for sure.

As a man I found him OK. He was an ex-footballer, he knew how to relate to players, you could sit down with him and have a chat and a laugh. I wouldn't say he was an ignorant man – but he *could* be ignorant at times. Like the night in Palermo when he refused to speak with me privately. But that was his style. And he was always big enough to back up his decisions and lead from the front. And in the end, those of us who played for Ireland in those years got to experience some of the best days of our lives. We all owe him a debt of gratitude for that.

Personally I think I probably underachieved as an international. I could have won more caps and I was a bit-player at two World Cups. That has left a sour taste. But there are consoling memories too and none more than Euro '88. The goal against Russia is a peak moment from a long career. And like every other footballer who reaches that level, a mountain of work has gone in to reaching that peak. But it's there, it's on film, it can never be taken away. It's almost my own personal

JFK moment. Most Irish fans, when I'm introduced to them the first thing they'll say is, 'I remember that goal against Russia.' And very often they'll tell me they can remember where they were when it happened.

I usually tell them that I can remember where I was too.

10

Old Head, Young Shoulders

We were flying home from Brussels the day after Heysel and I happened to be sitting next to Kenny and his wife Marina on the plane. The mood was heavy, everyone was shattered by the events of the night before, and I decided to change the subject.

We knew Joe Fagan was packing it in but we didn't know who the next manager was going to be. There were rumours going around, talk that it might be Phil Neal, and Kenny usually had his ear close to the ground.

'Who's the new manager? Any idea?' But he wasn't fully comfortable when I asked him. 'Don't know, not a clue.' I was getting a vibe from him that he knew more than he was letting on. 'Come on. You do know.' 'I don't!' 'You do. You definitely know something.'

And in the end I wore him down. 'OK, I do know.' 'Well, tell me so!' And he went, 'I can't, I'm not allowed.'

But I was badgering him now and eventually he came out with it. 'It's me. I'm the new manager.' 'Yeah, pull the other one.' 'No. It's true.' 'Seriously?' 'Yeah.' Oh. 'Well, can I be captain so?!'

Captain? Kenny wasn't long in the job when he was dropping me. It was one of the biggest kicks up the backside I ever got in my time at Liverpool. We were playing Tottenham in the stupid bloody Screen Sport Super Cup – designed by the FA to compensate those teams who would have played in Europe but for the UEFA ban – in December 1985. We were unbeaten in twelve games and had won seven of the previous eight. I'd played all twelve and assumed everything was ticking along nicely. We were getting off the bus at Anfield and I was coming down the centre aisle when Kenny got out of his seat and turned to me. 'You're sub tonight.' I smiled, I thought he was taking the mickey, but he wasn't. I was left on the bench against Tottenham, Kevin MacDonald came into centre midfield with Jan Molby and scored the first goal in a 2–0 win. I sat on the bench again for the next game against Aston Villa and wasn't even a sub in the following games against Arsenal and Newcastle. We were beaten 2–0 by Arsenal and drew 1–1 at Newcastle. This was one of those times when privately you saw the silver lining in a couple of poor results for the team. And sure enough, after my four-game demotion he picked me for the Manchester City match on Boxing Day. I mustn't have made much of a difference because City beat us 1–0. But I was back in the team and ended up playing fifty-seven games that season.

The thing that troubled me at the time, and for a long time after, was that Kenny never explained why he dropped me. I never knew whether he was just flexing his muscles for some reason, maybe sending out a message to everyone else in the squad. Or maybe he thought I'd become a bit blasé, or just that Kevin could do a better job than me in midfield. But not knowing why really kept me on edge: if he could drop me for no apparent reason once, he could do it again. Maybe he was playing mind games with me, I don't know, but whatever he was at, it worked. I got the fright of my life. And once I got back in the team I was never more determined to stay in it. I kept thinking *I can't let that happen again.* It taught me a lesson I should never have forgotten in the first place: don't ever take anything for granted in this game. It was one of the reasons why I played the best football of my career over the next three to four seasons.

There were players who didn't like Kenny, for the same reason I didn't like him in December '85: they weren't in the team. But as usual, we were only thinking about ourselves. We never looked at it from his point of view. He was thirty-four years old when he took over the biggest club in England and one of the biggest in Europe. He was still a player, for God's sake. And all of a sudden he had to stop thinking as a footballer who was only responsible for himself, and start thinking as a manager who was responsible for everything. No apprentice-ship, no couple of years as a number two, just straight in at the top – sink or swim.

Kenny brought Bob back to sort of mentor him and guide him but the buck stopped with the boss. It was a horrendous burden to place on his shoulders. Not just that, we'd won noth-ing in 1984/85 and he was under pressure to put silverware on the table as soon as possible. And I thought he showed unbe-lievable character the way he handled it. He had fantastic skills as a footballer but those skills almost hid the fact that he was hard as nails on a pitch. Kenny had real mental toughness and it came to the fore in that first season as manager of Liverpool Football Club.

He had to distance himself now from a load of lads he'd

been mates with for years. And we had to learn very quickly to change our relationship with him too. When he walked into the dressing room in the mornings there was a silence instead of the usual banter because he was the manager now and we didn't need him to know where we'd been the night before. That was just one example. We were used to calling him by his first name, or by his nickname 'Super', and we kept forgetting to address him as 'Gaffer'. It was awkward initially for him and for us. And he found team talks difficult too. He was fine when he was talking about an upcoming game, opponents and tactics and all that. But if there was a big team meeting about some issue or other you could see he was worried in case he'd say something wrong. Then the lads would start sniggering and winding him up. So he'd be choosing his words carefully for fear of making a mistake.

I know he developed a reputation for being very guarded in media interviews, sort of dour, giving nothing away. But with the players he was totally different. He was very approachable, you could go and talk to him. He'd sit with you and chat with you and still take the mick. Like Bob, he wouldn't be banging tables in the dressing room before games but, unlike Bob, he'd do plenty of shouting from the dugout. You'd hear him screaming, 'Sortitouuuth! Sortitouuuth!' But we were used to that because he'd been moaning at us for years on the pitch anyway. You'd look at one of the other lads and we'd both throw our eyes to heaven: there he goes, moaning again.

But Kenny must have had a lot of belief in his own ability as a manager from the start. A more insecure person might have been tempted to make a lot of changes to the squad, just to make a statement: I'm the boss now, this is me putting my stamp on things. But the squad he inherited from Joe, he did very little with it that first season. Steve McMahon was bought from Aston Villa in September – we were still trying to fill the void left by Souness – and that was Kenny's only big move in the transfer market. Alan Kennedy was moved on in September, Phil Neal in December; Alan was thirty-one and Jim Beglin was ready to take over at left-back; Nealy was thirty-four and Steve Nicol had been the heir apparent there for a couple of seasons.

Then we went and won the double. When Everton beat us 0–2 at Anfield on 22 February they went eight points clear of us and three ahead of Manchester United in second place. We had twelve games left: we won eleven and drew one. It was touch and go all the way to the last day. And then Kenny scored the winner at Stamford Bridge on the last day to clinch the title. If we didn't call him Super that day instead of Gaffer, we should have. Seven days later Rushie scored twice as we beat Everton in the FA Cup final.

It was fifteen years since Arsenal had won the double. It was twenty-five years since Bill Nicholson's Tottenham had won their double. Liverpool in 1985/86 became only the third team that century to achieve this milestone in the English game. It was a team that made history and yet it has been slightly neglected by history. It ended up sandwiched between the great sides of 1981–84 and 1987–90, and has remained in their shadow to this day. The reason why is fairly simple: it wasn't as good. It was actually a team in transition, there were a lot of players coming in and out of the first eleven, and it probably never really acquired its own identity. There was quite a bit of chopping and changing, especially in centre midfield where you had Sammy Lee, Steve McMahon and Kevin MacDonald vying for the slot alongside Jan Molby. Kenny was also rationing his appearances up front, with Paul Walsh stepping into the role. John Wark was also seeing some game time.

But it ended up with stats that bear comparison with any of the other sides that decade. Eighty-nine goals, twenty-six wins, ten draws, six defeats. There was no Souness, Kenny played only twenty-one league games and stalwarts like Neal and Kennedy had been moved on. It's a team and a season I'd forgotten about a little bit but we obviously had a very strong work ethic and enough know-how to win games in which we struggled. It didn't have a lot of star quality but it got the job done.

If anyone provided the bit of gold dust that season, it was Molby. He was the creative force in that side and he gave it whatever identity it had. A completely different centre midfield player to Souness, Jan ran the show with his range of passing off right foot and left. He had so much power and strength too, but he didn't use it in the tackle the way Souey could. Instead it made him very difficult to knock off the ball, as he proved with that fantastic goal against Man United in the League Cup that November. It was a fantastic individual goal and the way he raced half the length of the field with the ball at his feet surprised a lot of people: they didn't know there was always an athlete in Jan waiting to get out! But he was a ball player, first and foremost, and a brilliant one on his day.

A year after we won the title against Chelsea, we were back again at Stamford Bridge for the final game of the season, but this time the result didn't matter. Everton were already champions, they finished nine points ahead of Liverpool in second. Arsenal beat us in the League Cup final and Luton Town spanked us 3–0 in the FA Cup third round at Kenilworth

Road. And to cap it all, our goal machine was heading to Italy. We'd finished 1986/87 badly, losing five of the last nine and winning just three. I suppose it's another reason why the 1985/86 team isn't well remembered: we won nothing the following season and it more or less disappeared from view once the new era dawned.

People talk about the pressure on managers nowadays but it was fairly rough back then too – even more so for the manager of the leading club at the time. We had gone one season without winning anything and the pre-season stories going into 1987/88 included a lot of speculation about Kenny's future at the club if things didn't work out. His neck was on the block, apparently; there was also a gun to his head and, if that wasn't bad enough, he was under siege too. One thing was true: the team that had won the double a year earlier now needed surgery and this would be the first major test of his ability to build a team.

But Kenny had already started the process. Sammy Lee was sold to QPR in August 1986, Barry Venison had arrived in July and Steve Staunton, one for the future, was signed in September. John Aldridge was bought in January 1987 to take over from Ian Rush and Nigel Spackman joined a month later. Then, that summer, the two big coups: John Barnes arrived in June for £900,000, Peter Beardsley in July for £1.9 million. In October Ray Houghton was signed at a cost of £825,000.

The Beardsley deal was a new British transfer record. There was a lot of grumbling at the time about the amount of money Liverpool were spending. But people were missing a crucial point: it was one thing to buy these players, and another thing entirely to try and mould them into a team. Ron Atkinson had splashed the cash in his day too and hadn't been able to build a title-winning side at Man United. Liverpool learned the same lesson in later years when Gerard Houllier and Rafa Benitez waded into the transfer market and still couldn't get the job done. When you spend all that money on players, they still have to fit together as a unit; they have to have the right spirit and attitude; they have to stay free of injuries. Kenny had bought half a team in 1987 but there were no guarantees whatsoever that they would knit together into a championship-winning side.

But at least there was a clear logic behind his strategy. Ian Rush had scored forty goals in all competitions in 1986/87. Now he was leaving. Who was going to get you forty goals the following season? The answer was no one; Rushie was unique. But John Aldridge was a top-class finisher and he was surely worth a punt. And Aldo could only score goals if he got the chances. The two best creative players around at the time were Barnes at Watford and Beardsley at Newcastle. So Kenny brought them in. Ray Houghton was a clever player who never stopped running and the manager obviously saw a place for him on the right of midfield. Barnes on the left, Houghton on the right, Beardsley and Aldridge up front. Kenny had built a completely new forward line and the plan was to graft it on to the foundation that was already there: Grobbelaar, Nicol, Hansen, Lawrenson, Gillespie, Whelan, McMahon, Molby, Johnston. The squad was deeper now and it needed to be; Jan had a terrible run with injuries and Lawro's career came to an end in January '88.

With Barnes guaranteed his place on the left, a lot of people said it was the end for me. I'd more or less made the position my own during the previous five and a half seasons but I knew for sure that it wasn't going to be mine any more. But I hadn't much time to worry about it because Kenny was already lining me up to play alongside McMahon in centre midfield. It was a different role for me. I would be sitting in front of the back four while Macca got forward. It was a niche position, it meant the goals were going to dry up, but I didn't care about that. I was just happy to have survived the big transition that was under way. Me and Kenny never discussed how I'd play the role. As usual at Liverpool it was a case of, you're in the team, just get on with it. And I have to say I took to it like a duck to water. I just felt very comfortable there from the start. It took no time at all for Macca and me to develop a good understanding on the field – and we were good pals off it too. It turned out that our wives, Elaine and Julie, had been close friends at school, but it was purely by coincidence that they later met fellas who ended up playing centre midfield together for Liverpool.

Kenny didn't have long to wait to see how his best-laid plans would fare in the heat of battle. Arsenal had finished fourth in 1986/87, and George Graham was building a team that would win the championship in 1988/89. So Arsenal were going to be a major test for us at Highbury. It might have been the opening day of the season but this was going to be one of the biggest games of the season and, to prove the point, Arsenal had their first 50,000 gate in five years. Aldo got us off the mark after nine minutes and Nico got the winner with a great long-range header with just two minutes left in the game. I remember distinctly thinking in the dressing room afterwards *We've got a chance here with these players.* You could see that Barnes and Beardsley and Aldridge had struck up a good understanding, they were already operating on the same wavelength. But you didn't know if they'd stand up to the pressure of trying to win big games and now it looked like they could.

I think the win at Highbury set us up for the season. The confidence just flowed through the team after that result. But it could have gone the other way. Our first three games were away from home because of construction work going on at the Kop. A few bad results in those opening games and it might have damaged our confidence. A draw at Highbury would've been fine but Nico's late winner really got us buzzing. The goals started raining down: four against Coventry in the next game, three against Charlton, fours against Newcastle, Derby, Portsmouth and QPR. This team had only been together a wet week and now you were thinking *What can we achieve here? We can fill our boots with this team.*

We went the first twenty-nine games unbeaten in the league. If any Liverpool team I was part of ever came close to playing total football, this was the one. We became one of the best attacking teams the game in England has ever seen. The speed of the passing and movement; the full-backs bombing on; centre midfield in control (usually); the front four creating chance after chance; danger coming from every angle; confidence at an all-time high. And when we didn't have the ball we hustled like hell to get it back.

For that season and the next two or three, John Barnes was probably the best player in Europe in his position, if not the world. A lot of the time for us it was a case of get the ball out to Barnesy. Work the opening with a couple of passes in midfield, bang bang bang, now you can put him into space with the ball at his feet. Then he'd terrorise the full-back. And if the full-back got booked for bringing him down, just get it out to him even more. Ray Houghton on the other side was not as stylish but often was equally effective: very busy around the field, quick feet and a smart brain. Peter Beardsley was the same but with marvellous individual skills. Some of the goals he scored, some of the things he did – a wonderful talent. Aldo up front was getting a dream service: the result was twenty-nine goals in all competitions.

When people talk about that Liverpool team they don't call it 'the team of 1987/88'. They usually just call it 'Barnes and Beardsley'! That gets on my wick a bit. What about Hansen, Nicol and McMahon? Hansen and McMahon played forty-nine games that season, Nicol fifty. This was a very strong team, not a collection of brilliant individuals. Barnesy was a big star in other people's eyes, the fans and media in particular. But he was just one of us. And if he wasn't tracking back in a game we'd soon let him know about it. In fairness, he'd do the defensive part of his job when he had to but there were a few occasions when I ended up shouting at him – and he'd have a few shouts back at me for shouting at him.

And I know that Barnesy and Peter and Aldo would be the first to acknowledge everyone else's contribution to that season. Because apart from all the flair and entertainment, it was a genuinely united team. The spirit was great, the attitude was right and socially we got on well too. We were playing the football of our lives and we knew that we were all in this together, a group of young fellas who were striving towards the same goal. And once you were all in this environment together you had no prima donnas, nobody was a star among us.

I tell a lie. Steve Nicol was a star among us because everybody loved him. You'd see Nico and straightaway you'd have a smile on your face because you knew there'd be a bit of crack and banter to be had. He was daft as a brush, a really likeable fella, and you were always guaranteed a great laugh with him around. Being a Scot, and a bit younger, I think the rest of the Scottish mafia reckoned they could take the mick even more with him. Hansen, Kenny and Souey were very fond of him, in reality, it's just that they showed it by winding him up all the time. And, typical of the man, he always took it with a grin and tried to give it back.

I think Nico is the most underrated player of that whole era. He never got the credit he deserved at the time and I hope when people look back they will appreciate more what he did for the club. He was at Liverpool for over thirteen seasons. He played right-back, left-back, centre-back, right midfield, left midfield, and I might even be leaving out a few positions here. The point is that he was incredibly consistent wherever he played. He was very fit, very strong, he had a football brain and plenty of bottle. Sometimes he had too much bottle! Like going and taking the first penalty in a European Cup final in the Olympic Stadium in Rome. But he had loads of confidence and nothing ever seemed to get him down. Missing that penalty in Rome, if we had lost the European Cup as a result he would've got over it quicker than anybody. He just wasn't that type of person.

It doesn't do him justice to describe him as a utility man, even a good utility man. He was a very good player, full stop. Nico is up there with the top people I played with. You have Rush, Souness, Dalglish and Barnes – OK, they're up there at the very highest level. Then you have the next tier down, I suppose, the likes of Hansen and Lawro and too many others to mention, and Nico was right up there. He was such a good footballer. And I think people have glossed over it because he played in so many positions. When we won the double in

1985/86 Nico played forty-seven games that season, thirty-four in the league. In 1987/88 he played in all forty league games. He lost a lot of 1986/87 to injury, he played only fourteen league games, and that would've been a big blow to us. We drew a blank that season and Nico's absence was one of the main reasons why. By the time he was finished he had clocked up 468 games for Liverpool. To keep playing so many positions in so many games, year in year out, you've got to have something special.

Three teams:

The team of 1987/88: played 40, won 26, drew 12, lost 2. Goals for: 87. Goals against: 24. Goal difference: +63.

The treble-winning side of 1983/84: played 42, won 22, drew 14, lost 6. Goals for: 73. Goals against: 32. Goal difference: +41.

The legendary side of 1978/79: played 42, won 30, drew 8, lost 4. Goals for: 85. Goals against: 16. Goal difference: +69.

I think 1987/88 trumps 1983/84 – and both are trumped by 1978/79.

Let's have a bit more fun with the comparisons while we're at it. The team of 1978/79 would have been dominant in any era, unquestionably. And I believe the Liverpool teams of 1981–84 and 1987–90 were as good as any of the great English league sides that came after. The Manchester United team of 1993–97, their three-in-a-row sides of 1999–2001 and 2007–09; the Chelsea team of 2004–06; the Arsenal invincibles of 2003–04. We'd have beaten them all. Not every time we played them, but probably as often as they'd have beaten us.

We had the pace and intelligence and technical ability to play pass-and-move football at a very high tempo. We were similar in style to the modern Barcelona team, the way we kept moving the ball, the way we'd wait and wait until you'd worked an opening for the killer pass. We did it and, what's more, we had to do it on crap pitches most of the time. The ball bobbling off the rough surface, popping this way and that out of ruts and divots. To play the game we did on those surfaces, our control had to be spot on and it was. Put those Liverpool teams on the modern-day carpets and we'd have passed and moved even quicker and better.

That's the football side. We had the power and the bottle and the attitude too. Again, we had to have, because physically it was dog-eat-dog a lot of the time. Some of the tackles would be straight red cards nowadays. Referees let a lot of kicking and hacking go without blowing the whistle. So we could take care of ourselves, and we could dish it out too if it was necessary.

Roy Keane and Paul Scholes; Frank Lampard; Patrick Vieira; Graeme Souness was every bit as dominant – and a bit more as well. This is not being sentimental, it's not a case of all our yesterdays, I've no reason to be sentimental. All you've to do is look at the players we had and the standards they set: Hansen, Lawrenson, Souness, Dalglish and Rush; Barnes, Beardsley and Houghton. Most of the modern Premier League players wouldn't have lived with them. The only thing in a different league nowadays is the media coverage. When you see a goal on television in super-slow-motion from five different angles, the effect often exaggerates the quality of the goal. Then you have the commentators dramatising even ordinary passages of play. Newspapers and the internet have saturation coverage 24/7. So it's very difficult to see past the glamour and the hype.

But what I'm seeing on the pitch week in week out – even from
the best teams – if my mind wanders back to the '80s I usually
end up thinking *We were as good.* The game is quicker nowadays and the players are fitter. But are they any *better?*

In the first six months of 1987/88 I couldn't have been
happier: I was flying fit, I was loving my new role in midfield.
And then bang – the game gives you another sickener. I got
injured at the end of January and I was out for the next three
months. And of course the team sailed on without me. I played
the last four league games and figured I'd made it back just in
time for the Cup final against Wimbledon. I'd be disappointed
not to start but, even so, I'd have a good chance of getting a
run from the bench at some stage. About ninety minutes
before kick-off Kenny stood up at the team meeting to
announce the line-up. There'd been a lot of speculation because
he had plenty of options. He started with a preamble. 'You
know, picking a team for a Cup final, there's no room for sentiment.' As soon as he said the word 'sentiment' I knew I was
gone. Straightaway I knew. Because if he's talking about sentiment he's referring to a long-serving player. And it wasn't
Hansen so it had to be me.

And now I had a sinking feeling about the bench too. Craig
and Jan made the bench, Spackman would partner McMahon
in midfield. Jan had been injured all season, so I was sure I was
ahead of him fitness-wise. Craig had announced in the papers
a day or two before that Wimbledon was going to be his last
game for Liverpool. He was heading home after that. So in my
head I was thinking *Kenny's not going to pick him if he's walking
away from the club like that.* I actually believe Craig *was* a sentimental choice by Kenny, a sort of 'fond farewell' kind of
thing. Anyway, I still believe the gaffer got it wrong that day.

Now, you might think that if a fella has played hundreds of games and won plenty of trophies, he'd get over something like that pretty quickly. But the truth is you don't. Well, I didn't. I was greedy, we all were, and I badly wanted to play that day. I didn't want to miss a Cup final at Wembley; you weren't going to get many chances like that in your career and I hated missing out. It annoyed me for years afterwards, any time I thought about it. As it happened I did get the chance to play in another Cup final, a year later, and we got the right result that time. But it was won in the midst of so much grief that you genuinely didn't know whether to laugh or cry.

In 1989/90 we went back one more time for the league title. But I don't think we ever quite touched the heights of 1987/88 in the seasons after. We won 1989/90 with nine points to spare over Aston Villa and we still played some devastating football along the way. But we weren't as consistent. We'd conceded 24 goals in 40 games in 1987/88. Two years later we leaked 37 in 38 games. There was a lot of chopping and changing at the back and we didn't really find our groove until December. We went on a long unbeaten run then and just when we needed an extra push in the final furlong, up stepped the bold Ronnie Rosenthal. Ronnie appeared out of the blue and smashed a hat-trick against Charlton on 4 April. Talk about a hot streak! Ronnie scored seven in the last seven games and the man became a cult hero at Anfield for ever.

Me, I scored three goals that season and one of them was top drawer, even if I do say so myself. Unfortunately it was the own goal that is still remembered fondly by plenty of Manchester United fans – and even by those Liverpool fans who were able to see the funny side after we held out for the win. We were two up with about eight minutes to go at Old Trafford. The ball was headed out of our defence and I decided I'd slow the game down here by playing it back to Bruce in goal. So it dropped about twenty-five yards out and I caught it with a delightful half-volley that sailed right over Bruce's head – and into the top corner at the Stretford End. Ever have 40,000 people jeering you? It's not funny. I was absolutely mortified. And then we were under desperate pressure for the remaining minutes as United went chasing an equaliser. If they'd scored, I might as well have caught the first flight to Siberia. I was never so relieved to hear the final whistle in my life. And I got some abuse from the lads afterwards for putting them through the crapper like that.

Steve Staunton played left-back that day and I'm sure he was one of the ones giving me grief about it. Stan was no shrinking violet. Even as a young fella he'd take no messing from anyone. Earlier that season, in October 1989, he was pressed into emergency service as a forward. We were playing Wigan in a League Cup match at Anfield. He came on for Rushie at half-time. And blow me down, doesn't Stan go and score a hat-trick. Naturally he was chuffed with himself. He played the next game but the one after that, against Southampton at the Dell, Kenny put him on the bench and left him there. I was sitting beside him on the bus back to Liverpool and he was fuming, smoke coming out of his ears. Stan is from Dundalk, near the border with Northern Ireland, and he has the accent to prove it. And he said to me, in a real bitter tone of voice, 'Dalglish shhhit on me. The bawstherd shhhit on me.' And I was sympathising with Stan but inside I was cracking up. First chance I got I was regaling the lads with what he'd said. So we were training at Melwood on the Monday and we'd all forgotten about it. Next thing, a ball broke between Stan and Kenny, and

Stan just crippled him with a tackle. Kenny was poleaxed on the ground. And there was this stunned silence for a second or two. Then Nico piped up, in his best attempt at a Dundalk accent: 'Take that ya bawstherd ya.' And I followed up with: 'You won't shhhit on me again!' Now, Kenny's leg might have been broken at this stage but everyone was laughing too much to notice. Kenny was already a legend. He also happened to be the manager. And he was entitled to drop anyone he wanted. Stan was twenty at the time. But did he care?! That was Stan.

The only time I ever saw Kenny Dalglish openly change his mind as a manager was in December 1990. We were in the dressing room at Highbury and Kenny had announced his team. Barry Venison would be playing right-back, Steve Nicol right midfield. Then a little while later he said, 'No, Venners, you go right midfield, Nico, you go right-back.' I thought nothing of it at the time, nobody did. The following February, a few days after that famous 4–4 Cup tie with Everton, he resigned. It shocked us to the core. We never saw it coming. But we found out soon enough the reasons why. The man had been suffering inside and keeping it all bottled up. He'd been carrying the trauma of Hillsborough with him for almost two years. I suppose he was just worn down by it all in the end.

In hindsight maybe we should have picked up on it sooner. That little hesitation and change-of-mind at Highbury was perhaps a clue. Maybe there'd been other clues too if we'd been able to notice them. But we hadn't, because we were typical footballers and typical footballers are not the most sensitive of people. Looking back, I think the way Kenny kept going in the job for those twenty-two months after Hillsborough was heroic. He kept the show on the road even though there must have been times when he was churning up inside. I think he was just finally exhausted.

We didn't know it then, obviously, but Dalglish's managerial reign would be the last great era at Liverpool Football Club. No one could have dreamed at the time that we were facing a long wilderness without a title. As I write, it's twenty-one years and counting. The wheel came full circle when Kenny returned as manager in January 2011, twenty years after he walked away. He had nothing left to give then, but he has a lot to give now. I always believed that had the tragedies of Heysel and Hillsborough not happened, Kenny Dalglish would have gone on to become one of the great managers. Because of Heysel he didn't get to manage in Europe and because of Hillsborough he didn't get to stay long enough in the job. But, like Bob before him, he knew how to build teams. He packed a massive amount into his six years in charge.

Ronnie Moran stepped in as caretaker manager and the players, as always, moved on. About a week or so after Kenny resigned, we were all called to a meeting in the home dressing room at Anfield. Then Ronnie walked in with Hansen and Roy Evans. The three of them looked very serious. Ronnie told us he had an announcement to make. 'The board has asked Alan Hansen to be the next Liverpool manager and Alan has accepted.' We were all ears now. Hansen, said Ronnie, would be taking over with immediate effect. 'Alan, do you want to say a few words?' And Jockey stood up and said, 'Right, there's going to be a lot of changes round here. No more days off. Mondays we're all in. Thursdays we'll be looking at videos of the last game, Fridays we'll be looking at videos for the next game.' Then he looked around at a few of us and said, 'I know where you all drink in Southport, them pubs are off limits from now on.' Then he turned to a few others and said, 'I know where you drink on the Wirral, them pubs are off limits too. And the ones who drink in Liverpool, I know exactly where you all drink too and them pubs are also off limits. Right?'

You could've heard a pin drop. Hansen had his deepest Scottish accent on and he was already sounding like a serious manager. He went on to say that the training regime would be changing, that a lot of things around here would be changing, starting tomorrow morning at Melwood. And just before he left the dressing room he added another stinger. 'Oh, and by the way, Steve Nicol will be the new club captain.' Then he walked out and Ronnie and Roy followed him.

No sooner had they walked out than the bitching started. More training, no drinking, videos, new regime, what's all this shit about? Someone said, dead vicious, 'I never liked that Scottish twat anyway.' And I was badly put out because I was club captain at the time. So I decided to confront him head-on about it. I left the dressing room while the rest of them were still muttering and bumped into Marc Kenny coming out of the away team dressing room. Marc was another Home Farm graduate and was a young pro at Liverpool at the time. He went on to play with Shamrock Rovers in the League of Ireland. Anyway, he was heading somewhere in a hurry and I asked him where he was going. Turned out he'd been listening to the whole Hansen spiel outside the door. 'I'm going to phone me da and tell him to get down the bookies straight-away.' Marc had got the inside track. Hansen was the new manager but the word hadn't got out yet. He was going to pile on the readies and his da was going to do the same back in Dublin.

So he ran off and I went looking for Hansen. And as I went by the boot room I could hear a load of laughs coming from inside. I didn't even knock on the door, I just went straight in and there was Jockey and Bugsy and Evo sniggering away. I said, 'I'm glad youse three think it's fucking funny.' Then I accused Hansen. 'You should at least have had the decency to come and tell me to my face first.' And that just got them going again, they were in convulsions now. And it was only then the penny dropped. Ah, Jaysus. Caught rapid. I'd fallen for it hook, line and sinker. We all had. In fairness, Hansen was a brilliant wind-up merchant and this one was a classic.

When I came out of the boot room Marc Kenny had disappeared. I never found out if he got to back that sure thing with the bookies, or if his da had put the mortgage on Alan Hansen as the nailed-on next Liverpool manager.

11

The Liverpool Way?

You hear a lot of people talk about 'The Liverpool Way' these days. It's a phrase that's in fashion. It seems the only people who don't talk about it are the people who played for the club or managed it or coached there.

I can't remember if the term was even used back in the 80s. I know that we never heard it bandied around Anfield or Melwood. And we certainly didn't go out for a game on a Saturday saying, 'Come on, lads, let's do it the Liverpool Way.' If you came out with something like that, you'd be laughed out of the dressing room.

I'm still not sure I understand what it means, or what era exactly they have in mind when they talk about it. Maybe it means different things to different people. If I had to have a stab at it I'd probably say that it includes a certain style of play on the pitch, and maybe a set of values that the club tried to practise off it.

We obviously didn't invent the way we played, it wasn't unique to us, but at the same time you'd notice straightaway a player who wasn't schooled in that system. Like, a lot of players came into the club when I was there that you thought were good signings, but then they'd stick out like a sore thumb in our small training games. They just couldn't handle pass-and-move well enough. They'd be wanting another touch, they'd take too long on the ball. And even to this day, when we play in charity games or whatever, if there's a lad on your team, an ex-pro who didn't play for Liverpool, you will notice the difference pretty much immediately. Because he will run with the ball and then he'll turn back out and pass it to you when he could've done the same thing five seconds earlier. And in your head you're going *What are you doing, where are you running with it? Just gimme it and I'll give it back to you over there.* It wasn't always a crime to run with the ball, there were times when you had to do it, but you didn't run with it when you could pass it. That basically was the lesson Ronnie Moran dished out to me my first day at Liverpool.

There's no great mystery about pass-and-move. You had to have a certain level of technical ability, I suppose, before they signed you, and after that it was just drilled into you every day. You got better at it by pure repetition, doing it every day in small-sided games. It was basically nonstop motion: the ball had to be in circulation all the time and the players had to keep running. Then in a game situation your opponents eventually wouldn't be able to react quickly enough to what was going on around them, if you'd been passing it quickly enough and often enough – and always to someone in a red shirt.

Obviously, it's not as simple as it sounds, or as it looks. If the ball is being pinged around at that speed, all it takes is one heavy touch, or one pass slightly overhit or underhit, for the chain of passes to break down. Pass-and-move requires an awful lot of precision. And it needs a quick brain as well as quick feet. That was another eye-opener for me at Liverpool, especially when I broke into the first team – how quickly the likes of Souness and Dalglish could see a pass and execute it. Kenny told Rushie, when Rushie was getting into the team, 'If you move, I'll find you.' It was the same for me: if I moved they found me.

I remember being home on holidays in the summer of 1982 and still buzzing about the quality of players I was mixing with week in week out. I was going on about it to Matt Butler one day, just the pure pleasure of playing alongside lads who were that good. 'I get the ball when *I* want it now, not when *they* want to give it to me.' It's a crucial difference. And that to me is a football brain; knowing when to give the ball at the right time. You have to give the ball when he's ready, not when you're ready. You've got to make sure he gets it while he's got the time to do something with it. And these lads are not only doing that, but they're putting it in the space where you're going to be in a few strides, not where you are already. Measuring how far you are away, the speed you're travelling at, and the weight of pass required. I loved that they could do that routinely.

They seemed to have more time on the ball too. All top players give that impression because they're able to control it in a way that buys them more time and space. And if they have a choice of two passes to make, they'll make the right decision and choose the better option.

Liverpool liked to have players who could make a decision on their own. If you felt something needed changing you could try it. If it didn't work out you might get a bollocking but they wouldn't say, 'Don't do that again.' They wanted people to make their own decisions on the pitch. Over the years I saw players looking across to the bench if things weren't going well, as if to say, 'What do I do here?' Bugsy's answer would be fairly blunt. 'What the fuck do I know?! Sort it out! Just sort it out!' They wouldn't spend hours on the training ground explaining how you should handle a specific situation. Their attitude was, every game is different so what's the point? We can't tell you exactly what to do because the next game will be different. And good players should be able to make their own decisions in any situation. That's what you're paid to do.

That whole first season, 1981/82, was about getting used to these players, how they moved and how they thought. The likes of myself and Rushie just lapped it up. I know my brain speed on the pitch definitely got quicker after I went into the first team. I was seeing the options quicker and making the right decision more often. And I think we both cottoned on very quickly that if you moved, something would happen. There was always the possibility that if you made the run, someone would see you and something would happen. These lads had razor-sharp football brains.

I think maybe the modern game emphasises physical speed at the expense of mental speed. The emphasis on pace and fitness seems more and more to be producing athletes who can play football, rather than footballers first, athletes second. But that old saying about being a yard faster in your head – it's still an invaluable quality on a football pitch. The present-day Barcelona team epitomises for me the football brain at work. They play fantastic pass-and-move. Xavi and Iniesta run the show in midfield, they dictate everything, and neither of them has pace. But they've got magic feet and you can almost see their brains working every time they make a move.

Dalglish was no speed merchant either but between his ears he was lightning quick; he could spot a defence-splitting pass that no one else would have seen and execute it in the same moment. It doesn't just apply to creative players either. Alan Hansen generally strolled his way through games but he had this knack of getting to a ball faster than an opponent who would have beaten him hands down in a straight sprint. He could just read the play better, anticipate the pass and make his move earlier.

And I think that good, intelligent players will find a way anyway. With Hansen it wouldn't just have been a question of the brain ticking a little quicker, it would have been the competitor's streak in him too. I would have backed any of our lads to get to the ball that mattered, especially the team of 1981–84. There was major bottle in that team. It was the strongest I played on in terms of character and being hard to beat. They'd find a way to win the crucial ball. This quality was drilled into us too, as well as pass-and-move.

Alex Ferguson has drilled it into his teams over the years too, that willingness to run all day and fight for the result. You mightn't be playing well but you can still find a way to get a result out of a game. I think that attitude is the foundation of any great team.

I went back and had a look recently at the famous 5–0 game against Nottingham Forest in April 1988. I hadn't seen it in years and what struck me was our work rate when they had the ball. The speed and the energy that went into closing down the space and pressurising the player in possession. It was just relentless. That was something we did in training too. The nearest man to the ball was the first tackler and he had to close it down. Ronnie or Roy or Joe would be standing there screaming, 'Close, close, close! First man go, second man go, third man go!' You didn't worry about what was happening behind you; if you were the nearest man to the ball you went and closed it down. If he got the pass away, the next fella came and closed it, and so on. The first man usually wouldn't get the ball back but he had to put pressure on the pass and it might give an opening to the second man in; the second man would put more pressure on the next pass and it could be the third man in who'd get the ball back. With every tackle you're forcing them to play it quicker, until somebody makes a mistake and we have the ball again. It was systematic pressure and it demanded a lot of hard running. So, you could not be lazy in a Liverpool team, it didn't matter who you were. Everybody had the job of getting the ball back.

As a player, those were the boxes you had to tick at Anfield. Good technique, a football brain, a huge work ethic and a genuine heart. That was the formula. If that's what people mean by the Liverpool Way, so be it. But I think that all champion teams, probably in every era, possess the same qualities too.

One thing you could say was definitely unique to the Liverpool Way in those years was the boot room. Every club had a boot room, but not many clubs used it as a sort of breeding ground for future managers. The boot room has become part of the folklore of the club but as a player you weren't really conscious of its importance in the greater scheme of things. The main reason is that it was more or less off limits to us. You weren't barred from it but you knew it was where the manager and coaching staff hung out – it was their private place.

It was actually two rooms. There was a small room off it that had a boot stand and that's where the apprentices would clean and polish the boots for the first-team squad. You'd tie your boots together after a game at Anfield and leave them there to be collected. Each player had a number on his boots so the kids would know whose they were and they'd leave them back at your place in the dressing room, ready to be picked up the next morning. There was a door off that room that would take you into the bigger room, which was really a store room for gear and equipment. That was the boot room. There were a couple of large wicker skips in there that would be used to transport all the playing gear for away matches. It had shelves on the wall, maybe a chair or two, and bits and pieces of equipment from corner flags to nets and footballs. The manager and coaches would sit down on the skips, or whatever they could find, and this was where the real talking was done. Once in a while you might stick your head around the door to have a word with Roy or Ronnie, maybe on a Sunday morning if you were in for treatment and there was no one else around. But you wouldn't sit down and you wouldn't hang around.

I wouldn't have minded being a fly on the wall for some of their conversations but what was said in the boot room stayed in the boot room. I presume they talked about us a lot, our form, our fitness, how we'd played the previous Saturday, how we were performing in general. If we were on a poor run of results they had their books of training sessions going back years and years and they'd go through them for information and tips that might give them an idea or two. They'd break out the whisky too, and have a tot and a natter about things, probably sharing any gossip and crack going round the club. They were fairly hospitable too, apparently, to visiting coaches and managers, pouring the drink and plugging them for information. Little snippets: what's going on at your club, any good kids coming through, what sort of stuff do you do in training? I imagine they'd be looking for insights too about a team that they'd already played and that we'd be facing in the coming weeks. Knowing the lads involved, I'm sure they tried to pick their guests' brains while not giving too much away themselves.

I suppose the boot room basically was a sort of classroom where the assistants learned a huge amount from the manager, and where they in turn passed it down the line when they took over the top job. And I'm sure it was a two-way street: every manager must have learned a lot from them too. You can only imagine the store of knowledge and experience that was accumulated in that room over the decades. You had a lot of wise football heads in there, including someone like Tom Saunders, who was at the club for thirty years and who Kenny, for example, valued as a sounding board when he took over as manager.

Everyone in there must have absorbed so much knowledge about how the system worked at Liverpool, the style of play and the type of players that would fit within it. They were on the inside for so long, and they understood it so deeply, that they could be trusted to carry it on when the time came. So you had this amazing continuity from Shankly to Paisley to Fagan to Dalglish to Souness to Evans. It stopped working in the end, for all sorts of reasons, but it was unique to the club and if anything can be described as the Liverpool Way, this was surely it.

As far as values are concerned, people like Bob or Joe or Kenny never sat us down and gave us a lecture about 'the values of Liverpool Football Club'. That would've been far too pompous, it just wouldn't have been their style. But you learned how to behave from what they said and how they carried themselves. Not in a million years would you hear Bob puffing himself up in any way. He was probably the most humble man I ever met in football. And there he was producing the best teams in England and Europe and not saying a word about it. All lads when they're young need a bit of direction, I suppose, someone to set an example, and you took your cue from the likes of Bob and Joe and Roy and Ronnie Moran. They were the men behind all this success and they never made a song and dance about it. And if they didn't, then what right did you have to lose the run of yourself? Deep down they knew they were good, they had real confidence in what they were doing, but they let the success speak for itself. If you could sum up their way of working, it would be something like: excellence on the pitch, humility off it.

Even on the pitch, the veterans who were there when I broke into the team made sure you carried this message with you. They passed on that mind-set to us young lads. Again, deep down we knew how good we were, but you didn't rub it in to opponents who might be struggling. Even if we were winning by big margins it was a case of, just do your job, keep your head down, don't take the piss out of anybody. Sometimes we ended up humiliating them anyway, I suppose, by not letting up, by scoring more goals when the game was already won. But that was our job, it was nothing personal. You didn't go making smart remarks or laughing in their faces. I can't ever remember us playing keep ball just to give a team the run-around and have a laugh at their expense.

When we were on our way to beating Crystal Palace 9–0 that day in September 1989, I actually remember feeling a pang of guilt because the crowd at Anfield were enjoying every second of it and the Palace lads were obviously feeling more and more embarrassed. I said to Ian Wright at one stage, 'Look, don't worry about it, just carry on, try and keep playing.' Because personally I didn't want to humiliate anyone. But we were just on fire that day and it was coming so naturally to us that we just kept scoring and scoring. And fair play to Palace, they refused to lie down in the Cup semi-final the following April and beat us 4–3 against all the odds. That was another reason why no one at the club would've tolerated any big-time Charlies: you were only ever one game away from being brought back down to earth with a bang. So cop yourself on and if you get too big for your boots, son, there's plenty of room on the bench for you.

Mind you, I can remember a few teams rubbing our noses in it when they beat us. Coventry City caught us cold one day in December 1983, and gave us a right hiding at Highfield Road. That was the day Terry Gibson scored his famous hat-trick. Maybe it was a backhanded compliment but some of their players couldn't resist smiling into our faces and making a few remarks and celebrating right in front of us. They didn't show us much respect and we didn't forget it. They beat us 4–0 at Highfield Road and when we got them to our place the following May we made sure we scored five.

Generally I think we treated other teams with respect. Maybe they might have a different opinion, but we were conscious of behaving in a proper way with opponents and just getting the job done. For a lot of other fans, I think we were their second team, obviously not including Everton or Manchester United fans. But I think a lot of football followers around the country admired the way we played and the way we went about our business. We weren't saints, I'm not saying we were goody two-shoes all the time, it was just that the club had a down-to-earth culture that didn't tolerate arrogant behaviour.

If that wasn't enough to keep you in line, then our fans wouldn't be long about putting you in your place if they felt you deserved it. And sometimes even if you didn't deserve it! People seem to think that Liverpool players didn't get stick from their own fans – believe me, we got slaughtered sometimes. There was a stage in my second full season in the team when I got a lot of stick, especially from the Kemlyn Road stand. I was playing left side of midfield and if we were playing left to right in the first half, as you looked at it from the dugout, I'd be close to the fans on that side. Anfield was pretty compact, you could hear plenty of the comments. You'd pick up a ball two yards in from the sideline and someone would shout, 'You're shite! Go home to Ireland!' There were a load of lads down the front who were on my case during a lot of home games that season.

And I do remember one game, it must've been some time in 1981/82, and this bloke shouted, 'Get in the fucking game, Whelan, fucking Irish . . .' I couldn't hear the last word but I presume it wasn't complimentary. So I turned my head to look across the other side of the pitch, trying to ignore him. And there were Terry McDermott and Graeme Souness looking at me and giggling away. The reason they found it so funny was that the game hadn't kicked off. I was getting stick before the bloody game had even started! But that was all part and parcel of it, you developed a thick skin pretty quickly. Then when we changed ends at half-time I'd be getting slaughtered by Ronnie Moran on the other side. I don't know which was worse.

In fairness, that little bad spell apart, the times I got stick from the fans were few and far between. Most of the time it was the opposite: unbelievable loyalty and support and passion. When the Kop was in full voice you'd feel the shivers down your spine. You'd feel this wave of emotion rolling down on to the field. And it often hit you when you needed a lift and it just carried you along. You couldn't but respond to that sort of emotion.

It's not being romantic to say that there was a deep bond between the players and the fans. It was there and it was genuine. And one of the reasons is that we weren't strangers to them. This was the time before the Premier League, a time when players were neither millionaires nor celebrities. I think the vast salaries paid to players these days has driven a wedge between them and their fans. They're living in two separate worlds now. Footballers back then were paid a good wage but they weren't rich and they didn't live behind security gates and high walls in isolated mansions. We lived in nice suburbs but nothing out of the ordinary. We were still part of the community that paid our wages at the turnstiles. There was no 'them' and 'us' vibe. The club didn't have to arrange special meet-and-greets where we'd turn up and sign a few autographs for the fans and disappear again. We met them all the time. You'd meet them every day around Anfield, they were allowed in to watch training at Melwood, you'd chat to them in the pubs, you'd get to know lads who were mates with local players like Sammy and Tommo. It was just the natural way of things. I was part-owner of a pub for a couple of years, which my brother-in-law managed, and after games I'd bring some of the lads down and we'd have a few pints with the supporters who'd been at the game. They loved talking to you about the game and if you played bad, you'd walk in the door and they'd go, 'You were shite today, by the way.' You'd go, 'Well, not a lot I can do about it now! What are you having?'

We were well aware that thousands of those fans were on the dole and struggling to put bread on the table. You couldn't but be, you'd see it all around the city. Liverpool had the worst unemployment rate in Britain and we knew well that going to the football was an escape for them for a couple of hours on a Saturday. But money was so tight that an awful lot of fans had to stop coming to Anfield altogether or had to ration their visits there. If there was a midweek game the place would often be half-empty. The average league gate for the 1979/80 season was 44,500. A year later it was 37,500 and in 1981/82 it was 35,000. Fans chose their games because they had to.

The 1984 League Cup final was a Merseyside derby and it was a massive occasion for the city. Both sets of supporters travelled in their tens of thousands to Wembley and an awful lot of them had to scrape the money together to get there. Same with the FA Cup final in 1986. I saw a TV documentary at the time and fellas were saying, 'Well, we're gonna go down and enjoy it 'cos when I come back I've got no job to go to on Monday.' And it summed up what was going on in Liverpool at the time. The 1984 final was a damp squib, 0–0, and again they somehow managed to get a few quid together for the replay at Maine Road. I probably didn't fully understand at the time that if fans were giving you stick, they had a lot to be angry about anyway.

But we did feel a responsibility to them. It wasn't a token thing, it was genuine. We didn't make it a point of principle in the dressing room. No one ever said to the players before a game, 'You've got to go out and do it for the people,' but we knew that we had a duty to do our best. Us winning games wasn't going to change their lives but there was nothing else we could do about the situation. All we could do was go out on a Saturday and perform. They paid their money, it was up to us to keep our end of the bargain, because we were part of that community and it was part of us.

Maybe this is also what people mean when they talk about the Liverpool Way – that bond between the players and the people. Again, I don't think that bond was unique to our club. Maybe it was stronger and deeper there, at the time, than any place else. I'm not sure. But I'm pretty sure it would be no bad thing if players got in touch again with the people who pay their wages.

12

In Sunshine and in Shadow

It was a beautiful, sunny April day. We loved that time of year. The dressing room was always buzzing when April came round; summer was in the air and the season was building to a climax. You could set your body clock by it, year after year. There were trophies to be won and parties to be had before we broke up for the holidays. The same excitement would be felt all over the red half of the city as the weather turned warm and the games became a matter of winner takes all. When April arrived it always seemed as if happy days were just around the corner.

Those carefree times came to an end at Hillsborough. The tragedy makes you look back now and realise how innocent it all was before that day. And what a simple pleasure it actually is, just to be playing football, or following your team, and enjoying the good days if you're lucky enough to get them. It shouldn't have any bad consequences, doing something as harmless as that. And yet it had consequences that left families heartbroken and a community shattered.

The people who were in the stadium or on the pitch that day

all have their own stories to tell. I can only tell mine, and a lot of my story got lost in the shock and confusion of the days and weeks that followed.

Alan Hansen had picked up a bad knee injury in a pre-season game that was going to rule him out for most of the rest of the season, so Kenny appointed me captain in his place. When we walked on to the pitch at Hillsborough I didn't see anything to worry me on the terraces because I never looked at the crowd before any game. I was always nervous before kick-off and I'd just have my head down, raring to go.

The first few minutes were frenetic, players flying into tackles, and then Peter Beardsley clipped the top of the crossbar with a shot. It was just after that when the referee, Ray Lewis, came to me. Mr Lewis had a concerned look on his face when he came over. 'Ronnie, take the players off, get the players off towards the dressing rooms, there's trouble at the back of the goal.' I looked up and saw a supporter had come on to the grass at the Leppings Lane end. The referee then blew his whistle and I went round to the lads and called them off the pitch. I found out afterwards this was six minutes into the game. We made our way back to the dressing rooms and we figured at first it was just a bit of crowd congestion.

Inside the dressing room you couldn't hear anything, you couldn't see anything, we were completely cut off. For me it was Heysel all over again. We were being told over and over to keep ourselves warmed up, keep stretching, stay focused. 'Just keep yourselves ready, you'll be going back out. Just keep yourselves ready, you'll be going back out.' But I wasn't so sure about that. I was getting a bad feeling. The atmosphere wasn't right. You could sense the anxiety around the place.

The minutes ticked by. We were cocooned in that dressing room. We weren't allowed outside the door. We were told to stay there. Kenny was the only one of us going out and coming back. The first inkling we got was when the door was partly opened to let someone out. A lad was passing by, he saw us inside and he shouted in the door, 'You can't go out there, there's people dying.' What? What'd he say? We were looking at each other now and the mood became very tense very quickly. Most of us had family at the game. Were they OK? What the hell was going on? Eventually someone came in, I can't remember who, and told us that the game wouldn't be happening today; there'd been serious trouble.

It was only when we got to the players' lounge that we started realising what had happened. Everyone was white in the face and walking around stunned. Our wives were distraught, shaking and crying. We couldn't see anything down on the pitch from the players' lounge. The televisions were switched on and what we were seeing horrified us. We were seeing shell-shocked people wandering around the pitch, policemen, people being carried away on advertising hoardings, people everywhere in panic and tears. Reports were coming in every few minutes. There's been fatalities, many people are injured, and the numbers are expected to rise. I could hardly take it in. It was too big, I was bewildered, it was just too big to take in. From the players' lounge we went straight to the team bus and sat listening in silence to the radio reports on the journey home from Sheffield. More casualties, more fatalities, the story getting worse by the hour. The next day the phone at home was ringing off the hook and in between calls I just sat there in front of the television, numb from the scenes of grief and devastation.

And I was in a complete state of confusion. I couldn't think clearly at all. What do I say? What was I supposed to do? Do I leave the house? Is it wrong to go to Anfield? Will somebody please tell me what I'm supposed to do. In the end we got word that the players would be visiting the hospitals in Sheffield the next day. We met at Anfield, all the squad, and travelled up on the bus. We were all apprehensive – I was extremely nervous about walking into that situation. Because when you're a young professional footballer you think you're invincible. You're flying fit, you're in the prime of your life, you're living the dream. You haven't been around death, you haven't suffered major bereavement, you don't think about these things at all. Some of the lads handled it better than others but none of us really had the personal skills, or the life experience, to cope with what we were about to see.

We were taken from ward to ward. Some people were injured but were going to make a full recovery. In other rooms the scenes were harrowing. Every bed was surrounded by loved ones in terrible distress. There were people in comas, on life-support machines. At one bed somebody said, 'They're turning the machine off today.' The doctors and nurses encouraged us to talk to the patients who were unconscious. Just say something. Anything, I suppose, that might help. The families were so nice, they were happy to see us, but I felt useless. Again it was that confusion. Am I intruding here? Should I hang back? Am I in the way? What do I say? What could you say? 'Looking forward to seeing you back at Anfield.' 'Make sure to come and see us at Melwood when you get better.' We just whispered words of encouragement and shook hands with their relatives and wished them well.

There was one great moment of joy in all the sadness. One

young lad woke up while we were there. And when he got his bearings he saw a few Liverpool players smiling back and saying hello. You could see the look of surprise in his face. The relief and the happiness around that bed was just lovely to see. It was a ray of hope among all the devastation. We left the hospital badly shaken by what we'd seen. And it wasn't a fraction of what the families were going through. For many of them it was only going to get worse. The hospital that day was where the tragedy hit home for me. We'd come face to face with the human suffering that had been caused by the disastrous mistakes at Hillsborough football ground.

Coming back on the bus that day people spoke in whispers, if they spoke at all. I didn't say much and I wasn't able to shed any tears either. When we got back to Southport a couple of us decided to go for a drink. It was only going to be a couple of pints and we weren't even sure if we should. Would it be wrong to go for a few drinks? But we needed a few drinks, to be honest, after what we'd seen and heard. When I got home, my wife Elaine had the *Liverpool Echo* in her hand. She looked shattered. 'Have you seen this?' And on the back page was the story of Ian Whelan, a lad from Warrington who'd died, nineteen years of age. He was a huge Liverpool fan. His nickname was Ronnie and I was his favourite player. That was when I broke down. I completely lost it that night. I found it very difficult to take, reading that story. We eventually managed to get hold of a number for the Whelan family and I phoned them to say how sorry I was for their loss. I broke down other nights as well but that night was the worst. That young lad had gone to watch his football heroes and hadn't come home to his mum and dad.

I went to Ian's funeral, me and Jim Beglin. I went to another one with Alan Hansen. Once again the families couldn't have been more generous and once again I felt like an outsider intruding on their grief. But it was the right thing to do; it was only right and proper that we would be there to show our support. They had shown their support for us time and again over the years and I think, deep down, this was actually why I was feeling so awkward. It was guilt. You were a footballer, you were there to play a game, and the victims had come to watch you. I personally felt a lot of guilt, I don't know if other players felt it. And that's why I felt frightened, really, in the hospital, at the funerals, at Anfield.

We spent a lot of days at the football ground meeting people who just wanted to talk and cry and share their feelings. I could never find the right words, and at the back of my mind I'd be thinking *Is it my fault that someone you knew or someone you loved isn't here any more?* I had this dread that someone might say something really upsetting. But of course, no one ever did. They just wanted to find some comfort there. And Anfield had become this incredible shrine. Everyone remembers the sea of flowers on the pitch and on the Kop, it was an amazing spectacle. And those flowers came from all over the country.

The club made great decisions, it handled this awful time with such dignity and professionalism. The players were organised to go to every funeral; the gates were opened to let people lay their flowers on the field or just to walk on it and pay their respects. Kenny was magnificent through it all, the staff too, the players' wives – everybody rose to the occasion. Everton Football Club as well, and their supporters, were absolutely superb.

Kenny maintains that Hillsborough made us players grow

up and mature. Maybe it did, I'm not sure. I do know that it made me look at things differently. It helped me appreciate what I had in life a lot more. How precious your kids and family are. I had two young children by then. Ninety-six people died at Hillsborough. So many families had lost a loved one and having kids of your own gave you some sense of the pain they were going through. But I guess you could never come close to knowing how hard it was for them. And how hard it would be for them in the years after. It gave me some sense too of what the families of the Heysel victims had gone through four years earlier. Thirty-nine people lost their lives that night. But because they lived a long distance away, it was easier to move on with your own life. I know it shouldn't be that way, but that's human nature, I suppose. Now this tragedy had arrived on our own doorstep, it made you realise what the Heysel families had suffered and what they were still going through.

Nowadays people get counselling if they've gone through a traumatic experience. Back in 1989 I don't know how much help of that nature was available to people who needed it. A lot of people needed counselling a lot more than I did and it wouldn't have even dawned on me that it might help. What I needed, what the squad needed, was football. That was our therapy. That was the release we needed. But there was a time and a place for it and it would have to wait. We managed to fit in a little bit of training here and there but our hearts weren't in it, our heads weren't there. Eventually one day Ronnie Moran felt the time was right. Ronnie pulled us together at Melwood one morning and said the words that I think secretly we were all waiting to hear. 'Listen, this has been horrible, everything's been absolutely terrible. But you are professional footballers, this is what you do, we have to get back to it, we have to start playing again.'

Hillsborough happened on 15 April 1989. Fifteen days later we played Celtic in a friendly in Glasgow to raise funds. That was an emotional night but the game three days after that took it to another level: Everton at Goodison Park on 3 May. It was our first competitive game back, there were three points at stake, but it wasn't about a game at all. It was about a city in mourning, it was about mutual respect and gratitude and solidarity. On the pitch before the game you could feel the emotion hanging over the stadium like a cloud about to burst.

I remember saying to the referee Neil Midgley before kick-off, 'Midge, this is not a testimonial, don't let's treat it as a testimonial.' But I was only trying to kid myself. I was trying to get my head straight, I was trying to convince myself that this was just another game. But the atmosphere in the ground was telling me the exact opposite. It wasn't a normal match and it could never be a normal match. I tried to put my game-face on but in reality I didn't know how to approach it. I don't think any of the players knew how to approach it. We didn't know if it would be out of order to show you cared about the result when there were a lot more important things to care about. What if one side wins and one side loses? Is it appropriate to go and smash someone in a tackle, on an occasion like this? Would that be wrong? I think we were all walking on eggshells that day. Any betting man would have put his money down on a 0–0 draw.

It was totally fitting that our first game back would be against the other great Liverpool club. But as a footballer it wouldn't have been my choice of game. I would rather have played the likes of Manchester United where I could've got loads of frustration and emotion out, tried to kick someone or everyone. But that wasn't going to happen in this Merseyside derby. This was a game for the people of the city, not for the players. In hindsight I suppose it could be seen as the game that brought the period of public mourning to a close.

Our next game was the game that should have taken place at Hillsborough on 15 April. The FA Cup semi-final against Nottingham Forest: why should that game have ever brought about a tragedy of this magnitude, or any magnitude? There was a lot of debate beforehand about whether it should take place at all now. That a fixture that led to such a disaster should be abandoned for ever. I could see that point of view. Other people felt, and I was one of them, that it should go ahead, as a mark of respect to those who had lost their lives at the first game. You couldn't not finish it now. They had believed it was worth going to, so surely it was still worth play-ing. And we didn't just want to fulfil the fixture, we wanted to win it and we wanted to win the final in their memory. And once it was agreed, it became for us a mission. Once we took it on, we couldn't lose it. We had to get to Wembley now and get the job done once we got there. We put ourselves under a lot of pressure, but that was our small burden and we wanted to carry it.

The game took place at Old Trafford and I remember being very tense, unusually tense, in the dressing room beforehand. It was just unthinkable that we'd lose it. You knew there were so many people willing you on, but at the same time you had to try and keep a clear head and keep all the emotion at bay. Thankfully Aldo settled us down with an early goal. But Forest tried their damnedest to beat us and rightly so. Brian Clough was still manager and they weren't going to let us have it, they wanted to play in a Cup final at Wembley too.

We got through it and now we'd be facing Everton in the final. Was it fate? Who knows. But it was one of those extraordinary situations that made you wonder if sometimes these things are mapped out somewhere.

As everyone knows, Everton pushed us to the limit in the final. It was nothing we didn't expect, and there was no uncertainty about how the two sides were going to approach this game. In the twenty-four hours beforehand I don't think I ever felt pressure like it – before or since. It had become the Hillsborough final.

The pressure could have made us freeze but we seemed to channel it in a positive way into our performance. But I think it started to creep in on us as the game wore on and we defended our 1–0 lead, trying to edge minute by minute towards the final whistle. We thought we had done enough, we were just seeing the game out when up stepped Stuart McCall to take it into extra time. Now we had to do it all again, and normally the team that gets a late equaliser has the momentum in extra time.

But as badly as the Everton players wanted it, we wanted it a little bit more. We needed it, I suppose, a little bit more because it wasn't about us – it was about our supporters. I think it was this that pushed us on. Their last-minute equaliser was some kick in the guts to get but at the end of normal time there was only one thing in our heads: we've still got to win it. We have still got to win it. Then Rushie scored early in extra time and unbelievably McCall equalised again. And we were still thinking *We have to win it, we just have to win it.* Then

Barnes bent in a cross from the left, Rushie got his head on it and this time we had won it.

The two top moments of my Liverpool career – the twin peaks, if you like – are the 1984 European Cup final in Rome and the FA Cup final of 1989. The latter one, I suppose, is more personal for me. It goes back to my childhood in Finglas and a Saturday in May that came around every year. You'd park yourself in front of the television early that morning and you'd watch every minute of the coverage of the FA Cup final, from beginning to end. In fact you'd start with the Cup Final special of *It's a Knockout* and from there on you'd be glued to the build-up, which lasted hours and hours in those days. The team hotels, the player interviews, the wives and families, the action from the earlier rounds, the helicopter in the sky showing the team buses as they made their way to Wembley. And at the end of it all, the winning team climbing the steps, fans putting scarves around them, shaking hands with important people and the captain lifting the cup. It was unbelievably glamorous and exciting. It was the sort of thing you'd dream about but you wouldn't tell anyone for fear they'd laugh at you. Hansen played that day. He'd just made it back for the last half-dozen or so games of the season. But thankfully Kenny left me with the captaincy and when I lifted the cup that day it was literally a boyhood dream come true.

But that was a personal thing. For the squad and the man-ager and staff it was a huge weight off our shoulders. We'd kept our promise, we'd done what we had to do. And to do it in such dramatic circumstances, too. It made it even better that the Everton lads had made us fight for it every inch of the way. It was one of the great Cup finals. And it was played on another beautiful spring day.

Now, I think it would be far too presumptuous of me to say that winning it helped the bereaved families in some profound way. What they were suffering could not be fixed by the winning of a football game. But I'd like to think it helped for a little while, that it gave them a small bit of happiness that day. And I dread to think what people would have felt if we'd lost. The doom and gloom would have been terrible. Maybe losing would have made people feel a whole lot worse than winning made them feel better, if you know what I mean. But we didn't know how the result was going to affect people, we just knew that this was one game, above all games, that we had to win.

Back in the team hotel in London that night everyone was on a high. Then the exhaustion hit me, as it often did the night of a big win, and Elaine and I headed for our room. Elaine was in her dressing gown and I was already in bed when there was a knock on the door. Steve McMahon was there with Julie and a bottle of champagne and four glasses, big grins on their faces. They weren't ready to end the party just yet. 'Fancy one for the road?!' 'Sure why not.' I got back into bed with a glass of bubbly for company. Julie had a tight dress on that was killing her so she grabbed the hotel bathrobe from the bathroom and put that on. Macca sat on a chair and the two ladies were draped on the bed in their nightwear when there was another knock on the door. This time it was room service. We'd ordered tea and sandwiches earlier and in walked the waiter wheeling his trolley. It was hilarious, the look on his face when he saw the scene. The poor man did a quick about-turn and scarpered. We were in stitches laughing. Macca said it was like that George Best story all over again. 'Ronnie, where did it all go wrong?!'

The homecoming the next day was magnificent. The Cup final had been a special occasion for the city, both sets of supporters had taken over Wembley for the day and both teams had done themselves proud. The day couldn't really have gone any better and I think their pride was reflected in the homecoming parade. The streets were packed with supporters in blue and red and everyone had a smile on their face again.

Maybe our name was on the cup that season, after all that had happened, and maybe our name just wasn't on the league title. We all know what happened on the last day but the real damage was done in the first half of the season. At the halfway point our stats read: played 19, won 7, drawn 7, lost 5. In 1987/88 they'd read: played 19, won 14, drawn 5, lost 0. We had 47 points in the bag by then. In 1988/89 we had 28. The main difference was injuries to key players. Hansen was a pillar of the team and he was gone. Then Gary Gillespie was in and out with injuries and ended up playing just fifteen games in the league. Bruce missed a big chunk of the first half of the season too and finished with just twenty-one league appearances. That was the heart taken out of your defence and we got punished. It was a case of make-do-and-mend for a lot of games, the line-up kept changing, and that's what caused the inconsistency. We finally found some proper form in the new year and on 1 March we went on a run of nine wins from nine league games. The last of those was against Millwall at the Den on 11 April.

The postponed fixtures after Hillsborough meant we were facing a brutal schedule of eight games in twenty-three days. It began with that 0–0 match at Goodison Park on 3 May. On 7 May it was the replayed Cup semi-final with Forest, which we won 3–1. From then it went: 10 May – Forest again, Anfield, 1–0; 13 May – Wimbledon, Plough Lane, 1–2; 16 May – QPR, Anfield, 2–0; 20 May – Everton, Wembley, 3–2; 23 May – West Ham, Anfield, 5–1; 26 May – Arsenal, Anfield, 0–2.

After the Cup final we really only had a day to get ready for West Ham at Anfield on the Tuesday night. The extra time at Wembley had taken it out of our legs and there was the home-coming the next day when in normal circumstances we'd have been resting up. We didn't have enough time to recover, phys-ically and mentally. We scored five against West Ham but it wasn't a 5–1 game, far from it. We scored three in the last ten minutes. We were just dredging up reserves at this stage, almost playing from memory. We needed a break, we needed time to recuperate. But the powers-that-be in television apparently decided that the following Friday night would suit them best; the ratings would go through the roof. That's what mattered. Would Sunday afternoon have made such a big difference to them? Or Saturday? Stupid question. Our job was to be seen and not heard.

We were never sent out to play cautiously and we weren't that night against Arsenal either. But maybe it was the unspo-ken thought in the back of our minds: we don't need to win here, a draw will do. Even a 0–1 for Arsenal will win us the title. Maybe that thought infected our minds in some way, without us even knowing. If we'd needed to win we might have found an extra spurt of passion and adrenaline from some-where. But I don't think we were fully clear in our minds about what way to approach the game. On top of that we were phys-ically and emotionally exhausted. There was nothing left in the tank. I know I was running on empty. I was plodding along, trying and trying to get into the game, but nothing was getting me there. And once they scored after half-time they had all the momentum and we couldn't raise a gallop. I think we went into hold-out mode after that. Just contain them and maybe catch them on the counter. And we nearly, nearly, nearly made it. We were seconds away.

And then Mickey T goes and makes a name for himself! I could see it happening as it unfolded, almost in slow-motion. The ball going through the middle, Michael Thomas running on to it, Bruce coming out, Ray sprinting to get back. It was a difficult chance to take and I was thinking Bruce would get a block on it or Ray would get the tackle in or Thomas would take a bad touch. So much could have gone wrong with that chance. I couldn't believe it when the ball hit the net. Could not believe it. You're seeing something right in front of your eyes but you're not taking it in. And then the final whistle goes and the Arsenal players are going mad and some of our lads are stretched out on the ground completely stunned and miserable. But I didn't hang around. I must've been in the players' lounge five minutes after the final whistle. I ran straight to the dressing room and was stripped, showered and suited in minutes. I was just blank. I had no energy to cry or curse or feel sorry for myself. The only emotion I could feel was relief. *Thank God it's over. Thank God it's over.* It was the most draining, stressful season of my life at Liverpool and I was just glad that it was over.

The hurt started to seep in over the next few weeks when I couldn't stop myself any more from thinking about what had happened. To have it taken away from you like that. In the last seconds of the last game of the season. The Arsenal lads deserve every credit in the world for going to Anfield and taking the title from under our noses. It took serious bottle to do that. It's a legendary game now, but it still hurts and it looks at this stage like it always will. Six of us played that night who would've become the first players to win the double twice. That's something I'd love to have on my CV, and it's a regret that I don't. But I've always been able to live with it too. The regrets never ate me up inside. If it had been a normal season, if Hillsborough had never happened, it would've hurt me to the bone. I'd have been devastated. But I'd seen what real suffering was like in the hospital that day, and at the funerals in the days after, and I knew that what I was feeling just couldn't compare. And I think that's why the Liverpool supporters were philosophical about it too in the end. They gave the Arsenal players a tremendous ovation when the game was over. And they were brilliant with us too. They knew what we'd been through, they knew we'd given it everything in those eight games and they knew we had nothing left to give that night at Anfield.

And sometimes I'm inclined to wonder, was it in the stars, like the Cup final? Was someone somewhere saying, 'You've won the Cup, you can't have them all. It was Arsenal's day, it was Mickey T's moment.' That sort of thing.

It's now twenty-two years and counting since Hillsborough. I've had hundreds of conversations in the years since then with my team-mates who were there that day. And we have never talked about it. It's something we went through together and I guess no one wants to go back there. I suppose every one of us has thought about it and reflected on it in their own time and space. We all remember it, but we don't want to talk about it. Maybe we will some day sit down over a pint and discuss it; maybe we should. It seems a long time ago now but I suppose it's just still too raw to touch.

I don't think about it now as much as I used to. But in the years that followed it would often come into my mind, out of the blue. And when it did, I would think a lot about Ian Whelan and his family. These days it comes back into my mind from time to time, and when it does, I think about them still.

13

Rush & Co

John Aldridge's early goal in that 1989 Cup final was a clinical finish, stroked first time into the top corner. He made a difficult chance look easy.

Ian Rush had come back from Italy the previous summer and he struggled with injuries and form that season. But it was still no surprise that it was Rushie who stole the headlines on the big day. He scored his first goal early in extra time: a touch to control the ball in from Nico, shielding it on his chest with his back to goal, then the pivot and shot in one movement. And the winner: a delicate header, adjusting his body to get a glance on the cross from Barnes.

That was in May. The following September Aldo was gone to Spain. And it wasn't on his holidays. There was room for two strikers of that calibre in the squad, but Kenny obviously felt there wasn't room for both of them in the same team. Aldo saw the writing on the wall. He'd had first dibs on the jersey throughout 1988/89 and had made the most of it: 47 games, 31 goals. Rushie played 30 times for 11 goals.

But there was no doubt in Kenny's mind. If one of them had to give way, it wasn't going to be Rush. Aldo was one of the best centre-forwards of his generation; Rush was one of the best of the century.

There's very few strikers you look at and think, he's going to get us a goal today. It will happen. It's just inevitable that he will score today. Your opponents will know everything about him; they'll maybe put a man-marker to him; they'll want to kick him if they get a chance. And none of it will matter. He will still get us a goal.

Rush played 660 games for Liverpool; he scored 346 goals. So in reality it wasn't inevitable he'd score every game. It just felt that way. He scored a goal every two games and it was this phenomenal consistency that made you think *Rushie will get us a goal today.* No one could stop him scoring goals. He was a goal machine because he was as reliable as a machine. It is the hardest thing to do in the game of football, to score a goal, and he did it over and over and over. Tap-ins from two yards, belters from outside the box, volleys, headers, left foot and right – any which way the ball came to him.

He stole most of the headlines on the small days too. From the bread-and-butter games to the crunch three-pointers to the big gala occasions, he was there making his runs, ghosting in behind defenders, getting the ball in the net.

He was lightning quick. That's why he scored so many little goals, if you could call them that, because of his reflexes and his pace – he was there ahead of anybody over five yards, two yards, half a yard. And it would be a goal before anyone knew anything about it.

It can't be coached, that sort of nerve, that sort of instinct in front of goal. Aldridge had it too and so had Robbie Fowler,

whose first season in the team was my last. I never understood
how that instinct worked, but they had it. Like, why did the
ball always seem to drop to them? Why didn't it drop to me as
a midfielder? I hung around the box too on many an occasion,
trying to read the break of the ball and usually being in the
wrong place. Why were they so often in the right place?
They'd take a chance on getting in front of the centre-back
and it'd drop for them there; take a chance on getting behind
the centre-back and it'd drop for them there. Crosses, rico-
chets, fumbles – they'd be there to pick up the pieces. Thanks
very much, see ya later. I guess we'll just have to call it a sixth
sense.

Then there was the confidence. I was sat beside Aldo in the
dugout that day in Orlando when Ireland played Mexico at
USA '94. We were two goals down and I could hear Aldo agi-
tating to get on the field. He kept saying within earshot of Jack
Charlton, 'Put me on! Put me on and I'll score.' He believed
absolutely that he'd get a goal: he knew how to do it, he'd been
doing it all his life. In his head, a World Cup game against
Mexico in Florida was still just another game of football. It
held no fears for him. So he wasn't one bit happy being on the
bench when he was convinced that he'd score. Maybe it's part
of the psychology strikers have to have, never doubting that
they'll score. But he was chomping at the bit that day. Which
is why he famously bawled the official out of it who was delay-
ing his entry on to the pitch. Then six minutes from time, the
ball came across, Aldo met it with a textbook header and
Ireland had the goal that ultimately saw us through to the last
sixteen.

He went through long periods of his international career not
scoring because he was too busy running the channels for Jack.

But he kept showing up for chances. He wouldn't hide, he wouldn't not make the run in case he'd miss the chance. He was never frightened of missing chances. He wasn't frightened either of taking a boot to the head or sticking a leg out and getting it hacked, if it meant putting the ball in the net.

Aldo was twenty-eight when he signed for Liverpool and there were a few doubts that he could do it at the highest level. He'd scored plenty for Newport and Oxford but this was a different kind of pressure and he had big boots to fill. And it didn't faze him one bit. He scored sixty goals in his two full seasons and became a real folk hero. A lot of fellas were at Liverpool a lot longer and didn't end up half as popular. The fans loved him because he was one of their own; it was like he'd come down off the Kop and done what they'd dreamed of doing. Then he went off to Real Sociedad and continued scoring goals there.

Robbie Fowler was obviously another natural finisher. Our careers only overlapped for one season but long before he made the breakthrough you could see his class. He was showing it at Melwood practically every day. You could hear him too, as well as see him, because if there was any messing going on among the kids, he was usually in the thick of it. But when he drifted into the first-team squad he looked like he belonged straightaway. Lovely clean striker of a ball, unbelievably quick feet to buy himself half a yard, and ice cool in front of goal. He'd place a lot of balls past the keeper rather than lash them; he always seemed to have the angles worked out in his head so that he could steer his goals into the side netting, just rolling them inside the posts. And he could produce a piece of magic in a tight corner to slip defenders and get his shot off. Robbie was a very clever, instinctive scorer of goals.

All three of them were specialists and there wasn't much to choose between them when it came to the pure art of finishing. Rush had the most pace, Aldo was the best in the air, Fowler could improvise brilliantly.

But Rush was the greatest by a distance. The longevity and consistency of his career might never be matched at Liverpool. He broke Roger Hunt's all-time record and he broke just about every other record too. Then there was his work ethic and all-round team play. He was so prolific he could've gotten away with contributing a lot less than he did. But he had the ability to operate like a centre midfielder too: holding up the ball, linking the play, laying it off. Aldo was a poacher, he lived in the box and didn't do a lot outside of it. Robbie did a bit more but Rushie was streets ahead in all other departments – he just had a bigger game to offer the team.

And it's well documented by now how hard he worked as a defender. He never stopped chasing across the line, trying to put pressure on opponents in possession. He knew he was our first line of defence and he took the job seriously. If a centre-back was coming out with the ball, Rushie had this trick where he'd try and fake a lack of interest: go ahead, I'm not bothered chasing after you. But he'd be on red alert. And if the centre-back relaxed a bit, maybe just touched the ball that little bit too far in front, Rushie would be on to it like a shot. More often than not he wouldn't win the ball, but we could win it back because the centre-back might have had to clear it in a hurry. We generally got the ball back very early and often it was because Rushie had put the original pressure on. He was willing to do that sort of graft. He was selfish when it came to the business of scoring goals and he was totally selfless when it came to working for the team.

Ian's presence up front had another effect on us too. You didn't mind working your socks off to try and keep a clean sheet because there was always the chance that he'd find a goal at the other end. If a game wasn't going well and you were struggling to break the stalemate you'd be thinking *Keep a clean sheet here. Just keep a clean sheet and Rushie will nick us one.* Kenny, of course, could get us one too, lots of lads could, but with Rushie you went that extra yard to keep a clean sheet knowing that it could be late in the day before he'd get one.

There were times later on, in the early 1990s, when he missed a lot of games through injury or because someone else was selected, where you found it harder to keep holding out because you knew deep down you weren't going to score at the other end. It's not something you could keep doing week in week out, you'd soon get pissed off with the whole thing. *Bloody hell! We're not scoring goals and we've got to do this again, try and get something out of the game.* Having Rushie up front always gave us hope that we'd get the vital goal.

He has often said himself that he got great service. He and Kenny obviously had a brilliant understanding; they were a world-class partnership. Barnes, Beardsley and Houghton when they came along; they all knew how and when to slip him the through ball that would put him in the clear. And me and Rushie went back a long way too. We had a good understanding, especially during my days on the left of midfield. It wasn't a thing we ever practised in training. We never really talked about it much. You'd get on the ball and you'd look up and you'd be reading his movement and his body language. There'd be no words but he'd be saying, 'Just put it there. I'm ready to go, just put it there.' Other times it'd be, 'Don't play it yet, hold it a tick, I'll go offside if I move now.' So you'd wait a tick and then it'd be, 'OK! Get it in here now!' And you'd put it where he wanted it. The centre-back probably just wouldn't see enough of him and by the time he'd react, it'd be too late.

He'd pick his times to make his move. He would switch on if Kenny or some of us got on the ball because he'd be thinking *One of these will see me.* But there were other times when he'd sort of knock off a little bit when someone else had the ball because he'd know he wasn't going to get it exactly the way he wanted it.

The lads gave me plenty of stick over the years for always being first on the scene to celebrate his latest goal – or to celebrate anyone's goal. Well, I wasn't *always* the first, but I'd usually be there pretty quick all the same. Which is why I ended up in a lot of newspaper photographs the next day or in the TV pictures on *Match of the Day* that night. But I swear, it had nothing to do with that; I never ever in my life thought about bloody cameras or photographs or anything like that. I was just happier than everyone else – what's wrong with being happy?! What's wrong with celebrating a goal?! Because I'd get so nervous before a game, I used to love the relief that came with a goal. I'd be, 'Yessssss! Rushie, ya good thing ya! Brilliant!' And I'd be running after them and jumping up on top of them and all that carry on. And you always wanted to acknowledge the guy who'd laid on the goal too. 'Great ball, you saw the pass, well done.' And the goals I scored, if somebody had picked me out with a great ball, you'd want to give him a nod, make sure he knew you appreciated it.

Now, while we're on the subject, and I hope I'm not turning into Victor Meldrew here, but is there anything more stupid these days than a fella taking his jersey off after he's scored? You're going to get booked, you clown, and you *know* you're going to get booked. Like, it's in the rules! You can celebrate, you can run like mad, you can do triple somersaults if you want, but don't take your jersey off. Can't fathom that at all. Oh, and don't start kissing the badge on your shirt either. If another club offered you another ten bob in your wages you'd be out the door in a flash. Kissing the badge does my head in.

And so do pre-match huddles. I don't see the good it does. You see teams doing pre-match huddles and then they're stuffed four-nil. You see teams doing pre-match huddles every week and they're second from bottom in the league. What good is it doing them? We'd have scoffed at it if someone ever suggested it. Whatever bonding was needed was already done. A few words in the dressing room – now let's get out and do it. Save your huddles for your missus.

I was best man the day Rushie got married to his missus. I hope Ian and Tracy weren't regretting it when I stood up to make a speech that would qualify for the worst best man's speech in the history of best man's speeches. I had to apologise to the happy couple afterwards. I think I had to apologise to the priest too, for a joke that wasn't, as Kenny Everett used say, in the best possible taste. It wasn't the greatest performance of my career but what can I say – I was never the best when it came to public speaking.

Rushie gave me the honour because we'd been good mates at Liverpool from day one. I arrived in September 1979, he arrived the following May. We were the same age, just a month between us, and I think we bonded because we both found ourselves in the same boat at Anfield. Shy, quiet lads, a bit intimidated by our surroundings and struggling to find our feet. We came into the first team more or less at the same time and we both felt like outsiders in that dressing room for a while. So we had a lot in common and we stuck together. The two of us did most of our socialising together, went out for beers many a time and had many a laugh. When he scored his goals I was happy for him and if I provided the assist I was happier still. You can still see old TV footage of the team celebrating a Cup final at Wembley, the lads running around doing their lap of the pitch, and usually at the back of the group you'll find me and Rushie just walking along and having a chat.

We started out living this dream at eighteen years of age and it lasted another fifteen years. That's a long time and there were a lot of ups and downs. We were there during the triumphs and the tragedies, went through some bad days and celebrated a lot of great ones. There's a lot of shared history there, I suppose. You don't make a lot of real friends in football but I'm glad to say that I count Rushie among mine.

14

The Man Comes Around

Seven years after leaving for Italy, Graeme Souness walked back into our lives. He still had the 'tache and the tan but a lot of other things had changed. Souey had managed Rangers for five years and had made a major impact: big moves in the transfer market, lots of controversies and four Scottish championships.

I thought he was exactly the manager Liverpool needed. I was thrilled he was coming back. There was no one better to take over from Kenny. We all thought the same, especially the old pros who'd soldiered with him during his playing days. He was steeped in Liverpool. He knew how the club worked. He knew how we played the game. He had five years of high-level management under his belt. He was the ideal man. Sad to see Kenny go, but this was a new era and we were going to win things; I had no doubt about it.

That was April 1991. Fast forward to April 1993. Blackburn Rovers have turned us over 4–1 at Ewood Park. Souey went ballistic in the dressing room afterwards and he was well entitled to because we'd been absolutely stuffed – and by a team, as it happened, that was managed by Kenny. But Souey had been feeling the pressure long before that game. We'd now won just four of the last fourteen. The losing streak included a 0–2 defeat to Bolton – who back then were playing in the third tier of English football – at Anfield in the Cup in January. That result had really turned up the heat on him and us. And now we'd been torn apart by Blackburn.

I'd played the four previous games having come back from an injury: we'd won three and drawn the other one. I was making a difference, and I had a decent game against Blackburn too in centre midfield. So when Souey started ranting about 'the older players' in the Ewood Park dressing room that day, I took exception. He didn't name us but he was referring to me, Nicol, Barnes and Rush. The rest of the team was David James, Mike Marsh, David Burrows, Steve Harkness, Ronny Rosenthal, Don Hutchison and Mark Walters. Souey's accusation was that we weren't doing enough to help them along. Not just this game but every game. He was giving out stink and his analysis of the situation boiled down to one problem – the older players. He had a bee in his bonnet about us for some reason, and it didn't just start at Blackburn; he'd raised it as an issue several times in the months before that.

And here he was again banging on about it. I was fuming inside because, number one, there was no acknowledgement from him that he might be at fault too. And number two, it wasn't true: I knew from personal experience that some of the young lads wouldn't listen when you tried talking to them in training. And if you shouted at them in the heat of a match, one or two of them would turn round and tell you where to go.

Eventually I had enough. I said to Souey, 'Look, it's not as simple as that. You try talking to them and they tell you to fuck off.' That only made him worse. 'Who? Who tells you that? Who tells you that?' I just shrugged my shoulders. 'Tell me who they are and I'll back you up!' He was losing it now. 'Tell me who they are and I'll back you up!' And I said, 'Just like you're backing me up now?' He flipped after that, started screaming. 'You tell me!' And I wouldn't reply. 'You tell me!'

And it just descended into a shouting match. I'm putting my tie on at this stage and I've my back turned to him, looking in the mirror, hoping he'll let it go. But he wouldn't let it go. He kept challenging me. So I snapped back at him. 'Ah, just fuck off and leave me alone.' And he's still shouting, 'You tell me!' And every time he says it I say back, 'Fuck off, Souey.' 'You tell me!' 'Fuck off, Souey.'

It just got silly in the end. You can imagine the silence around the room.

And I remember distinctly, when all this was going on, looking over and seeing Ronnie Moran and Roy Evans. And I'm a hundred per cent sure that the two of them were nodding their heads at me as if to say, 'Yeah, we know, you're right.' Souey was saying he'd back me up but I wasn't convinced about that! It was the older lads I wanted to back me up against him. But none of them did. I was getting shot down completely and no one backed me up, which was a bit of a sad situation really. Maybe they didn't feel the way I felt about it, but I wasn't going to take the blame for all that was going on. There was a lot more going wrong than just the older players supposedly not helping the younger players. Five weeks later we finished sixth in the league. In January 1994, nine months after that bust-up at Blackburn, Graeme resigned.

The first thing that should be said is that Souey got some things right, even though people – and I was one of them –

thought they were wrong at the time. I can remember going into training one winter's morning and looking forward to my bacon-and-egg toastie in the canteen at Melwood because it was cold and I was hungry and a nice hot toastie would do the trick. But I was told it was off the menu. What?! You're joking. 'Sorry, love, we're not allowed any more. We can toast a slice of brown bread if you like?' Ah here. Come on now. Toasted brown bread? You might as well give me a slice of chipboard. A different diet was soon part of the new regime. The menu was changed. The days of your bacon, sausage and egg breakfast – with toasted *white* bread – were gone. Even if they wanted to, the dinner ladies would be wary of doing us a fry in case they'd get into trouble. And you weren't going to be getting your chicken and chips and beans for lunch either. It was fish and salads and boiled chicken and pasta. Get it into you and stop moaning about it. But of course we did plenty of moaning about it. Where is he going with his chicken and his pasta and his rabbit food? Didn't Souey himself win plenty of trophies on steak and chips and lager? Now it's feckin' pasta and Perrier water.

To be fair, he didn't impose a drinking ban. Maybe because it wouldn't have worked. He was more into emphasising the importance of good nutrition; eating the right food, taking the right supplements, drinking enough water. It was the Italian influence. He'd learned a lot about the football culture in Italy during his two years at Sampdoria. He'd adopted the lifestyle of the professional footballer there and that included their diet, which was obviously a lot stricter than ours. Now he was introducing it to us and with our typical insular attitude in British football, we thought it was a load of cobblers.

He brought in a lady dietician one day early on in his

regime, to try and enlighten us. She sat us down in the players'
lounge at Anfield and began by asking some questions. She
wanted to emphasise the importance of restoring fluids and
nutrition to the body after a hard ninety-minute match. 'So,
what do you do straight after a game?' And Nico said, 'Well,
we usually go to the players' lounge and have a pint.' And I
could see Souey out of the corner of my eye folding his arms,
looking a little bit uneasy. 'That's OK,' she said, 'a pint after a
game is fine. And what do you do then?' And Nico told her,
'Well, we have another one.' And a few of the lads were giggling now. 'And then another one.' And Souey was looking
down at the floor now, getting more uncomfortable with this
conversation. And then she said, 'Well, when do you eat after
a game?' And Nico said, 'About half-two in the morning you'd
have a Chinese.'

The lads were sniggering, she was trying to hide her shock
and Souey was trying to hide his embarrassment. He had a lot
of work to do with us on the refuelling front. But it was just
that in England he was ahead of his time on this issue. That
was 1991. I don't think many clubs were preaching the importance of a proper diet back then. Everyone takes it for granted
now.

He also decided to change the traditional routine for daily
training. Instead of meeting at Anfield and getting stripped
there first, we'd all go straight to Melwood. Since Shankly's
time it had always been Anfield first, then Melwood, but the
time had come to change it. Anfield was getting too busy, there
was too much going on around the club day-to-day with corporate events, various meetings, visitors, people coming and
going. It was hard to get a car park space a lot of mornings now
and it made sense to change the routine.

Souey was moving the whole operation to Melwood and one major casualty was the boot room. That caused a lot of controversy, abandoning the boot room and having it converted into a press room. But he couldn't pick the boot room up and physically transfer it to Melwood. And I'm not sure, but apparently the board of directors had previously drawn up plans to have it converted anyway. Whatever the truth, times had changed. The original boot room men were gone. It wasn't Bill Shankly and Bob Paisley and Joe Fagan and Reuben Bennett (the only original boot room member who never managed Liverpool) sitting there any more. It was Souey and Phil Boersma. But the boot room had an aura about it and when Souey's reign started turning sour on him, getting rid of the boot room became a sort of symbol, I suppose, of the way things had gone wrong.

But in those early days Souey was a man in a hurry and there was no room for sentiment. He wanted to change things and he wanted them changed now. We saw it first in pre-season training. Ronnie and Roy were looking to do it the old Liverpool way, tried and trusted over the years. A load of 440m and 880m runs, done at intervals, rest periods in between. Graeme had brought Phil with him down from Rangers as his assistant cum fitness trainer. And they wanted to put their stamp on things, so we effectively ended up doing nearly two pre-season sessions every day. Bugsy and Evo would put us through our paces and we'd be knackered after it. Then we'd face into twenty minutes of envelope running as ordered by Boey and Souey. Across the back of the goal, reach the corner flag then a long diagonal run to the flag in the bottom corner, up the side of the pitch, reach the corner flag then a long diagonal down to the other corner; half-pace, three-quarter

The Double : 1986
The Reds Return To Liverpool Following Victory Over
Everton in the 1986 FA Cup Final.

May '86: the Double is in the bag, the boys are back in town.

Probably my proudest moment in Liverpool red:
lifting the FA Cup and fulfilling a boyhood dream.

October '87: the new era is underway and the goals are raining down. John Barnes scored twice against QPR that day and as usual I was first to arrive on the scene.

Euro '88: the three amigos go wild in Stuttgart.
Yes, Ray, we all know who put the ball in the England net.

The goal. Ireland v USSR, Euro '88: wasn't bad, was it?! I mean Mick's throw-in. They don't throw them in like that anymore. That's me hitting the deck after making the volley. I still didn't know at that point where the ball was going to end up. I found out soon enough.

The greatest ever homecoming: a nation descends on Dublin to welcome us back from Germany.

October '89: Lansdowne Road – the ball is on its way to the Northern Ireland net.
I've got the shot away before Norman Whiteside (white shirt) arrives;
Kevin Sheedy, Ray Houghton and John Aldridge are in the vicinity.

November '89: Aldo in the famous red shirt of . . . Malta. We've just beaten them 2–0 in Valetta to
qualify for Ireland's first World Cup. Aldo scored both goals, I was captain – Italia '90 here we come.

CHAMPIONS
Liverpool FC Celebrate A Record 18th Title
1989/90

April 1990: the last Liverpool squad to win the league.

The Christmas party – what are we like?! Bruce, me and Spackers.
And an unidentified female friend.

When we were friends: Jack and me in happier times.

April '92: Portsmouth at Highbury, FA Cup semi-final. The scoreboard operator hasn't reacted yet, but it's 1–1. Best tap-in of my career. I get injured in the replay and miss the final.

USA '94: not seeing much game time but I'm making the most of it anyway. Paul and Ma and me at one of the after-match parties in America.

Beauty and the bloke: Elaine was the star on our wedding day, I scrubbed up best I could.

Two daughters and a daddy: Georgia (left) and Elizabeth join in
the celebrations on my testimonial night at Anfield.

All grown up now: Paul, Ma and me; Rosemarie (left), Janice and Ann.

pace, jog across the back of the goal, and repeat the process for twenty minutes. It was the new manager laying down a marker: I mean business here. There's going to be no shirking around here. But it led to injuries. It was obviously too much because a lot of players early on started getting niggles and strains, hamstrings and groins, and a few ended up getting bad Achilles injuries that needed operations.

To be fair, Souey in general had rotten luck with injured players throughout his time in charge. It made it that bit harder to get consistent performances week in week out. But I don't believe the lack of success had anything to do with the changes he made. A lot of it was good and needed to be done. He also improved facilities and he modernised our medical treatment too.

Souey failed for two reasons: his judgement of players and the way he handled players, both young and old. You live and die by the players you bring in – and also by the players you let go. After that, you need good man-management skills, and at times his were terrible.

Between summer and Christmas of 1991 the manager got rid of six players. That was a statement in itself. Peter Beardsley, Steve McMahon and Steve Staunton were among them. Stan was twenty-two, he went on to have seven great seasons at Aston Villa and became one of the best left-backs in the country. McMahon still had plenty more to contribute. Beardsley went to Everton and had two brilliant seasons there before moving to Newcastle where he put in another three or four great seasons. Gary Ablett was also sold to Everton and had four good years with them. Gary Gillespie was thirty-one and troubled with injuries so, fair enough, Gary was probably going to move on.

Mark Wright was the big-money signing who was going to anchor our defence. He wasn't a Hansen or a Thompson or a Lawrenson, but players of that calibre are hard to find anyway. But he was the England centre-back so in theory at least he looked like a good choice. But we found ourselves having to adapt to a new style of play with the back four, rather than the back four adapting to the Liverpool style of play. They didn't operate the way the likes of Hansen and Tommo and Lawro and Gary Gillespie did, which was to push up and hold the line behind you. I was the one sitting in front of the back four and I was used to the lads pressing high up and leaving no gaps between us. You'd close down the opposition midfielders, somebody would play a ball past you and one of our centre-backs would usually be there to step up and intercept the ball or get tight to the centre-forward. Now you'd turn around and the defenders would've dropped fifteen yards back and there'd be a big gap for a centre-forward or a runner from midfield to exploit.

We'd never had to do patterns of play in training, everybody knew the system. But now we're doing patterns of play and it's another thing the manager has to deal with. Graeme was doing a lot of coaching and explaining, trying to iron out problems like this. 'If our midfield is closing down their midfield, the back four shouldn't be dropping off.' But the back four was dropping off and suddenly there was a lot of disruption to the way we played and it had a knock-on effect. It's a bit like a golfer changing his swing, I suppose: even small adjustments can destabilise the whole thing and leave him struggling for a long time. Trying to change from one system to another in a team takes time and leaves the team vulnerable. And if it leads to a few bad results it will affect confidence and then you're quickly into a downward spiral of more bad results and lower levels of confidence.

When managers moved on players it never upset me because in one way it was none of my business – you just had to get on with it. We still had to play no matter who was bought or sold. But of course it *was* our business, more than anyone else's arguably, because we had to play with them and deal with the consequences if they weren't doing the job. So if the manager was selling somebody the one question you'd be asking yourself was, 'OK, is he getting someone better in?' Souey sold Beardsley for £1 million and brought in Dean Saunders for £2.9 million and Mark Walters for £1.25 million. That was a net outlay of £3 million. I liked Deano and Wally but between the two of them they couldn't do what Beardsley did. The answer to the question in this case was: 'No.'

Rob Jones arrived from Crewe in October 1991 and Rob was a player; he was the real deal and a terrific signing. Mickey Thomas arrived in December and was one of Souey's better signings too. To be fair to everyone, I think we'll just draw a discreet veil over the signing of poor old Istvan Kozma. It's probably best for all.

But you had a team now that wasn't stable and united. There was a lot of individual play. Different players were doing different things. They weren't fitting into a system. It wasn't just the defence; a lot of things weren't right. We had our moments, times when we clicked and looked pretty impressive. But the reality was we were a team that wasn't hard to beat. I'd played with a team that was one of the hardest to beat there's ever been. And I played in a team that had so much flair it could go and win a game out of nowhere. Souey's team was neither one thing nor the other. Wally, for example, was one of those players who could produce a piece of magic in a game, but not often enough to help you win the league. And that's pretty much how the team performed as well. A lot of good moments but not consistent enough to win a league. And that's the standard we should be talking about at Liverpool. You want to be looking at players who are good enough to win a league and we weren't bringing in players of that calibre. We didn't gel as a team and it never really happened for us that first season.

And I don't think we ever recovered. The clear-out had been too radical. He had changed too much too soon. There was no stability there. Souey was always scrambling after that to find the right combination. He was flailing around in the transfer market, buying and selling without much rhyme or reason, trying to find the winning formula. In the summer of 1992 Houghton, Venison and Glenn Hysen were sold. In September Saunders was sold to Villa. In came David James, Paul Stewart and Torben Piechnik. Things were going from bad to worse now. In the summer of 1993 Mike Marsh and David Burrows were swapped to West Ham for Julian Dicks. Nigel Clough and Neil Ruddock also arrived. Stewart, Dicks and Ruddock were bought because Souey wanted strong, hard men in his team. And that's fine – Souey was a strong, hard man too. But he was a top class ball player as well.

Time and again his decisions in the transfer market left us shaking our heads. Some of the lads he brought in, they looked good prospects, and even though they didn't work out you could understand why he bought them. Others, you didn't even need to see them playing before you knew they wouldn't be good enough. It seems to me that the more the pressure on him increased, the more his judgement deteriorated. Souey signed fifteen players in two years. He tore up the tried and trusted way of doing it, which was to make one or two changes per season, building a new side patiently and carefully. The template had been there for decades, and no one knew it better than himself. But this was a manager who was going to do it his way: I'm getting my own players in and I'm going to succeed with these players.

Apart from Rob Jones, it'd be hard to say that any of his signings ever really worked out. Some players would have one good season, maybe two at a stretch, and after that it would all fizzle out. He has made a lot of excuses over the years about why it didn't work out for him at Liverpool, and he has thrown around a fair bit of blame. It was the squad Kenny left him; it was players looking for more money; it was the older players hanging around for testimonials; it was players not showing enough pride in the jersey. Let's say for the sake of argument that he's right about all this. OK. Now, could he please take a look at the players he signed? How many of them were good enough for Liverpool Football Club? His dealings in the transfer market were pretty abysmal. We finished sixth in the table in 1991/92, eighteen points behind Leeds. It was Liverpool's worst finish since 1964/65. A club that hadn't been out of the top two for ten years was back with the also-rans. We finished sixth again in 1992/93, twenty-five points behind Man United. We finished eighth in 1993/94, thirty-two points behind United. I rest my case.

I also believe his man-management skills could have been a lot better. With Souey it was my way or the highway. In fairness, he wasn't confrontational all the time. He was confrontational when things weren't going well. So I suppose he was confrontational a lot of the time – and in a bad mood the rest of the time. But I honestly know that he wanted it to work. From the bottom of his heart he wanted it to work. I would have loved if he'd succeeded, and I wanted to help him as much as I could. He was an old mate, after all, and I had nothing but admiration for him as a player. But I was just plagued with so many injuries. I missed huge chunks of his first two seasons. Maybe I was a bit naïve, thinking that we could have a closer relationship than he might have had with the younger lads, seeing what we'd been through together as players. And I never forgot the tribute he paid me on television after we beat Aston Villa in the FA Cup. It was March 1992, I'd come back after a long injury and played fairly well; Souey said I epitomised what Liverpool Football Club was all about; he said I'd given my heart and soul to the club over the years; it was a really nice thing to say and it gave me a great boost at the time.

But sadly it was all downhill from there. I lost the captaincy to Mark Wright soon after and he had the honour of lifting the FA Cup at Wembley later that same season – the one trophy Graeme did bring to the club and which shouldn't be overlooked either. Then the Premier League kicked in at the start of 1992/93 and everybody was issued with squad numbers.

Players have a thing about the number on their shirt. Ray Kennedy had worn the No. 5 shirt so I got it when I took over from him. I didn't own the number, I also wore 8 and 10 over the years. But early in 1982/83 I was out injured and not playing great when I got back into the team. Then in September 1982 we played Dundalk in the first round of the European Cup at Oriel Park. Before the game I asked Ronnie Moran, 'Can I wear number five today?' Bugsy grunted back at me, 'Wear whatever you want.' So I wore the No. 5, I scored two goals that day, and it was always my lucky number after that. I tried to get it as often as I could and eventually I wore it more or less constantly for seven years. Then I found out in the 1992/93 pre-season that Wrighty would be the permanent captain now and that he'd be wearing the No. 5 shirt. I'd be wearing No. 12. A manager with half-decent man-management skills would've gone to a player who'd been there all his career, whether it was me or anybody else, and explained the situation. No big deal: just show a bit of respect and courtesy to a long-serving player, that's all.

In September 1993 Everton beat us 2–0 in the derby at Goodison Park. It was another setback and the mood at the club was bad. I had a poor game on the day and I wasn't the only one. A few days later I was in the corridor by the dressing room and I saw Souey coming from the opposite direction. I looked at him to say hello or something but he just put his head down and passed me by without a word. Totally blanked me. I think I'd have preferred if he'd just hit me a good punch. But it was very petty. There was no need for it. As a manager you don't just blank a player like that. He obviously felt I was one of the main culprits for the Everton result and I was dropped from the squad for the next game, against Fulham the following Wednesday. The next game would be against Chelsea at Stamford Bridge and by now I was training with the reserves. I wasn't involved with the squad at all.

On Friday morning after training the squad would be travelling down to London; they had their overnight bags and their suits with them at Melwood. Someone came to me on the training ground and said I was wanted in the manager's office. Souey was at his desk. One of the first-team players had picked up a knock in training. 'We need you to travel down to

Chelsea with us. Can you go home and get your suit?' Naturally enough the atmosphere between us was fairly frosty. I said
OK but as I was walking out the door I couldn't resist having
a snipe. 'You must have a lot of fucking injuries if you're asking
me.' I didn't wait for the reply. I went home, got my gear and
travelled down with the team. An hour before kick-off Souey
named his team and subs and I wasn't even on the bench. I was
stunned. What was that all about? Was it because I'd given him
a bit of lip in his office?

One way or another, it wasn't something you'd do to a kid,
drag him all the way to London and then leave him there in his
civvies. And it certainly wasn't something you'd do to a veteran.
I was thirty-two years of age, I'd been in the first team for
twelve seasons, I'd played something like 460 games at this
stage. Again it was poor man-management, a basic lack of
respect. He knew it wasn't the done thing. He could've said
something, made some gesture, 'Sorry about that.' But he
never said a word.

He'd done the same thing the previous season with Bruce
Grobbelaar, except in this case he dragged Bruce all the way
back from Angola. Bruce was out there to play two World Cup
qualifiers with Zimbabwe. David James was injured, so
Graeme contacted Bruce to tell him he was needed. He could
fly back in on the Tuesday, play the next night and fly back out
again on the Thursday. So Bruce hauled himself back from
Africa only to be told that Mike Hooper would be playing.
Souness maintained apparently that he never told Bruce he'd
be playing. But I don't think Bruce would have come all the
way back from Angola if he didn't believe a hundred per cent
that he was going to be involved. Again, it was shabby treatment of a veteran who deserved a lot more respect than that.

The game in question was that infamous replay with Bolton in the Cup.

These were small incidents in the greater scheme of things; he was only antagonising a few individuals here and it would be kept in-house, as these things always should. It was a lot more serious when things went public and it was Souey himself who went public on the tensions in the camp after that Bolton game. He couldn't contain his frustration any more. He went on a rant to the press afterwards. 'They (the players) don't see playing for Liverpool as the pinnacle of their careers. They are only interested in getting another move or another lump sum of money and that's totally unacceptable. You can have players with all the ability in the world but when they go out not wanting to run around and fight for the ball as much as other teams then you're going to lose.'

And as a manager you're going to lose the dressing room if you come out with stuff like that to the press. This was his man-management at its worst. He broke a cardinal rule here, slating the players like that. He was basically calling us greedy and gutless in front of the public. It was a reckless thing to do. The irony was he'd signed six of the players who played that day himself.

Melwood was not a happy place in those days. We were losing games, we were dropping down the league and we were always uptight in front of the manager. You couldn't relax and enjoy your football, everyone was walking on eggshells around him. Players are at their best when they're happy and content. When they're not, it shows on the pitch too. The fun had gone out of it.

I think Souey went into the job the way he used to go into tackles, full steam ahead, not caring whether he hurt himself or anyone else. Everybody was sorry to see him go when he left as a player; I'm not so sure it was the same when he left as manager.

Now, all of this would've been water under the bridge a long time ago if it weren't for comments that Souey made in a book which I cannot let go unchallenged. They concern the Liverpool veterans who were still there when he was in charge. We were all long finished playing by the time he made these comments; but he was still having a go at us and he was still making excuses for himself.

'While I was manager,' he says, 'Nicol, Whelan, Rush and Grobbelaar had testimonials, and Jan Molby and John Barnes were waiting their turn. It seemed to me that the passion for the club had disappeared and that was a massive shock for me.'

The implication is that we'd stopped caring about Liverpool Football Club. That we were just hanging around, punching in time, waiting for our testimonials; then we'd just take the money and run. I can't speak for the other lads but I can for myself. He's wrong. It's untrue. His comments are offensive. And as recently as 2010 he was rehashing this stuff on Irish radio.

I never kissed the badge on my shirt, and I never made big statements in public about what the club meant to me. I hope and I believe I showed it through my actions on the pitch. I loved playing for Liverpool and its supporters. The place was a second home for me. I was happy there, I felt I was family there. I never once thought about leaving. I never once made the slightest inquiry about a transfer.

Even the most cynical pro in the world would have to feel something for a club where he'd spent virtually his entire career. And if he'd had some of the best and worst times of his life at that club, he'd develop a bond with the place that goes far beyond the terms of his contract. I wasn't, I don't think, a cynical person; I spent fifteen years at the club; I had some of the best and worst times of my life there. You couldn't but have an emotional bond with the place that went far beyond the terms of your contract. There was too much history there. Too much of my life had gone into the club to be able to stop caring about it, even if I wanted to.

Apart from questioning my 'passion' for the club, Souness was questioning my integrity as a professional too. If you're only hanging around waiting for your testimonial it means you're not really trying any more; you're not being honest; your commitment isn't genuine. As a kid the one thing I wouldn't get away with was not trying; my Da wouldn't tolerate it for a second. He always said, 'If you give a hundred per cent no one can criticise your commitment.' It goes without saying that you wouldn't get away with it at Liverpool either. I got my share of criticism over the years but it was never for a lack of commitment. And now apparently, once I reached my testimonial age I dropped the habits of a lifetime and turned into a dishonest pro? It's bullshit. Graeme should never have said those things.

September 1989 was my tenth anniversary at Liverpool, nearly two years before Souey took over. If I'd wanted to take the money and run I could've done it then. In fact I didn't get round to holding my testimonial until August 1993. Obviously, I deliberately waited until Souey was manager. You see, I always knew Kenny was going to suddenly walk out on us one day and that Souey would be the man to take over from him; it was a cunning plan all along, just to piss him off.

Bruce, Nico, Rushie and myself were the only survivors still around from Souey's playing days. We didn't pull our weight, allegedly, when he was manager, and I discovered from his book that we apparently didn't pull our weight when he was a player either. 'Six years earlier as young players,' he says, 'they could do it because in those days they had a few guys on the pitch who could lead them by the nose. The bottom line was that they were no longer good enough to win the major trophies.'

I'm not saying for one minute that Souey wasn't a leader in that team. He was the general and I for one was willing to learn from him and hoping to emulate him. There was a hierarchy in that team and I respected it. But the young lads, we all could play, we all had bottle and we could run forever. Souey led from the front but he didn't carry us; we carried ourselves. We learned fast, too, and by the time he left in 1984 we were well able to look after ourselves. We'd long completed our apprenticeships.

When he moved to Italy in 1984 I didn't criticise him for doing it, and I'm not criticising him for it now. He wanted a new challenge, he wanted to develop as a player, and good luck to him. But it was also a huge move for him financially. Football salaries in Italy were way ahead of England at the time. We didn't have that luxury. We were nearing the end of our careers and we needed testimonials to boost our savings before retiring from the game.

Despite what Souey says, the trophies didn't stop coming when he left either; we somehow managed to win three more championships and two FA Cups without him.

The trophies, bar that one FA Cup in '92, only stopped coming when he came back. It was all such an anticlimax in the end. We had ten years of success and we wanted more. That's what we were about: winning things, celebrating another trophy and another and another. We were greedy, all right, but it was for medals. That's what we were hanging on for, not frigging testimonials.

I don't bump into Graeme much these days; he doesn't live in Liverpool, we've pretty much gone our separate ways in life. I meet him from time to time in RTE, the Irish TV station, and we get on no problem. When we played together I didn't socialise in his circles because he was older than me. But we got on well. I liked him as a bloke and admired him no end as a player. The only time we came to dislike each other was when he was the manager, I was a player, and we just didn't see eye-to-eye on what was happening at the football club. And it looks like we still don't see eye-to-eye on it. I guess we'll just have to agree to disagree and hopefully remain friends. Life's too short and none of us is getting any younger.

Occasionally you will hear him say, if he's being interviewed about that era, that he has his regrets. That he learned a lot more about management in the years after, and that he'd do things differently if he had his time back. And that's fair enough. I mean, wouldn't we all?

15

Crocked

The day I walked away limping from that tackle with Paul Davis in April 1990, I didn't know it was going to cost me a World Cup.

There were a few other things I didn't know either until I went for a bone scan a week later. Ronnie Moran had seen me hobbling around at training and eventually he told me to go off and get a scan. The nurse injected the dye as per usual, I waited the necessary few hours for the dye to go through my body, and then they did the scan. Wherever the damage was, it would show up in a hot spot on the scan. When the nurse came back she had four hot spots to show me. 'There's a bone broken in your foot, all right. Just there you can see a small fracture on your instep. But,' she added, 'you've also got two broken toes and a fracture in your heel.'

It was news to me. The toes had been hurting me for weeks but I thought they were just bruised. With the other injury I knew there was something wrong but I reckoned it was the Achilles. It had been giving me gyp for months and every morning I'd be limping around at the start of training until it warmed up. But it was a fracture in the heel that was actually mending itself by the time I found out about it.

Injuries were the bane of your life and an absolute curse. They were a daily hazard but you had to go about your work as if they were never going to happen. It was, and is, the only way for a player to deal with it. You could never start worrying about it because if you did, then you were only one negative thought away from pulling out of a tackle. And if someone starts doing that, he might as well pack it in because there is no worse sight in football than a player pulling out of a tackle.

So, you never ever dwelled on the possibility that the job you loved might only be one bad injury away from coming to an end. You didn't want to go there in your head, not for a second. Even when you saw it happening to others, you figured it would never happen to you. Maybe it's like young fellas tearing around in fast cars; they see other young fellas being pulled out of a crashed car but they never think it'll happen to them. We were the same, I suppose. Some day somebody's number will be up, but it's not going to be me. Nah, definitely not me.

I'm sure Kevin MacDonald and Jim Beglin thought the same, if they thought about it at all; they wouldn't have dreamed that it was going to end the way it did. I was on the pitch at the Dell that day in September 1986 when Kevin's career was basically destroyed with a broken leg having just come on as a sub. It was a desperate moment of bad luck. I was on the pitch at Goodison Park four months later when Jim's leg was broken in a terrible tackle. He never played for Liverpool again. Both lads had been part of the double-winning squad the previous season; they'd played in the Cup final. Kevin was twenty-five the day it all changed for him, Jim was twenty-three. We were all gutted for them at the time but we all reckoned they'd be back. You weren't thinking that those two moments were going to have life-changing consequences for them; it was the furthest thing from your mind. But you might've been thinking at the back of your mind *There but for the grace of God* . . . And then you moved on to the next game still convinced as much as ever that it would never happen to you.

By then I had buried the memory of my own brush with the nightmare scenario. For seven months through 1983 I woke up every day with the fear that my career might be over before it had properly started. I was starting to think about jobs out there in the real world. I had no qualifications, no trade, and I was looking at factory work as a realistic alternative. Elaine's dad worked in the Ford plant in Liverpool and I talked to him about maybe finding me a job there if the worst came to the worst. That's how I was thinking at the time, that's how bad it got.

I'd been troubled with groin problems for months. I had constant pain, it felt as if I was carrying this heavy weight around the pelvic area all the time. I couldn't run freely in the beginning and eventually I was struggling to run at all. The doctor looked at the first x-rays and said it was a groin strain, nothing worse, take a few weeks off. Eventually I went to see a specialist. As it happened, Rushie was also troubled with a groin injury and we were both sent on the same day to meet the specialist. More x-rays were taken at the hospital and we carried them back to the waiting room. I started messing. I grabbed his x-ray and held it up to the light. 'Christ, Rushie, you're in serious trouble here. Don't like the look of that at all.' Turned out I was right. But it was me who was in trouble, not him, because we'd got them mixed up. I was holding his x-ray thinking it was mine, and vice versa.

The specialist inspected my x-ray and told me that the pelvis wasn't properly aligned. It was tilted at a weird angle. He said I'd have to let it rest and hope that it would right itself over time. I rested it right through the summer and when I started back running in pre-season it was still no better. They said it needed more rest so I went back to doing nothing for another two months. I made another attempt at a comeback, same story; it was getting very worrying by this stage. The doctors kept saying, 'There's nothing we can do, you have to wait until it rights itself.'

I'd heard before of players having to retire with pelvic injuries and I was getting very anxious. Elaine and I were married now, we had a big mortgage on a house; what would happen if the club just let my contract run out? I didn't handle it well, I wasn't the best person to be around at that time. I'd go into training every morning, just to be doing something, but there was very little I could actually do. I physically couldn't do anything apart from lifting a few weights. For the first time in my life I started to put on weight. The long lay-off meant I was putting on the pounds and this wasn't helping my mood either. I was at a complete loss. The games were coming thick and fast and the team was doing fine without me. Lawro was playing in midfield and I heard a whisper that they were looking at Craig Johnston to replace me on a long-term basis. I was in a state of panic after that. Were they thinking that my career was possibly over? Were they moving on without me?

I couldn't keep the dread out of my head: is this thing ever going to come right? Maybe this is it, maybe I *am* finished? On the way home from Melwood it was a case of, 'Might as well go in for a pint, I've got nothing else to do.' And then you'd have another pint and another pint, drowning your sorrows until you'd arrive home the worse for wear. I was scared, Elaine was scared, it was a horrible time.

Eventually a surgeon, God bless him, suggested an operation. But he told me it would be the last throw of the dice. If this didn't work, then he didn't see what else could be done. I told him to go for it – I couldn't stand the worry any more. He snipped the tendons in my groin on both sides and it worked like a dream. The pelvis straightened itself out, the pain disappeared and I started running freely again. Relief at last! I could nearly feel the big black cloud over my head floating away. I was never more happy to hear Moransco bawling me out of it on the training ground.

Joe Fagan later that season, after I'd played a good game, told the press that I'd done really well to come back from what had been a career-threatening injury. But did it change me? Did it make me stop and think? You must be joking! As soon as I got back into the swing of things I forgot about it. You didn't want to be thinking about scary things like that. I just reverted to the tried and trusted footballers' mentality. An injury ending your career? Nah, that'll never happen to me. I suppose the least I could've done was contact my career guidance teacher back in Patrician College and said to him: 'You know what? You had a point! I should've got myself something to fall back on.' But I was out of the woods and I never looked back.

And anyway, if all else failed, there was always Bugsy's magic sponge to rely on, wasn't there? To be honest, the medical facilities were a bit on the primitive side in those days. You were expected to have a high pain threshold – all players were – and generally the less said about injuries the better. Just get out and get on with it. Everyone seemed to be carrying some sort of a knock most of the time. You learned to get to know your own body and how far you could push an injury. You'd be all the time monitoring your ankle or calf or whatever part was sore, testing it and feeling it, weighing it up to see if it could take ninety minutes. *Will I be able to start? Yeah, once the adrenaline kicks in I should be able to get through it.* That was it a lot of the time: first ten minutes it'll hurt, then it'll warm up and you'll be okay.

I had a cracked rib once. Anybody who's had a cracked rib knows how painful it is. I told Moransco one day at training. 'Bloody killing me, this is.' Of course, Ronnie dismissed me straightaway. 'It's only cracked – it's not broken, is it?' OK, Nurse Moran, if you say so. Before the game I got an injection to kill the pain but it only lasted half an hour; I was in agony for the next hour and all I got afterwards was him telling me, 'You were a bit slack there today, lad.' What?! Are you taking the piss? It was killing me even to breathe out there! Moransco was lucky his magic sponge didn't end up wedged up his arse that day.

I got my share of cortisone injections over the years but, to be fair, they were conscious of not overdoing them. People were starting to understand that there could be long-term damage. A lot of players in the '70s had taken too many cortisone shots into ankle joints and knee joints and all they were really doing was masking the pain. Fellas would go out and play with these injuries and some of them ended up with bad enough problems in the years after they retired. By the '80s if you got a cortisone injection you wouldn't train the next day, you'd let it settle down for forty-eight hours and see if it had helped any bit.

But you swallowed painkillers and anti-inflammatories like they were sweets. Voltarol in particular was popular; it was the footballers' friend. You took the tablets as a matter of course. Moransco would hand you a batch of them to take home for the weekend if you asked. A lot of footballers ended up with stomach problems because they took so many of them. I was on them night and day during my long lay-off because the groin was constantly sore. In the end I was prescribed suppositories, as they were supposed to hit the spot quicker. I'm sure Moransco told me, in no uncertain terms, where to stick them. So I did – and for all the good they did I might as well have been taking Smarties.

But the truth is, you didn't care how many tablets you had to take because you wanted to play every game. I don't know if modern players will carry injuries into games the way we did; and maybe we weren't as tough as the hard men who played in previous generations. But financially we had an incentive to play that maybe current players don't have; they're still going to be pulling down a massive pay packet every week whether they play or not. We wanted our win bonuses and if it meant swallowing a few mouthfuls of painkillers along the way, you did it.

And, of course, you didn't want to lose your place either. That was the ultimate incentive. There was always someone breathing down your neck. I played thirty-three games in the 1987/88 season but when I was out of action for three months, in came Nigel Spackman and he ended up with thirty-three games to his credit as well. I missed the famous 5–0 game against Forest at Anfield in April and he was brilliant that day.

It was one of the greatest Liverpool team performances but, as usual, if you weren't playing you weren't exactly celebrating. I remember watching it and thinking to myself at the final whistle *Bloody hell, the way Spackers is playing he could keep Maradona out of the team, never mind me.*

So there was every incentive to stay out of the treatment room at Anfield. And another incentive was the treatment room itself. It was a depressing sort of a place; it wasn't designed so that you could enjoy your stay. They didn't bring you flowers and chocolates. You weren't even allowed to bring in the newspapers with you, in case you'd get too comfortable sitting there on the machines reading the sports pages. And we weren't lavished with the greatest expertise either. It was usually Ronnie or Roy or Joe. I'm not saying they were quacks – but I don't think they spent too much time at medical school either! Needless to say, they didn't have the most gentle bedside manner. You wouldn't mistake any of them for Florence Nightingale. They'd give you a rubdown, do a bit of deep massage on the muscle or ligament, and tell you you'd be right as rain by tomorrow. And they never told anybody how long an injury would take. They hated doing that because they reckoned if they said, 'That'll take three weeks,' the player would get it into his head straightaway that he was gone for three weeks. So don't tell him how long and he could be back in ten days.

Bob was the only one who had permission to give you a time line. Bob had trained as a physio back in the day and he still liked to come in and deliver his expert opinion. 'What's wrong with you, lad?' 'Hamstring, Gaffer.' 'Right. Give us a look.' He'd dig his fingers into your hamstring and tell you, 'That'll be a ten-dayer' or 'That'll be a two-weeker'. I was in the treatment room one Sunday morning when a Liverpool scout from over on the Wirral brought a young lad in, about twelve or thirteen, for treatment. He must have been a good prospect to get this sort of special attention. Next thing Bob came in. He asked the kid what was wrong. 'It's me knee.' The kid was overawed that Bob Paisley was standing there in front of him, actually talking to him. 'Right. Give us a look.' So Bob examined the knee. 'When does it hurt you?' 'Well, walking up the stairs it hurts a lot.' Eventually the kid left the room and the scout turned to Bob. 'What should I do with him, Bob?' 'Tell his mum to buy a bungalow,' said Bob as he walked out the door, chuckling away to himself.

A few years later the club brought in a specialist physio. But he'd usually only come in at lunchtime. Once he'd diagnosed the problem he'd leave a note for the lads for next morning: 'Put him on the laser machine for twenty minutes'; 'Give him some ultrasound on his ankle for ten minutes'. And Ronnie or Roy would hook you up to the machine the next day. We assumed they knew what they were doing. They sounded like they did anyway.

But there was one time when Paul Walsh had a bad ankle and he was getting ultrasound for weeks but it was still a bit slow to heal. And one day me and Walshy were in the treatment room when a technician came in to give the machines a service. The ultrasound machine had a sort of hose attached to it and at the top of the hose was this metal head, almost like a microphone. If you had a torn calf muscle, say, they'd smear a bit of gel on the calf and then they'd rub the metal head part over and back, sending the sound waves into your muscle. If the machine was working properly and you dropped some water on the metal head, it would sizzle. So the technician did this – and nothing happened. It was stone cold. The machine was broken. And he looked at Walshy. 'How long have you been using this?' 'Couple of weeks.' And your man went, 'Well, I'm afraid it hasn't been doing you much good.' The look on Walshy's face was hilarious. 'You mean they've been treating me for two weeks with a lump of fucking metal?!' They had, and no one had copped it. They might as well have been rubbing his ankle with a crowbar.

The ultrasound machine was supposed to be the modern, high-tech approach. It was much more sophisticated than the old-fashioned wax treatment. In the corner of the treatment room was this thing called the wax bath. It was basically a box filled with wax and if you had a bad ankle after a game you'd come in on the Sunday morning – and you wouldn't be looking forward to it. They'd plug in the box and heat the wax until it was melting hot. Then you'd stick your foot in it for as long as you could bear it and pull it out. You'd have this coating of wax on your foot and ankle. And you kept putting it in and taking it out until you had this big lump of wax hanging around the bottom part of your leg. And then they'd wait a while and cut it off and drop it back into the box. And that was your wax treatment done for the day. But you didn't want to be coming in the next day getting your foot scalded with hot wax. So you'd strap your ankle up and say it was feeling much better now, thanks very much. There was method in their madness sometimes. They just wanted you back out on the training ground a.s.a.p. God knows what it did, the magic wax, but I presume it did more for your ankle than a dead ultrasound machine. It might have helped, it probably didn't do any harm. I'm just glad Moransco didn't make me use it when my groin was acting up.

I suppose if you spend every day of your life for twenty years, more or less, running around a field, it's going to catch up with you – unless you are very lucky. And I wasn't one of the lucky ones. I didn't escape, the wear and tear got to me in the end. My first nine seasons in the Liverpool first team, I played 419 games, an average of 46 a season. My last four seasons I played 71 games, an average of 17. That tells its own tale. Slowly but surely my body was breaking down. I never had hamstring injuries, then I started getting hamstring injuries. I missed the 1992 Cup final because of a bad hamstring. I broke my leg, broke my foot, and was plagued with a thigh injury that kept recurring. It kept filling up with scar tissue. It would usually hit me around Christmas for some reason. I'd have a minor operation to get rid of some of the scar tissue and it would build up again over a period of months and then I'd have to have the same procedure done again. Eventually, around Christmas 1993, the surgeon said I'd have to get a full clear-out done on it. I ended up with fifteen staples down my thigh after that last operation. But it solved the problem and for the first time in three years I had a long run of games without interruption. In the second half of my last season at Liverpool I was flying fit. I went to USA '94 in great shape but by that stage it was too late, Big Jack had written me off.

It was much too late for Souey too. His era had come and gone and sadly I'd only been a bit player for most of it. That was the most disappointing period of my time at the club. Play a game, miss five games, play a game, miss another load of games. I was crocked, and I was tearing my hair out with the frustration. Nico was having a bad time of it too and we often ended up in the treatment room at Melwood, sharing our woes.

One morning the pair of us were really down in the dumps; all we had to look forward to was another bloody physio session while the lads outside were running around, playing ball and having a laugh. The team would be heading down to London for a game afterwards and we'd be left there hanging around. We were due two physio sessions that day, one at half-nine, the other at half-one. So we had our morning session and then we went out for a chat with the lads before they boarded the bus for London. They left and suddenly the place was dead quiet. We turned and looked at each other. We were both thinking the same thing at the same time. Nico had a glint in his eye and I must've had too. 'Fancy a ...?' Mmmmm. 'Not a bad idea!' 'D'you think we should?' 'What time is it?' 'Half-ten.' 'Sure, the place won't be open.' 'We can try.'

And in our wisdom we decided we would try. So we went across to the Derby Arms and knocked on the door. And the landlord came down and opened the door and got a bit of a surprise when he saw two well-known Liverpool players looking back at him at this hour of the morning. 'Sorry to bother you, we know it's a bit early, but any chance of a few pints?' He wasn't mad about the idea, but he didn't want to turn us away either. He stuck his head out and took a quick look, left and right. 'Come on.' He bolted the door, pulled two pints of lager and we sat there delighted with ourselves, like two kids skiving off school. 'Cheers, Nico!' 'Cheers, Ron, me old son!' Then Nico got a pang of guilt. 'Jeez, I hope Souey doesn't find out about this!' I said, 'Don't worry about that. If Souey says anything I'll just mention the day he played half-pissed against Middlesbrough.' Nico still wasn't convinced. So I said, 'I'm sure Souey'll understand.'

The two of us cracked up. Eh, two more pints there, please, when you're ready. We got back to the treatment room for twenty past one and were lying on the tables when Paul Chadwick, the physio, came in to hook us up to the machines. When he came back a half-hour later we were fast asleep. Sweet dreams.

As I write this I'm approaching my fiftieth birthday. The big Five-O. And I'm in pretty good nick all told, I'm glad to say. I was always lightly built, I never had weight problems when I was playing, I didn't have a heavy frame to carry around. So I think long term I escaped without too much damage. I get my share of aches and pains. The hip gets sore if I'm sitting too long; getting up in the morning my ankles need a bit of warming up before they're comfortable; and now and again the knee will lock. I'll get this big click coming out of my knee. There's wear and tear, all right, but it's not too bad, considering the amount of hard miles I put up on the clock. Overall, I think my body served me well, despite the problems of my final years in football.

And if I'm ever tempted to moan about it I can still hear the words of Ronnie Moran echoing in my head. 'There's nothing wrong with you, lad – get out there and get on with it!'

So I do. And I'm happy that I can.

16

Assassins

OK, Cally, I'm sorry. I shouldn't have done it. It was mean, it was nasty, and there was no need. But you shouldn't have done me first! Now I know that isn't an excuse. And, in fairness, you just kicked me, there was nothing vicious about it. But the minute you did it, I was annoyed. I was thinking *Why is Cally kicking me?* But I let it go. Or I thought I did. Then the chance came along to kick you back. And I just couldn't resist. Didn't even think twice. So, Cally, once again, I'm sorry. Even though I can hear you saying, 'It's a bit late now, Ron!'

I was a bit late on the night too. It was November 1988. We were playing Millwall at Anfield. Hansen was injured, Gillespie was injured, Venison was injured, I was playing right-back. And playing on the left wing was a tricky winger with a sweet left foot by the name of Kevin O'Callaghan. I knew Cally and I liked him, we were mates from our Ireland days under Eoin Hand. But we were in direct opposition that night. In the first half I got on the ball and as Cally came in to tackle me I pretended I was going to knock one down the line. But I cut inside instead and as I did,

Cally caught me with a kick. *Mmmmm. Wasn't expecting that from Cally. Ah, it was harmless, no problem.* Forgot about it, played on.

In the second half Cally got a ball on the left-hand side and took on Ray Houghton, I think it was. He skipped past Rayzor and cut inside towards the byline as I went to close him down. But he took one touch too many and overran the ball; it was going to run out of play. But he went stretching for it and in that instant I knew I had an opportunity to do Cally good and proper. I went straight through as if I was stretching for the ball but I wasn't stretching for the ball at all. He wasn't wearing shin pads and I ripped him down the shin. Left poor old Cally in a heap on the floor. He had to get five or six stitches in his shin afterwards. And I regret it to this day, I genuinely do. There were people I didn't regret doing and others I'd have loved to have done, but never got the chance. But I was sorry I did it to Cally because he was a friend, and a real nice bloke as well. I didn't feel good about it afterwards.

What can I say? It was the typical footballers' mentality, I suppose: he kicked me, I'm gonna kick him. And there was also the consideration that, if I did him then I wouldn't have to worry about him for a while. I was playing right-back against a very skilful player who could make a fool out of you in the blink of an eye with one of his shimmies. If I caught him right, that could be the end of my problems for the day.

Roy Evans reckons I was 'a bit of an assassin'. One of the quiet ones. That's probably overstating it: I wasn't *that* bad. Or, to put it another way, I wasn't that good. If I was, I'd have caught Falcao good and proper that night in Rome. But Roy says, watching from the dugout over the years, he saw a fair few fellas limping away out of tackles with myself. It's probably true. I could put my foot in – and leave it there. I think it was usually fairly subtle, apart from the time I caught Graeme Le Saux so high, during that 4–1 Blackburn game in 1993, I must've left stud marks on his stomach. Don't know how I didn't get sent off for that one. The ref didn't even book me. And because Le Saux came squaring up to me afterwards, *we* ended up with the free kick.

I was blessed with quick feet and you generally got the better of a tackle if you had quicker feet than the other bloke. It was more of a help, though, in not getting done yourself, rather than doing someone else. I saw an old newspaper quote from George Best recently. 'Great players don't take serious knocks, not many anyway. They smell defenders coming in with heavy tackles and know when and where to move.' There was no one better than George at skipping out of tackles just in the nick of time. I was never a great player, far from it, but I could 'smell' someone coming in to do me. My nose must've been blocked the night Falcao did me. But usually I was quick enough to get out of the way. That's why I always said, any time I did get caught, that it was my own fault. If I'm not quick enough to see him coming and get out of the way, it's my fault; I deserve to be kicked. And if they're not quick enough to see me coming, it's their fault. That was my policy, anyway. It's me against you, who's the quickest? Who's going to come out on top here? And if you can't handle it, you shouldn't really be playing.

Some games, you knew you had to win the battle first before you could start playing ball. Wimbledon in our day had a reputation for turning every game into a battle. But I can honestly say I never worried about them at all. They'd try to rough you up, all right, especially down at Plough Lane; put the ball in the air and try to catch you with elbows and knees and what-ever. But the only thing you had to worry about was the way they disrupted your style of play. They'd take great pleasure in getting in your face and harassing you for ninety minutes. But I never felt I'd get badly done against them because basically they weren't good enough to do you. They were better at talk-ing about it, going round shouting about what they were going to do to you. But all they were doing was giving you a warning well in advance. The likes of Vinnie Jones never worried me at all because I reckoned that if Vinnie was going to catch me, I'd have to be very slow.

It was the likes of Jimmy Case who worried me, because they never said anything. And they knew how to do you if they got half a chance. Jimmy Case and Graeme Souness were the two most ruthless men I ever saw going into a tackle. And I didn't have to worry about Souey because I never played against him. Jimbo was an iron man. And he was deadly. I played against him many a time when he moved to Brighton and then on to Southampton and he was *the* hardest player I ever came up against. He caught me once at Anfield, I thought he'd done the ligaments in my knee, but luckily it was OK. We played Southampton in an FA Cup semi-final at White Hart Lane in April 1986 and in one incident the ball bounced up between me and Jimbo. In those situations the best form of protection was to go in full-blooded. If you committed fully to the clash you had a better chance of not getting hurt. Needless to say, Jimbo knew this too. We both knew what was coming, we both went high with the studs and neither of us got near the ball. It just rolled away. Jan Molby said afterwards, 'It was just a case of which one of you was higher!' No one was hurt, we just said nothing and carried on. After a game Jimbo would be the first to shake your hand, have a chat and a joke. But then, first minute of the next game, you knew if there was a ball to be won and he had a chance to catch you, he'd do it. So you had to have the same attitude.

Apparently the Millwall lads weren't happy with me after the Cally tackle. Kenny Cunningham was there as a young pro and he told me they had a photo of Cally's wounded shin pinned up on the notice board in the dressing room. We had to play them twice at the Den later that season and Tony Cascarino was playing with them at the time. I remember Cas telling me years later that a few of them talked about getting some revenge. The words 'Let's do Whelan' or 'Let's get Whelan' were being bandied about. Anyway, they never got round to it.

I don't blame them or judge them for thinking that way. If someone had done me half as bad as I did Cally, I'd remember who it was too. And I'd be hoping to get in a bit of retaliation somewhere down the line. Could be the following season, it didn't matter, you'd be waiting for your chance. I certainly wasn't going to forget John Trewick's hatchet job. It was September 1985, we were playing Oxford United at the Manor Ground. It was the 2–2 game that's remembered now for Alan Kennedy's late own goal in what was his last game for Liverpool. But I was gone after twenty minutes, replaced by Paul Walsh. John had split my forehead above the eye and I have the scar to this day. The ball came out of the box and it bounced up. I headed it away and he followed through with the studs up high – very high. It was a bit of a kung fu job, like Cantona's kick on that supporter at Crystal Palace, except this one was straight at my head. The claret was flowing and I was brought in to get stitched up.

Then after an hour Rushie was carted off, concussed from a bang on the head. I came into the dressing room to check up on him; he was lying down, a doctor was attending to him. He was more or less out for the count but he was coming round when I arrived. And he looked at me, he was still trying to focus his eyes, and my face must've been a mess because he put on this real woozy smile when he saw me. His voice was groggy and he was going, 'Awwwww, what happened to you?! What happened to you?!' I said to him, 'Rushie, you saw what happened! You were on the pitch when it happened!' But he couldn't remember a thing. He was just lying there laughing his head off at the sight of me.

Anyway, I filed away John Trewick for another day. The return match with Oxford at Anfield was the following March and I figured they were going to get relegated that season so if I wanted a bit of revenge, it'd have to be this game. But the game just never presented me with a proper opportunity. Then in the last minute or so I spotted a half-chance and reckoned it was now or never. John was chasing a ball into the corner and I made a run from midfield to get there. But it was a sad attempt at a hatchet job. He played the ball and I came sliding in and wasn't even close. Missed by a mile. It was never really on. That's the thing about trying to do someone: it has to happen spontaneously, you can't really plan it or force it to happen. I never got John Trewick back and, to be fair, he was really the only player I ever deliberately went after.

The day I caught Lloyd McGrath was more typical; I spotted a chance and I took it. Lloyd was one tough nut. Any time we played Coventry City, he was always up for the scrap. He was prepared to kick, and to be kicked. He never said anything, just got stuck in. And you just couldn't hurt Lloyd. No matter how much you tackled him or kicked him, he'd come back for more. A part of me respected him, another part of me found him very annoying!

One time he clashed heads with Steve McMahon at Highfield Road. It was right on half-time and everybody headed for the dressing rooms not knowing Macca was flat out on the field. Roy Evans went over to him and got him up and back into the dressing room. And a few of us started laughing because he had this big lump on his head; he was like a cartoon character with this egg sticking out of his head. It may well have been an accidental clash but Macca wasn't happy about it. The next time we played them Macca went into a 50-50 with Lloyd and as usual there wasn't a bother on Lloyd. The two of them were on the ground but the ball was right beside Lloyd. So I just thought to myself *I'm never going to have a better chance to hurt Lloyd McGrath.* So I dived in two-footed off the ground and got some of the ball and a lot of Lloyd. I didn't want to do serious damage, I didn't target the legs, I think I caught him around the ribs. But I have to admit, I got some satisfaction out of seeing him down and the physio coming on to treat him. I'd finally hurt Lloyd McGrath; it was well worth the booking that I got.

Liverpool were a big scalp in those days. There was always somebody looking to have a go. Teams took great pleasure in beating us and individual players took great pleasure in dishing out the dirty tackles. They seemed to think that any Liverpool player was fair game if the chance came along. We had our own system for dealing with this. Macca and myself, for example, had an understanding that if one of us had already been booked, and was looking to have a go back at someone, the other one would do it on his behalf. I learned this from my time playing with Souness. 'You're booked, just leave it for now, I'll see what I can do.' If I was booked and someone had done me, Macca would be, 'OK, I'll have a look.' I wouldn't need to say anything.

Now, I'm well aware that these stories don't reflect particularly well on me. Looking back from this perspective, I can see I was guilty of some nasty stuff. Not a lot, if you spread it out over the course of nearly five hundred games. But some. I'll hold my hands up and admit it.

I can see the bigger picture now. But I didn't see the bigger picture then; I didn't care about seeing the bigger picture. I don't think any of us did. We believed every game was a dog-eat-dog situation. Professional football was dog-eat-dog. You'd been trained from a young age to fight for your place in the team. Once you did that, you fought your way into the next team and the next team. And when you got into the first team at Liverpool, you fought to stay in it. You did that by trying to win the battle with your opponents every week. Twice a week, a lot of the time. You saw your opponents as the enemy; they want to beat us, we want to beat them. That's where your head was as a player.

There was a lot of alpha-male stuff going on too. I'd say if David Attenborough was describing footballers he'd call us a territorial species. That's what we were doing with all those tackles and confrontations – marking our territory. Claiming our ground. It was some sort of male-dominance ritual, I suppose. And if you wanted to win matches you often had to win the fight first. Then we could start playing our football.

Souness was peerless in a 50-50 tackle, he had such power and timing. There's an art to the 50-50. And you can disguise your real intentions if you want to. Some players are very good at letting the opposition player get there first, which is when you're going to hurt him. You get there just that split second after he gets there; he gets the ball, you get him. That's how my friend Falcao did me in Rome. It looks as though that's how Souey caught Tony Galvin in the 1982 League Cup final against Spurs. He marked his territory that day with Tony: 'This is my part of the pitch, if you want to come in here, you're gonna get hurt.' Tony was hurt in that tackle and we didn't see him much in the game after that. Tackles like that had a purpose, they could have a real effect on a game. Tony was going to take a while to get back into the match, which would give us a bit more time on the ball. That's what it was all geared up to achieve. It wasn't just to hurt someone for the sake of it, not usually anyway; it was to give us the time and space to play our game.

The Tottenham midfield that day was: Hoddle, Ardiles, Hazard and Galvin. Ours was: McDermott, Lee, Souness and Whelan. They were technically more talented but I don't think they had the same sort of appetite we had for winning balls in midfield. And we could play a bit too, once we had the ball. The blend was better in our four. Their manager Keith Burkinshaw said afterwards we were the only team in England who managed to nullify their midfield.

If you timed your 50-50 tackle well, you could make it a 51-49 job – in your favour. It was a case of who could look after himself better. And it was easy to con the referee. Two players sliding in for it, one is going to get hurt, a referee in those circumstances wasn't often going to book you, especially in the 1980s. You could get away with an awful lot more back then. Elbows, knees, boots: a lot of times you'd see a centre-back or centre-forward finishing the game with a black eye or a split forehead or a busted nose. There were more two-footed tackles and you had a bit more licence to go through the back of somebody. You'd get up, hold your hands up and say, 'Sorry, ref, I went for the ball.' He might have his doubts about you but he couldn't be certain; and they were slower to reach for their notebooks anyway.

These days you can't fart on a football field but the refs are reaching for their cards. You won't be surprised to hear me say that I think the game has gone too soft. That's what old pros are supposed to say, isn't it?! The rules are much stricter and, to be fair, a lot of these changes have been for the better. I'm not sorry to see the tackle from behind gone. Going through the back of someone was a nasty job, that was the coward's way of doing you. But the 50-50 tackle – don't take that away. Supporters loved a full-on 50-50 and the players I knew didn't mind them either. It sickens me when you see a good 50-50 challenge and the referee blows up and gives a free kick and tells the players to calm down. Let them at it, for God's sake. Let them at it and see who comes out on top. If someone gets hurt, they get hurt. That's part and parcel of the game. But the whistlers nowadays, they're more like health-and-safety officers than football referees. And if they have a sense of humour, they keep it well hidden.

You could talk more to referees back in the '80s. They had a sense of humour – some of them anyway – and they enjoyed a bit of banter. Neil Midgley was great, we all had good time for Midge. He has since passed on, sadly, but he was one referee you liked to see in charge of your games. And you couldn't con him either; he knew the tricks of our trade. But you could have a go at him and he wouldn't take offence. He'd turn around and go, 'Ronnie, you're not playing too good yourself either, mate.' 'Aw, fuck off, Midge.' 'Don't you swear at me!' And suddenly the two of us would be smiling. So you'd go again. 'Aw, fuck off, Midge.' 'Right, you fuck off as well then!' And off we'd go on our merry way.

I can't say we didn't try to gang up on them, especially at Anfield. I reckon that we got a few home decisions over the years that were borderline, to say the least. Kenny used to have a good go at the referees. Michael Robinson used to try and butter them up. 'How are you? Everything good? How's the kids?' The one night we really needed a home-town decision, we didn't get it. Alan Smith's goal for Arsenal on that night in '89. I had no idea whether Smith had got a touch with his head or not. But we surrounded the officials and tried to make it as difficult as possible for them. I was questioning the linesman, trying to undermine his nerve. 'Did you see him head it? Did you see him head it? Indirect free kick. Ref had his hand up. No way.' And the linesman was nodding his head, definitely a goal. 'No way. How can you be sure?' They did very well that night, the referee David Hutchinson and his officials, because they let the goal stand. They stood their ground under such intimidating circumstances – a league title on the line at Anfield. When I went for the toss-up before the game, maybe I should've asked Mr Hutchinson how the wife and kids were – I'm sure it would've made all the difference.

There was another incident which I'd forgotten about until I was reminded of it years after I retired. I was at a function one night and got chatting to one of the men in black from our playing days. It was John Lloyd, the Welsh referee. He told me about one time we were playing Derby at Anfield, I think it was September 1987. One of the Derby players came in and did Steve Nicol and we were furious. I could remember the tackle, all right, and Nico writhing around on the ground after it. A load of our lads ran in and there was the usual jostling and pushing and grabbing. I couldn't remember this part: Lloydy ran in blowing his whistle and shouted, 'Let me take care of this, I'll sort him out!' And he got a tap on the shoulder and it was me. And apparently I said to him, 'Lloydy, we'll sort him out.' And Lloyd said, 'OK, you sort it out. You've got one chance.' Meaning we had one chance to exact a bit of revenge and after that, no more nonsense.

But some games needed to be kept on a tight leash by a strong referee and none more so than our annual battles with Everton and Manchester United. Those were the games where you had your real dust-ups in midfield. We got to know each other as opposing players because we clashed so many times. There was a lot of mutual respect. We wouldn't go out to do them, they wouldn't go out to do us. You'd have a running battle with them for ninety minutes but they were honourable battles.

At Everton you had Peter Reid and Paul Bracewell in the engine room and it was a pleasure to play against them. They were fair and they were hard. Reidy was magnificent, a major influence in that Everton side. He didn't complain if you whacked him in a tackle and you didn't either if he whacked you. You'd come away from those games tired and sore but you knew you'd been in a fair fight. The combat was left on the field. You'd have a beer in the players' lounge afterwards and there'd be no animosity carried over.

Likewise Bryan Robson at United. Robbo was the best I ever played against in England. The influence he had on his team was huge. Defence, attack, passing and tackling, all-round inspiration – Robbo was the man. And if he hit you in a tackle you knew all about it. The United team those years had a lot of power and attitude. Norman Whiteside, Mark Hughes, Paul McGrath – those lads knew how to win a 50-50 ball. I loved those games. I think we all did, anyone who was privileged enough to play in them. If I get nostalgic at all, it's for games like those, where you never felt more alive with excitement and adrenaline and determination.

I got a few doings in Merseyside derbies over the years but not from Bracewell or Reid. My first ever derby was a reserves match at Goodison. The pitch was a bit of a mud heap and I slipped and fell at one stage. Next thing I was getting raked down the leg by some new Scottish lad they'd signed. Turned out to be my future next-door neighbour and all-round sound bloke, Graeme Sharp. Adrian Heath got me the same way in a first-team derby, raking me down the back of the leg. I wouldn't mind but there wasn't a ball anywhere to be seen – we were standing around waiting for a corner to be taken!

And the worst injury I ever got from an opponent was also against Everton. I ended up with a broken leg. So which assassin managed to do that? Should I name and shame? It was Peter Beagrie, actually. Peter feckin' Beagrie. Now Peter had many qualities; but when it came to the hard stuff, he was no Stuart Pearce. This one was a complete accident. He was there in front of me with the ball, doing all these fancy stepovers. And I just stood there because the ball wasn't moving. Then he ran into me – and I was carted off with a broken leg. Just like that.

Maybe there was a sort of poetic justice in it, getting hurt by another tricky winger who wouldn't harm a fly, after what I'd done to Cally. It pissed me off badly at the time, needless to say, because he hadn't even tried to do me. He just ran into me. Or maybe it was the most subtle hatchet job ever executed on a football field. But I doubt it.

Anyway, I couldn't complain. You weren't supposed to complain. If you dished it out, you had to take it when it came your way, be it from Bryan Robson or Peter Beagrie. Because as the wise man said, back in the day, all is fair in love and war.

17

Underrated

I scored fourteen goals from midfield during my first full season in the Liverpool team and sometimes I get the impression that my career was all downhill from there.

Personally I'm more than happy with the way it turned out. But I've read and heard a lot of comment over the years, and I've met thousands of Liverpool fans in that time, and I know there are some people who reckon I never quite lived up to expectations.

And there are others who defend me by saying I was the sort of pro who did a good job in a quiet way to a consistent standard. Basically they say I was an underrated player in the end. And that I'm still possibly underrated when the Liverpool teams of the 1980s are being discussed.

And maybe the others say that, with hindsight, I was overrated at the beginning. That the goals in the 1982 League Cup final, my attacking play that season and the next, proved in the long run to be something of a false dawn.

I'm actually not sure if that's how they see it, and I have very little control anyway over how other people assess my career. I do know that I was never underrated by the people whose opinions mattered most to me – my team-mates. Within the dressing room I always felt appreciated for the job I did.

As for the other end of the argument, that I never went on to become the star player those first few seasons suggested – that was never going to happen. There were reasons why, to do with what Liverpool wanted from me as a player, and with my own make-up as a person.

But I suppose that the first season, in particular, sent expectations soaring. I'd already scored on my debut for the first team in April 1981. I didn't become a fixture in the team until Christmas of that year. I scored thirteen goals from the left side of midfield between Boxing Day and the end of the season and was billed as the next big thing, the latest sensation, the new Liverpool hot shot – all that nonsense. I received the Robinsons Young Player of the Year award at the end of that season and the general consensus seemed to be, 'This kid is class, he can do anything.'

Bob Paisley was quoted as saying that I reminded him of the great Peter Doherty. I didn't know who Mr Doherty was but I found out he'd apparently been a brilliant inside-forward from Northern Ireland who was famous before the war for his goal-scoring exploits at Blackpool and Manchester City.

While doing some research for this book I came across a cutting from an old football magazine – *Shoot* or *Match*, I'm not sure. Phil Thompson had a column in it at the time and in 1982 he wrote: 'I just have enough space to single out one very special young man. Ronnie Whelan is the nearest thing to a perfect player I've seen. He reminds me of Martin Peters, the 1966 World Cup winner whose manager Sir Alf Ramsey said was ten years ahead of his time. You name the skill, Ronnie's got it!' (Cheers, Tommo, but crikey, I must've turned out to be a big disappointment!)

Anyway, that was all fine at the time. It didn't bother me much one way or the other, I was just on cloud nine right through the second half of that season. It only dawned on me years later that maybe people looking in from the outside were disappointed that I didn't go on to be a more crowd-pleasing, flamboyant sort of player. But at the time I wasn't thinking that way at all. It wasn't like I deliberately made a decision to sacrifice that side of my game – if I had that side of my game to sacrifice. It didn't even occur to me that I had a choice to make – and anyway I don't believe that I did. Instead, I had a job to do. That was the one thing that was very clear in my mind. I was taking over from Ray Kennedy in the wide-left position and my job was to hold that position. That was what Bob and the coaching staff wanted from me and that was what I set about doing.

I remember the 5–1 game against Stoke City at the Victoria Ground that season; I scored our fifth. The reason I remember it is that Peter Doherty was asked by one of the newspapers to come and give his opinion on the lad who was supposed to be the new Peter Doherty. Afterwards he said that I was a good player but that I should be looking to get on the ball more. I should be looking to exert more of an influence on the game. But my main job was to hold the wide-left position and I wasn't the type to ignore team instructions just so I could spend more time on the ball. I was there to keep the game wide and make space for the others to play in. And when we broke forward I should be following the play, ideally arriving late to get on the end of a cross or a loose ball in the box. And that's exactly what I did in the very next game – against Tottenham at Wembley.

I spent six seasons playing the wide-left position and I scored sixty-two goals from that position, an average of more than ten per season. So I never felt, not for a minute, that I wasn't being allowed to express myself. But the rave notices I got in the first season faded away after that, except for the odd goal at Wembley or for a few nice finishes from outside the box. Otherwise I came to be seen pretty much as a cog in the machine. And I was fine with that too. In fact I felt privileged to be considered good enough to be an integral part of that system. We were playing devastating football season after season and it was brilliant just to be surrounded by great players, all of us working in harmony for the team. I loved that. I loved it when the flowing moves came off and the ball was in the net and you were on your way to another three points and another trophy at the end of the season. When it worked, it worked like clockwork, and you had to be good, if I may say so, to fit within that system.

Bob was also quoted as saying that in time another Liverpool manager would build a new team around me. Again, that was in the early years. But I think you had to be truly exceptional, like Souness, to have a Liverpool team revolve around you. From time to time you'd hear talk, gossip really, that another club was going to make a move for me and make me the main man in their side. The money would be great, the team would be built around me, I'd be the star, etc. etc. Nah. No chance. Not a hope in hell. Nothing could beat the satisfaction I was getting from playing the way we played and winning the trophies we did. Very few Liverpool players were poached by other clubs in those years. I'd imagine that very few managers even thought it was worth trying: the player wouldn't want to leave, the club wouldn't want to let him go.

When Kenny moved me to the holding role in centre midfield for the start of 1987/88, I knew my goal-scoring days were more or less over. Steve McMahon would be the one getting forward, I would be the one screening the back four. Given my own stats, I suppose I could have questioned why I shouldn't be the one getting forward. If I was averaging over ten goals a season I could, in theory at least, have finished my career with a hundred goals from midfield. But I never asked, Kenny never explained, and I never wanted an explanation. I averaged two goals a season for the next four seasons. I wasn't bothered. This, for me, was a more senior position. And it gave me a new lease of life. It was a fulcrum role, I had more responsibility, I had a chance to control the tempo of a game now.

It meant I was moving further away from the young lad with the alleged star quality who'd burst on to the scene six years earlier. I'd been a cog on the left flank back then, now I was being slotted in deeper into the machine, at times almost invisible if you weren't watching closely. Out on the left you might have to take a few more touches before connecting with a team-mate; or you might have to take on the full-back. Now my job was to break up attacks, win the ball back and get it moving as fast as I could to Houghton and Barnes and Beardsley who could go and do their dribbling further up the pitch. One touch or two was usually sufficient. The net effect, really, was that you stripped your game down to the basics – no frills at all.

I don't know when or where he said it, but I found an old quote from Sir Alex Ferguson where he said Whelan 'did the simple things better than anybody else in the game'. I don't know about doing it better than anybody else, but doing the simple things was my role now. And it wasn't a role that made you stand out on a pitch. Sometimes you'd notice, on the TV highlights that night, if the team had put a chain of passes together the commentator wouldn't mention your name at all because you'd moved the ball on so quickly.

But basically I was playing a more conservative role now and as a result I became a more conservative player. Maybe it's why some people feel I failed to live up to expectations, and why others feel I was underappreciated in the end. All I can say is that, as a footballer, it was the most fulfilling time of my career. You were in the engine room and you were seeing an awful lot more action here: tackling, tracking, blocking, passing, starting moves. You were never far from the ball, whereas out on the left, if the right-back had it you were waving at him from sixty yards.

And even though it was mostly the simple pass, I still had chances to find Rushie or Aldo with attacking passes. I ended up with very few goals but a fair few assists along the way. I had the experience to play the role too. I understood better the need for structure in a team. We had loads of attacking flair but one midfielder at least had to shield the defence, break up the other team's attacks and start ours. And if I didn't get the ball back, who was going to do it? The answer to that one is easy: someone else. They'd have found someone else and I'd have been forgotten about. But I happened to be there at the time and they didn't have to go looking for anybody else to do it.

And, to be fair, it wasn't just the players who appreciated it – a lot of the Liverpool supporters did too. They knew their football. Sometimes they'd tell you they noticed you more when you weren't in the team. You were only missed when you weren't there. I think it was a compliment. And look, we all like to get a compliment every now and again. People shouldn't underestimate how vulnerable you sometimes feel out on a pitch. Footballers feel they are under scrutiny all the time. Your work is held up for public inspection every time you cross the white line for a game. You do develop a thick skin but you still feel a bit thin-skinned, if you know what I mean. No one likes being told they're bad at their job. So if you're scoring goals fairly regularly it takes the pressure off. If you're doing a job that doesn't involve scoring goals or creating goals, you can disappear off the radar. That's why the approval of my team-mates meant a lot to me in those years, and still does.

Sometimes, if I'm really questioning myself about my career, I'll think *Yeah, maybe I could've been a bit more ambitious. Maybe I could've expressed myself more. Maybe I could've got forward more, maybe I could've got on the ball more instead of passing it all the time.* But then you ask yourself, how much more? It's impossible to quantify these things. So it's a bit of a pointless exercise. You can't go back through every game and wonder if you should've carried this ball or that ball rather than laying it off to Barnes; or if you should've taken a chance on joining an attack, knowing you were leaving a big gap in midfield. It's ifs and buts and maybes.

The bottom line was the team. We all had to serve the team. When Bob Paisley wanted me to hold the position wide left, I did that; he also wanted me to get forward and score goals and I tried to do that too. Kenny Dalglish wanted me to defend the midfield, I defended the midfield. Various managers over the years asked me to play left-back, right-back, right midfield and I did that too. When Paul Walsh was injured I was asked to play up front with Rushie for a run of games and I did that too. No big deal: you were asked, and you did it.

I suppose this might sound like I just took my orders and carried them out without questioning them. To which I'd say: so what? Maybe a player with a bigger ego might've thrown a tantrum if he was asked to play out of position. Now, I had an ego too; we all did. But I wasn't a hothead; I had a fairly rational streak. And it always seemed a no-brainer to me that if they asked you to play somewhere, it was because they had a good reason. Players were injured, we still needed the points, so it was in my interest as well as theirs to try and do the job. And if you threw a tantrum you'd still have to do the job anyway, so why bother? No, once I was in the first eleven I was happy to play anywhere.

This attitude was more to do with my make-up as a person than my opinion of myself as a player. I wasn't a confrontational person by nature. The bust-up I had with Souey that day at Ewood Park was totally unlike me; and it took a lot out of me. I didn't mind confrontation on the field but I didn't like that sort of confrontation with people. I was never one of the louder voices in the dressing room. If someone had a go at me and I thought they had a point, I'd take it. If someone had a go at me and I disagreed, I'd have a go back. But that was usually as far as it went. In later years I would intervene more in the dressing room talks, I felt I'd earned the right to have my say. But I didn't have an extrovert personality and I never liked standing out in a room full of people. I wouldn't be pushing myself forward to be noticed.

Some players have a personality that enables them to stand out on the field, even if their football ability is pretty ordinary. In my case, if my football didn't do the talking, nothing else did. And even if I did play well, my personality was such that sometimes you'd be overlooked anyway. I remember after one game someone getting the man-of-the-match award and Joe Fagan asking, 'Why didn't Ronnie Whelan get man-of-the-match?' But I didn't like that sort of attention. I was more comfortable just doing the job and disappearing afterwards. I was never comfortable talking to the press in those days and would avoid the TV cameras.

Team captains tend to have dominant personalities and when Kenny made me captain in Hansen's absence for 1988/89 I felt the only way I could do it was to try and lead by deeds not words. I wanted to make the first 50-50 tackle if the chance came. Even when I wasn't captain it was often left to me to have a look at the first tackle, especially during Kenny's era. It was said plenty of times: 'We need to start quick and set the tempo, so get it going with the first tackle, OK?' And if you were playing at home there was no better way of lifting the players and getting the crowd going than by smashing into someone in the first minute. You'd hope then that the players would follow your lead after that. I didn't do speeches, and they weren't much in demand at Liverpool anyway. But I hope I did show leadership in my own understated way.

In the end I believe I became the player I wanted to be, if not the player other people thought I should be. I wasn't the most naturally gifted player you were ever going to meet, and I didn't specialise in one particular skill. I couldn't dribble like John Barnes, couldn't tackle like Graeme Souness, couldn't spray the ball around like Jan Molby, couldn't head a ball like John Toshack. But I could do them all to a proper technical standard. I had a football brain, my touch was correct, I could use left and right foot comfortably; I could pass, tackle, shoot and score goals. I don't think I was brilliant at any of them but I was sound at them all.

It's probably why I didn't become an individual star; it's probably why I fitted smoothly into the Liverpool system of that era. And I believed in the system; I was willing to serve it. I think serving that system is what kept me at Liverpool Football Club for fifteen years.

18

Brass

An Agreement made the 21st day of September 1979 between Peter Beckett Robinson of Anfield Road, Liverpool L4 OTH in the County of Lancaster, the Secretary of and acting pursuant to Resolution and Authority for and on behalf of the Liverpool Football Club of Liverpool (hereinafter referred to as the Club) of the one part, and Ronald Andrew Whelan of 48 Abbotstown Avenue, Finglas West, Dublin 11 in the County of Dublin, Football Player (hereinafter referred to as the Player) of the other part whereby it is agreed as follows: –

1. The player hereby agrees to play in an efficient manner and to the best of his ability for the Club for the period of 3 years (hereinafter called 'the initial period of employment') from the 24th day of September 1979 to the 31st day of July 1982. Unless the initial period of employment shall either be (a) previously determined in accordance with the provisions of one or other of Clauses 10, 11 or 12 hereof or (b) terminated, extended or renewed as provided by Clauses 17 and 18 of this Agreement.

I recently found my first contract with Liverpool Football Club in the attic. Never knew I still had it. It's a four-page document all contained on one fold-over sheet of firm blue paper.

It was a simple contract. I would be paid £150 per week. The club would pay for my accommodation at a rate of £50 per week from 24 September 1979 to 17 November 1979. The club would pay the return air fare from Liverpool to Dublin four times each year, 'to allow the player to travel home to see his parents'. And I would receive a 'signing levy' – my signing-on fee – of £250 in three instalments: £84 upon signature of contract, £83 on 24 September 1980, £83 on 24 September 1981.

When I broke into the first team eighteen months after signing they offered me a new contract and doubled my weekly basic to £300. Eighteen months later they doubled it again. That was how it worked. Call you in one day, usually without any prior notice, and offer you another two years on double the money. 'Is that OK? How does that sound?' 'Yeah, grand, no worries.' 'Great! You can just sign here.' The whole procedure would be over in minutes. By the summer of 1983 I was on £600 a week; by the time Kenny took over it was £1,200; and so on through the 1980s.

There was also your signing-on fee. Later in my career I think it was something like a hundred grand spread over three years, broken down and added to your wages each week. For every point accumulated there was a £125 bonus, so in 1987/88, for example, we would have earned an extra £11,250 for finishing on ninety points. There was also a crowd bonus, so many pounds for every thousand people over 30,000 – or was it 25,000? I can't remember, I was never sure how it worked, and I haven't kept any old pay-slips. Finally there were your trophy bonuses: league, League Cup, FA Cup, European Cup. It was five or six grand a cup and this went straight into my pension.

When the American basketball star LeBron James took a minority share in Liverpool FC in April 2011, a quote of his I saw in the newspapers caught my eye. 'The first time I stepped on an NBA court,' he said, 'I became a businessman.' I was thinking *The first time I stepped out on a professional football field I became a wage-earner, like my da before me.* We were all wage-earners in those days, even the most famous players in England. Our weekly pay was well ahead of the industrial wage but we were still wage-earners. We were comfortable but we were far from rich. A successful Premier League footballer nowadays is rich. They still talk in terms of a player's weekly pay but if you're earning £100,000 a week you're not a wage earner any more, you're a businessman.

If I'd known back in the '80s what I know now, I might have been more aggressive in my negotiations for new contracts. But I was naïve and I probably undersold myself; I probably wasn't earning what I was worth. But to be honest, I'm still not sure about that either. I don't feel hard done by. It's just that I could perhaps have paid more attention, planned the negotiations better. Basically I could've asked for more money. I did do that towards the end of my career but for the first eight years or so I more or less took what they offered and didn't question it.

I was a working-class lad, as most of us were. I hadn't grown up around money and I wasn't comfortable dealing with money or talking about it. I had this vague idea all along that if you were considered good enough to be a professional foot-baller, you'd get paid to do it. This would be the reward at the end of a long apprenticeship that stretched back to your child-hood. But I never once sat down and thought about what those rewards might actually be. As in, how much money will I earn if I make it to the pro game? I was so obsessed about the process of making it, that I never thought about the reward. A bit like the old football cliché that if you take care of the performance, the result will take care of itself. I was all about the performance and nothing about the result.

In my head, if I thought about it at all, the result would be to become a professional footballer, full stop. Not, how much money can I make if I do become a professional footballer? That's an important distinction. Just being a pro was enough for me. I just had to keep getting better and better at football until one day someone from England would offer me a contract and solve all my problems.

So when John Smith and Peter Robinson offered me terms on my eighteenth birthday I was so relieved and so grateful that I wanted to snap the pen out of their hands and sign the contract before they had time to change their minds. I didn't care what the money was. Just sign my name and I'm in, I'm there, I've made it to the other side. After that it would be a case again of process not reward, performance not result. Make the reserves. Make the first team. Stay in the first team. Win trophies. It wasn't until I reached my mid-to-late twenties that I started thinking long term: *I need to start saving as much as I can in the years I've got left.*

But at the same time, I never went in and banged the table looking for massive increases. I still wouldn't have been comfortable doing that. People reading this might say, 'Come on, don't tell lies,' but I promise you it's true. I can't speak for the other lads I played with over the years but I believe it was the same for most of them too. We got such a buzz out of winning that we wanted to capture that feeling again and again. It became a self-perpetuating thing. We loved being the best. We took pride in it. It was a big ego trip for us, sweeping aside teams, being acclaimed as champions, bringing back trophies to the city.

Maybe if the whole bandwagon had collapsed and we'd stopped winning things, we might've started brooding about stuff, wondering if the club was penny-pinching, getting paranoid about our rates of pay. But we were enjoying it too much to start getting bogged down in that sort of attitude. Personally I was happy: I didn't have money problems, we were winning things – everything was good.

So when you went into the boardroom to sign a new contract you never really stopped to ask, 'Hang on, could I do a bit better here?' Well I didn't, anyway. I know now it's a basic rule of any negotiation that you always ask for more, if only for the sake of it. If you'd had an agent he'd have done it, he'd have been happy to get a bit bolshie with the men in suits across the table. But we didn't have agents. And the men in suits were John and Peter, people we liked and trusted. We had no reason not to trust them because they were fair; we got on with them and we knew they were doing a great job running the club.

So it wasn't really the done thing to have a big barney with them over money. And even if you wanted to, it was back to this thing of not really feeling confident enough in yourself to say, 'No. I think I deserve a bit more.' I guess I didn't know any better at the time. Maybe I should have, because I saw how Da handled our negotiations the first time I ever sat in the boardroom at Anfield. He wasn't afraid to ask for more. And he got what he asked for too. John Smith and Peter Robinson weren't daft, they were no pushovers, but that day, while I was shaking with nerves outside the boardroom, they weighed up the deal my da was looking for and decided to go along with it. There was a lesson in that for me but I was too young, I suppose, to heed it.

And the other thing is, I didn't feel the need to ask for more. I was happy with what I was getting. I never felt cheated or exploited in any way. At Liverpool nobody ever seemed to fall out with the club over money. There wasn't much dressing room jealousy that I can recall either. That was probably because we never knew what anyone else was earning. It just wasn't discussed. Maybe we had all been brought up with that old-fashioned mentality where it wasn't considered polite to talk about what you earned. We'd hear rumours from time to time that the top players at other clubs were on more than us and if it was ever broached with the club, we'd be told that our win bonuses were better or whatever. It'd be fobbed off like that and we wouldn't bother to inquire any more about it.

But it would probably have helped, when it came to our own negotiations, if we'd known what our team-mates were on. You could go in and say, 'Well, so-and-so is on X amount so I want the same.' But from the day I started at Liverpool to the day I finished, nobody ever talked about contracts. I didn't think much of it at the time but, thinking about it now, it was probably a taboo subject for some reason. It just wasn't a thing you talked about. If you went up to one of the lads and asked, 'What're you on?' it'd be, 'None of your business what I'm on.' And footballers' wages were rarely mentioned in the newspapers like they are today. You didn't have agents who could go and leak it to the press. Everybody was called in at different times, they signed their own deals and none of us was any the wiser.

It wasn't, I think, until the late 1980s that we started being a bit more proactive. I signed a new contract around that time and I knew that Rushie had brought in an adviser for his negotiations. Not an agent, a solicitor I think, and I decided I'd recruit him as well. And by now the broader financial world was also taking an interest in the football business. One of the big City firms, I think it was Touche Ross, had done a report on Liverpool's finances which outlined the salaries of all the staff. It didn't name names but you could make an educated guess at who was on what, starting with the manager and working your way down the pay scale. So myself and my adviser made the comparisons, figured out what the players in my category were on, and went in and asked for more. There was a bit of hard bargaining that day until we reached an agreement. I remember Peter Robinson remarking to me months later, 'You had a good fella with you that day! I was impressed with the way you handled it.'

Once a deal was signed I was happy to forget about it and get back to playing. There was no point moaning about it if you heard that someone else was getting ten grand a year more and you figured you should be on the same money. You had your chance, you were happy with the deal when you signed it; you now had a contract to honour and you couldn't go back in looking to tear it up. But as you went into the 1990s you could sense that it was becoming more of an issue in the dressing room. Players were being signed for big money in the transfer market and you couldn't avoid the speculation about what sort of wages they were getting. It never led to any unrest but it was on the agenda now. Some of the veterans who'd been there a long time were starting to feel a bit overlooked or undervalued. I remember having a chat with one of the long-serving players, he was grumbling about it at training one day. Personally I wasn't put out about it; I just reckoned that that was how the game had always worked. The latest big signing was always going to have more leverage in any negotiations: other clubs were bidding for him, he was a star, he could ask his price.

The biggest contract by far that I ever signed was my last. It was a two-year deal that would take me up to the end of the 1993/94 season. The Premier League had been launched at the start of 1992/93, more or less the same time as I signed my last deal. The money was tiny by comparison to the fortunes that were later to be made, but it was still massive compared to what it had been just ten years earlier. In 1982 I was earning £300 a week plus bonuses. The deal I signed in 1992 would come to about £300,000 a year all in, about £6,500 a week. But it was conditional on appearances. My injury problems meant the deal was structured in part on a pay-per-game basis. If I didn't make the team or the bench on a given week, I'd be down £2,000 that week.

Two grand is chicken feed for most Premier League players nowadays but it was still a heck of a lot of money in our time. I was thirty-one now and for the first time in my life I was starting to worry about money because I knew that my best earning days were coming to an end. As soon as I stopped playing my income would fall off a cliff. I didn't have enough money in the bank not to be concerned about that. The truth was that I'd be leaving the game with a modest enough financial cushion for the lean years that lay ahead. Contracts for

£150, £300 and £600 a week, plus bonuses, meant that my earnings through the first half of my career were pretty moderate. You couldn't put together much of a nest egg on those wages, and at the time I wasn't thinking much about the future anyway.

My wages accelerated from the mid-80s on – they were brilliant compared to the average industrial wage – but we were also paying between 50 and 60 per cent in tax straight off the top. So while the top line looked good, when you got to the bottom line it literally didn't look half as good.

When I signed my last contract I asked an expert who Alan Hansen knew to check out my PFA pension. It turned out that the pension was disappointing. It would be a help, but not much more than that. I could start drawing it down when I was thirty-five. If I wanted to withdraw the maximum amount every year, I think it was something like £50,000, it would expire within ten to fifteen years. If I wanted it to last until the age of sixty-five, say, I'd have to restrict it to something like £20,000 a year. Basically, the less you took the longer it would last and the advice was to touch as little of it as possible. One way or another I knew that a big shortfall in my annual income was looming. And Elaine and I had three young children to bring up and put through school and college.

This was why, under the new deal, I wanted to play as many games as possible. Even if I'd wanted to rest on my laurels, as Souey alleges, I couldn't afford to. Every time I played it was another two grand in the bank for my retirement. Injuries were now going to cost me like never before and, to tell the truth, I would have willingly taken cortisone injections to play through the pain barrier. I was running out of time to make myself and my family as financially secure as I could. In 1992/93 I made eighteen appearances. If I'd been fit and selected I could have made a further thirty. That's a lot of money I missed out on.

I remember being on the bench for a game in October 1993. It was Arsenal at Anfield and we weren't playing well. At half-time Souey came in and told me to get warmed up. 'You're going on second half.' But Ronnie and Roy looked at him a bit surprised. 'You can't make a substitution *now*. Give it another ten minutes, see if anything happens.' Souey agreed, but told me to get warmed up anyway when we went back out. We improved after half-time but I was still up and down the side-line getting ready to go on. After about fifteen minutes I figured I wasn't going to get on so I went back to the dugout. Ten minutes later Souey told me to go out and get warmed up again. So I did. And I was running up and down for another ten minutes but there was still no sign of me getting the nod. Suddenly there was about five minutes left and I realised I wasn't going to get a run. I was too pissed off to go back to the dugout so I just ambled down to the Anfield Road end and sat on the advertising hoardings there. With about a minute to go I went back down to the bench, steaming with Souey. And I was thinking *I didn't get on, but I still got my two grand. So to hell with you, Souey.* But that was just short-term bitterness. We still had a long season ahead of us and I needed game time. I needed every chance to show him that I still deserved my place in the team. Sitting on the bench wasn't going to help me. But the first half of that season was pretty much a write-off; I ended up playing twenty-three games in total that final season.

I left the game with money in the bank and the need to make a living. I was far from financially secure. But that was fine; no complaints; I did OK. The next generation would be set up for life by the time they left the game – and good luck to them too. It's all relative. We were much better off than the generations who had gone before us.

Both 'the Club' and 'the Player' fulfilled the terms of that first contract. They paid me my £150 a week and my £50 for digs and my flights home and my £250 signing levy. In return they obviously decided that this particular pro had played 'in an efficient manner and to the best of his ability'. I think both sides kept their part of the bargain in the contracts that followed too. And whatever money I made, I hope it can be fairly said that I earned it.

19

The Generation Game

After the confrontation with Graeme Souness that day in April 1993 I went up to the players' lounge in Ewood Park to meet my wife and family. I was still rattled by what had happened and Elaine could see it. 'What's wrong?' 'Nothing.' 'What happened?' 'Nothing.' I didn't want to talk about it, wasn't able to talk about it.

Then I got a tap on the shoulder. It was Torben Piechnik. And he says to me, in his Danish accent, 'You are a very brave man.' I said to him it wasn't about being brave, it was about being totally pissed off. But I could tell he was uncomfortable talking about it; there was a lot of tension hanging in the air among the other Liverpool players too.

It only dawned on me a long time afterwards that there hadn't been a row like that in the Liverpool dressing room for years. You didn't get that sort of ferocious argument any more. The younger lads in the squad hadn't come up in that culture. Torben Piechnik had probably never seen the likes of it before.

I realised that Souey and me were old-school by then. We'd

tackled our differences the old-school way. I'd seen him come face to face with the likes of Dalglish in the dressing room when I was a young fella. I'd seen Ronnie Moran have a hundred arguments. I'd seen the likes of Hansen, Thompson, Neal get stuck into an argument if things got heated. I'd even seen Tommo arguing with Bob Paisley. It was a rough and ready environment. Raw things would be said; the language would be industrial, swear words bouncing off the walls. You'd have fellas jabbing their fingers and accusing each other of not doing enough or not doing it right or not doing anything.

No one doubted back then that this was the way to sort things out. If you were angry about something they preferred that you came straight out with it. Get it off your chest, sort it out and move on. But most of that generation was gone now or going. Only Bruce, Rushie, Nico and myself were left.

But it wasn't just the personnel who were changing, the times were changing too. Young lads seemed a bit more sensitive. They were a bit more thin-skinned. I remember Alex Ferguson saying one time that the new generation were a bit more fragile and he had to change the way he handled them. The famous hair-dryer treatment wouldn't work any more. The days were gone when he could tear strips off a player the way he once did at Aberdeen and in his early years at United. I could identify a bit with that.

Maybe it was a society thing, I don't know. Maybe in our day, rough and all as it was, we'd been treated a bit more gently than the generation before us had been treated. I'm not sure. I suppose these things are changing under your feet without you even noticing them.

But there were little telltale signs that the football culture in general was softening up a bit. As a kid at Liverpool you were always told, if you got done in a tackle, to get up and get on with it: you couldn't show your opponent that you'd been hurt. It would give them an advantage, they'd think they were getting on top – so no lying about on the ground unless you were in serious pain. Now it was going to the other extreme and these days it's hateful to watch, fellas feigning injury left, right and centre.

And back in those days, if you were dropped you were dropped. No one gets dropped any more – they are 'rotated'. It's cushioned a little bit for them. In the '80s, if you were dropped no one tried to sweeten the blow for you. You felt singled out and a bit exposed. You'd be angry about it and you'd be bursting a gut to prove them wrong and get back in the team.

Anyway, the time had probably come by the 1990s to show a bit more consideration for the feelings of younger players. Maybe managers and staff had no choice in the matter any more. Young lads wouldn't put up with it; they'd answer back.

The only downside, I found, was that they wouldn't listen as much to the experienced pros. They thought they knew more than they did. As a manager, Souey found it frustrating dealing with the new breed of footballer. As a player, I found it frustrating too. Maybe I didn't say things the right way. But I thought it was foolish of them. If the likes of Tommo or Nealy were telling me what to do, I wouldn't be inclined to contradict them. These fellas were weighed down with medals, for starters. And you'd learn a lot from them if you kept your mouth shut and listened to what they had to say. We looked up to those players. I never got a sense that the next generation really looked up to anybody – the manager included.

Maybe it was the trappings: some of them were already on good money even though they were just starting out. There was a bit of the big-time Charlie about some of them – even before they'd hit the big time. It's important to say they weren't all like that. You had the likes of Mike Marsh, for example. Mike was a Liverpool lad through and through and he had a great attitude. He listened, he wanted to learn. Marshy would want to know exactly what you were saying, he'd want to do everything right.

Then you had a few other players. Whatever you said, they could take it or leave it. They didn't really want to know. You'd talk to them in training about doing something and you could sense a sort of dismissive attitude coming back at you. 'OK, yeah yeah yeah.' Yeah, whatever. If you had a go at them in the heat of a game it'd be, 'Ah, fuck off.' Then they'd turn around and ignore you.

That was what I was trying to say to Souey that day at Ewood. Maybe we had more in common than we thought that day. We were both at the wrong end of the generation gap. The Liverpool tradition of continuity, the young guard learning from the old guard and carrying it through to the next era – it was breaking down. We ended up with a sort of 'them' and 'us' split between the younger lads and the older lads. It wasn't the only problem there at the time. You had this mishmash of per-sonalities and backgrounds and ways of behaving and it all clashed. You could cover over those cracks in lots of games but they'd always surface again, often in crunch situations.

But after Souey left, the future still looked bright for Liverpool given the sheer raw talent of some of the players coming through. Steve McManaman, Robbie Fowler and Jamie Redknapp looked set to take over the reins and deliver more trophies throughout the 1990s. But in the end I don't think that they, and quite a lot of other players, had the drive and desire for it. That's the X factor in any championship-winning team and, to be fair, it's hard to quantify. It's not something you can measure in the stats.

They were likeable lads, good blokes, and just because a person has a laid-back nature, it doesn't necessarily mean that he lacks for hunger or ambition. So I can't be certain about it, but sometimes I got the impression that winning a championship didn't mean that much to them at the end of the day. Or perhaps it meant a lot to them – but just not enough. We can all *say* how much it would mean to win one, but what are you going to *do* about it? How far will you go for it? Are you prepared to get hurt in a tackle for it? Will you put your head in the way? Will you burn your lungs to get back and defend an attack? And will you do that in every game, or just most games, or just when you feel like it? They all add up, those tackles, those runs, those hard yards. They're the difference between one point and three, between one point and no point at all.

I wouldn't say for one second that they didn't take their football seriously. They did take it seriously, and they loved winning games just as much as anyone. The acid test for me was their attitude to defeat. They were serious about winning, I don't think they were as serious about losing. Did it hurt them enough when we lost games? I'm not sure. I'm only going by my own experience. The bus journey home after a defeat didn't seem as quiet or subdued as it used to be. I noticed with the younger lads that you'd hear them laughing and joking and chatting away. In the '80s you had a pretty quiet bus after we'd lost a game. There'd have been the usual recriminations in the dressing room and then this sort of brooding silence on the way home.

The younger lads, they seemed to get over a defeat a bit too quickly for my liking. It seemed it wasn't the be-all and end-all for them when we lost a game. It wasn't hurting them so deep down that it was going to be a completely different performance the next time we played a game. And if it doesn't hurt enough, it will happen again. And it seemed to happen too often in those years. It's one reason why you end up finishing sixth in the league and eighth in the league.

Liverpool played some cracking football in those years too, it should be said. It was often highly entertaining and brilliant to watch. But for me there was more style than substance about it in the end.

These were extremely talented footballers. But for all their talent, they left the club with not a lot to show for it in terms of medals, anyway. It's as true now as it was then: you get out of it what you put into it. The only question for me is: did it hurt enough?

Part of the problem was the celebrity culture that spread through the game like a virus once the Premier League era began. I played in the first game of the new era, Liverpool versus Nottingham Forest on 16 August 1992. Already you could see the change. There was a lot of razzmatazz and bells and whistles that day.

In the years that followed, money started pouring in, the media coverage went ballistic, the game became part of the entertainment industry. Football used to be just ... football. Now it was show business. You were starting to hear a new line when it came to the verbal exchanges between players. In the old days it was show me your medals, now it was show me your money. One day I heard a fella sneering at an opponent during a game, 'I pay more tax than you get wages.'

The game was losing touch with its working-class roots and so were the players. A lot of them had their heads turned; they lost the run of themselves. To be fair, it must have been hard for them to keep their feet on the ground. They were young; and now suddenly they were rich and famous. It was designer watches, designer clothes, champagne instead of lager. But still, it didn't mean you had to turn up for an FA Cup final in white designer suits, as our lads did in 1996. By then I was back to watching cup finals at home in front of the telly. I nearly choked on my sandwich when I saw the get-up they were wearing that day.

But it was nothing to my reaction, years later, when the story came out about the pound coin or piece of jewellery or whatever it was. I couldn't believe it at first, thought it was a wind-up. The idea that the players would be passing a coin around during a game at Anfield, just for a lark, and that the last man holding it would have to pay for the drinks that night. Lining up a wall, supposedly defending a free kick, and passing this coin around. Like it was all just one big joke? When I heard that story, it was beyond my comprehension. That people playing for Liverpool Football Club could show such contempt for the supporters and management. I still don't know whether to fully believe it or not, it's that bad. But if it happened, it was a complete and utter disgrace.

The long decline was well under way by then. There was no sense at all when we won the championship in 1990 that it would be the club's last title to this day. Not a hint, not a clue, nothing. It was just business as usual. Why should next year be any different? When Kenny resigned I was sure Souey would pick up where he left off. When Souey left I was sure it would happen under Roy Evans.

When Gerard Houllier took over from Roy I wasn't so sure any more. There was too much upheaval in the game in general to be sure about anything any longer. The English game was going global. Players were arriving from all parts of Europe and beyond. The finances were crazy, the hype was ridiculous, managers were coming and going at a rate of knots. Players were becoming more like rock stars, the media were plastering them across the front pages as well as the back.

The game was still the same one I had played, but it wasn't really my world any more. I'd had my time. We'd missed the gold rush, our generation; we were the last of the old soldiers, I suppose. And now there's a generation of football fans who hardly know that the game existed before the Premier League came along. But it did. We don't have the money to prove it but some of us are lucky enough to have the medals.

20

The Formby Bypass

I was in a good mood because I'd made my mind up and I was happy with my decision. I drove into Melwood that morning ready to sign and ready to play football.

It was August 1994 and I was out of contract. I was nearly thirty-three and I'd been holding out for a two-year contract. Roy Evans was manager now and Roy had told me the board was prepared to offer me just a one-year deal.

There was a bit of toing and froing between us. I was thinking *I'm here fifteen years, surely they could be a bit more generous than that.* They were thinking *He's been injured an awful lot the last three years, we think a one-year contract is fair.* What they wouldn't have appreciated is that I was flying fit again. The last operation on my thigh around Christmas 1993 had finally solved the problem. My first game back was Roy's first as manager, away to Norwich in February 1994. I played fifteen of the last sixteen games that season, went to USA '94 with the Ireland squad and came back for pre-season in great fettle.

I hummed and hawed over the offer for a couple of days.

Eventually it was a case of, 'Sod it, I'll sign it.' I went into Melwood and had a word with Roy on the training ground. 'Listen, I've thought about it, I'm gonna take the deal, it's better than nothing.' Evo went, 'OK, I'll tell the board.' I came in the next day full of the joys and went on to the training ground; Evo saw me and came over. He had a very uneasy look on his face. He came straight out with it. 'I'm sorry, Ron, the board have withdrawn the offer.' *What?* 'What d'you mean? The one year?' 'Yeah. I'm afraid so.' I stood there looking at him. Shock was setting in. 'They've withdrawn it?' 'Yeah.' I was frozen to the spot. I can't remember if I uttered another word. Roy mentioned something about still coming in to train, if I wanted to, until I'd found another club. Then he just drifted back to where the first-team squad was training. And I turned around, went back into the dressing room, threw my clothes into my kit bag and walked back towards the car park.

I headed for home in a daze. As I drove, the enormity of what had happened started to sink in. It was over. It was gone. My life as a Liverpool footballer was over. I could feel myself starting to unravel a bit. The more it hit me the more the emotions started welling up inside. I pulled into a lay-by on the Formby bypass and stopped the car. I just sat there staring out the windscreen. And then I burst into tears.

In football they don't give you a gold watch and a nice send-off when your time is up. You're there one day, you're gone the next, the show moves on. It's a story as old as the game itself. There's thousands of ex-pros out there with the same tale. Everyone knows how cold and ruthless the game came be. Kids are told at fifteen or sixteen that they're not good enough, veterans are told they're not wanted any more, managers are sacked, staff are let go at a moment's notice.

You *know* that it is like this. But it doesn't mean you're prepared for it when it happens to you. Especially when you don't see it coming. In my case it was a bolt out of the blue. The board had offered me a one-year deal. Then they took it back. It was the speed of it that left me a bit traumatised. Fifteen years ended in fifteen seconds. No handshakes, no goodbyes, no word of thanks for services rendered. You just turn on your heel and you walk away. The lads are playing a game just twenty yards away and you can hear them calling for the ball and talking and laughing the same as any other day. But you might as well be a million miles away. Suddenly you're an outsider now. You've gone from the inside to the outside in a matter of seconds. You're not part of the gang any more.

I felt I deserved better. I would've liked to have seen the end coming, if only to have been a bit better prepared for it. I would've liked to have been treated a bit more like a human being. But, I suppose, on a number of occasions in this book I have described the Liverpool team as a machine and myself as a cog in that machine. And when you think about it, that's how I was disposed of in the end: a worn-out part that needed replacing and that ended up where worn-out parts usually end up – the scrapheap. It's where every pro eventually ends up but I thought the club would do it with a little bit more decency. It hurt a lot at the time. I was angry, I swore, I called people names.

And then, after feeling sorry for myself for a few days, I swallowed my pride and went back to Melwood. They didn't need me but I needed them. I couldn't afford to mope around. I needed to get fit because I needed to find another club. So I went back and trained every day for a couple of weeks with the apprentices until Peter Taylor, the Southend United manager, offered me a one-year contract. Goodbye Anfield, hello Roots Hall. Goodbye Premier League, hello Endsleigh League. But I was kind of in survival mode now. It was a case of getting on with it and looking on the bright side. It was Division 1 of the Football League, the second division in old money, but it had a lot of big clubs with good crowds every week, competing to get back to the big time. What mattered for me was that I was still in the game. Playing football was the only life I knew, it was the only job I could do, and I wasn't ready to leave that world. It's the fear of the unknown, I suppose. I'd been inside this cocoon since I was eighteen; it was the place where I found my niche in life; I felt secure there and wanted to hang on for as long as I could.

I don't think I brought any airs and graces with me to Roots Hall. The Southend lads didn't have the same ability as the Liverpool players but they were still footballers. They spoke the same language, they were good for a laugh and it took me no time to feel part of the gang again. But the signs were everywhere that you had come down in the world. The home dressing room was small, the away dressing room was even smaller, and no one washed your kit for you any more. You had to bring it home and wash it yourself. But I didn't mind, I wanted to get stuck in and look forward, rather than looking back at the way it had all ended for me at Liverpool. I got over my anger pretty quickly because deep down I knew there was no point: it was just how the game worked. There was nothing personal. They buy you, sell you, drop you, pick you; they pay you well, renew your contract and pay you more; then they let you go and they don't have to say goodbye or thanks or anything. It's a conveyor belt that never stops.

When they throw you off it, you have to dust yourself down and get used to your new situation. Because when you leave a club the size of Liverpool, it's like a safety net has been taken away from you. A whole support structure goes with it. A hundred little details were taken care of for you when you were there. I found myself forgetting where I'd put my passport because at Liverpool they held it for you. You'd sail through customs and security at every airport because someone had sorted all that out. Now I had to queue up like everyone else and have my tickets and passport ready like everyone else. I have to transfer to another terminal at the airport – well, how do I do that?! Somebody always had that arranged.

I'd used the club doctor at Liverpool for fifteen years. He was always there for you for every ache and pain. Now I had to go and find a doctor. I'd never had to worry about cars. The first car I ever drove was the Rover 2000 that Robinsons gave me as part of the Young Player of the Year award back in 1982. After that I had a sponsored car from Ford pretty much for the rest of my career, several top models over the years. I drove home from Melwood that last day in a sponsored car. I had to hand it back and buy one like any normal Joe. Everything that was there for you on a plate was taken away. It's like losing a whole family of friends and people who can help you.

You'd have to include in that group most of your team-mates too. Most players go their separate ways when it's all over. They have their own families and friends, their own lives to lead. I don't think you get many lasting friendships out of the dressing room. It's like most workplaces in that regard. People tend to forget that footballers don't spend a great deal of time together. In most workplaces, be it office or factory, they do an eight-hour shift. Footballers do ninety minutes, more or less, every morning and that's them done for the day. They play a game at the weekend, maybe another one midweek, and they'll spend a fair amount of time together on the road, in hotels and airports, travelling here and there. But overall it's still well down on the amount of time people spend together in most other work environments.

On top of that, players are coming and going at clubs all the time. I was very fortunate in that I got to spend the vast majority of my career at one club, but I've lost count of the amount of players that came and went during that time. You're laughing and joking with them one day on the training ground, the next day they're gone and you never see them again.

The big difference, I suppose, between our line of work and most other kinds is the emotional bond that teams have to cultivate if they want to be successful. The players share the same excitement and anxiety before a game and the same happiness or disappointment after a game. They are highly dependent on each other to get the job done. But that's what it is: a job. You're paid to win football matches, as a group of players, and after that you're not expected to be bosom buddies off the pitch. There *is* an emotional bond between you but it's still a professional relationship. You will go through some unbelievable highs and lows together but whatever emotions are there at the time, they generally don't last. The bond is created to help get the job done and that's about as far as it goes; it's really only skin deep.

As it happens, we have a very active Liverpool ex-players' society. We have our golf days and our charity matches and various functions and every time we meet up we have a good laugh; it's like we revert to being team-mates again. And we rarely talk about old games or great wins or some brilliant goal we scored. It's usually the comical stuff we remember; something stupid that someone said or did, the funny yarns and stories. Then we all go our separate ways again. The 1984 team that won in Rome, people might think we have some sort of special bond because of what we went through that night, but we don't really. I'd see Hansen and Kenny a bit more often because we live in the same area but I might meet the rest of the lads just a couple of times a year. I play golf with Gary Gillespie a fair bit because Gary also lives nearby. I'm good friends still with Rushie and Steve McMahon, and I think most of the lads from those teams in the 1980s still get on well whenever we meet up. But life moves on, it's all a long time ago now and, let's be honest, footballers aren't the most sentimental of people anyway. I think the game, and the football industry in general, hardens you up from a young age.

When it leaves you behind, you hope to have enough money to be comfortable and, more than anything, a family of your own to fall back on. I felt very alone and vulnerable when I left Melwood that day in August 1994. Then I arrived home and there were my daughters, all smiles and hugs to see me back early from work, and you had no choice but to start smiling again. Elizabeth was nine, Georgia was six, and for those few minutes all was well with the world again. Elaine was holding Amy, our four-month-old baby, and once again she was there to listen as I poured out my woes. It wasn't the first time I drew such comfort and security from my family and it wouldn't be the last. My family was a rock for me through all the ups and downs of a long career in a rough business.

It began with a reserves game one midweek night at Anfield in 1980. Me and Sammy Lee went for a drink afterwards. We moved on to a nightclub called Snobs, of all things. Sammy bumped into a girl he knew called Julie, the Julie who went on to marry Steve McMahon. Julie had a very pretty friend with her by the name of Elaine Connolly and we got chatting. A few weeks later we bumped into them again in the same club. Numbers were exchanged, phone calls were made, and before long we were going steady. We were young but we got serious pretty quick; I think we both knew from early on where it was going. We bought a house in Southport, where we live to this day, and in the summer of 1983 we married.

In those days managers liked to see a player settle down early into family life, but at the same time they didn't want family life to be getting in the way of his football either. So, for example, if your wife was due to give birth, they'd take a look at the fixtures schedule around the due date and see if the baby could arrive at the most convenient time for them! In other words, straight after one game, if at all possible, and well before the next game. At Liverpool they even had a gynaecologist to work with the players' wives. Mrs Francis was a big Liverpool supporter and she was the gynaecologist to all the footballers' wives. She had actually delivered David Johnson, who played for Liverpool in the late 70s and early 80s, and in time delivered David's kids too. In truth, we were all happy to co-operate with the fixtures schedule, including our wives, and when our time came in 1985 Elaine and I met Mrs Francis to arrange the arrival of our first-born. Liverpool would be away to Coventry but I could get back from Highfield Road in two hours and Elaine would be induced that night. There would be a week to the next game, I would get a day or two off from training but apart from that it would be business as usual. I had no problems with this and neither did Elaine. We just took it for granted. And if by chance she happened to go into labour early, I'd still have been expected to play the game first before rushing back to the hospital. That's how it was. We had both grown up with the traditional values around work and family and it was fine by us. It was the mid-80s but this was still before the era when the husband was nearly expected to have the baby himself, or the next best thing to it. I wasn't what they call nowadays a 'new man'. And if you took a look around the Liverpool dressing room in those days, you wouldn't have found too many 'new' men there at all. Elaine was induced, Elizabeth was born, I played the next game and we were over the moon with our new arrival.

But still, nothing could get in the way of a footballer's routine. Everything revolved around his career. I'm sure Elaine and her friends among the Liverpool wives had many a conversation about this. I'd train in the morning, sleep in the afternoon, and Elaine would frequently take the baby away to make sure I wouldn't be woken up. When we left on Fridays for away games they'd be left with the kids on their own. If we had a home game I'd normally go to the team hotel on the Friday because I'd be no use about the house anyway, getting uptight and anxious and irritable.

But eventually, and sooner than you think, the day arrives when there are no more games to play. I did the season at Southend, Peter Taylor stepped down as manager and the club offered me a two-year deal to take over as player-manager. But I busted my knee at the start of 1995/96 and that injury more or less ended my playing days. We finished mid-table in my first season as manager, we were relegated the following season and I was out of a job.

I was out of work for ten months until one day I got a call out of the blue from an old pal from my schoolboy days at Man United, Scott McGarvey. The much-travelled Scott had contacts in Greek football and knew of a manager's job going at the Athens club Panionios. I did a year there and we ended up getting to the quarter-finals of the European Cup Winners' Cup. Lazio stuffed us over the two legs but the tie generated huge excitement in Greece at the time. Unfortunately the season turned sour. Greek football can be a fairly chaotic environment. Money dried up, players weren't getting paid, they went on strike and we started dropping down the league. Then the fans turned on us and it wasn't much fun sitting in the dugout when there were half-full plastic bottles raining down and frightening the life out of you. So I bailed out after one season and was offered the job at Olympiakos Nicosia in Cyprus, where I had three very enjoyable years. The family enjoyed the lifestyle there too but, once again, the realities of the football industry kicked in. We were second in the league in my last season there, with three games to go, and I was sacked, just like that. It was probably for financial reasons but no one ever gave me a proper explanation. The club didn't have much money but I'd built a decent squad, we'd qualified for Europe, and all of a sudden I was left in the lurch. It was really disappointing, the way it all finished. I ended up having to go to court to get paid what I was owed. I then did six months at another Cypriot club, Apollon Limassol, but I'd had enough; I'd had a bellyful of it at that stage and wanted out. We came home to Liverpool.

I started picking up a few gigs in television as a pundit and that has since developed into a busy media career. I also do some after-dinner speaking, corporate work and golf days. I enjoy the work, it keeps me in touch with the game and I get to meet a lot of players from the old days along the way.

I don't have a football to kick around in the back garden because with three girls growing up there was never much demand for one. I do have a ball in the house, in fact I have three, but they're very old and wouldn't be much use if tried to practise my old keepy-uppy routine. They are match balls, one from the 5–0 against Coventry at Anfield in April 1986. I scored a hat-trick that day against my old mate from the Liverpool reserves, Steve Ogrizovic. The second was used in the Charity Shield game against Wimbledon in 1988 and the third is from the 1989 Cup final. That one is special, signed by all the players who played for Liverpool on that historic day. I intend holding on to those mementoes; they're family heir-looms, I suppose.

When it comes down to it, a football was all I had to help me make my way in the world. I set out to master it as best I could when I was a kid. I trained to be as good as I could be at every skill. And making that commitment took me all the way to the top of the game in England. In return the game gave me an unbelievable amount back. It gave me and my family a secure life. It gave me confidence and it gave me status. It took me all over the world. It allowed me to play in great stadiums, on great occasions; it allowed me to play at World Cups and European Championships. It helped me to express myself, to channel my skill and my aggression and my personality. I belonged in that environment. I was nowhere more comfort-able than with a ball at my feet on a rectangle of grass. I could be myself there in a way that I couldn't really be in a room full of people. Learning how to use a ball properly transformed my life.

I even got to meet the Pope because of it! Researching this book I came across an old profile from *Shoot* magazine. They were previewing the 1982 League Cup final and they asked me to do the traditional footballer's questionnaire. What car do I drive? *Don't have a car.* Nickname? *Dusty.* (Because the wits in the dressing room reckoned I pronounced 'Just' in a funny way.) Favourite player? *Bryan Robson.* Favourite food? *Steak and chips.* Favourite drink? *Tea and milk.* (That's what I told them, anyway.) Favourite actor/actress? *Paul Newman/ Sophia Loren.* Favourite TV show? *The Professionals.* If not a player, what job would you do? *No idea.* What person in the world would you most like to meet? *The Pope.* And eight years later I met him, at Italia '90, along with the rest of the Ireland squad. Because I was handy with a ball, I even got to meet the Pope.

On 7 May 1994 we played Aston Villa at Villa Park. If I'd known it was going to be my last game I might've got all the lads to sign the match ball and kept that one too. Then again, I might have just booted it over the stand. Maybe it was a sign of the times, but we lost 2–1 and I was taken off with eleven minutes to go. My last game at Anfield was a week earlier, against Norwich. We lost that one too. And in another sign of the times, it would be the last game played in front of the famous standing terrace that was the Kop. A few days later the demolition crew moved in and work on the building of an all-seater stand began. It had been an absolute thrill and a privilege to play in front of that magnificent terrace for thirteen years. Now it was going, and I was gone.

So many people over the next few years asked me if I missed the buzz and the excitement of top-flight football. Like, where are you ever going to find that feeling again? Scoring a goal at

Wembley, scoring a goal at the Kop end, winning another trophy? But we're hard-headed people, footballers, and you know from a long way out that it's not going to last for ever. So I wasn't thinking *What will replace that feeling?* I was thinking *What am I going to do now? Where am I going to go?*

What you miss is the camaraderie; the crack and the banter. Because there was something different every day; someone always had a yarn, someone else had done something silly that had us in stitches. There was no end to the laughs. But I didn't miss the worry and the nerves I felt in the days coming up to every game. I knew I had to have that feeling if I was to play well; I accepted it as part of the job and learned to cope with it. But fifteen years is a long time to be going around with a knot in your stomach.

I played 493 games for Liverpool Football Club. I would've liked to have made the 500 mark. But I am grateful for what I got. Six league titles and four runners-up places in ten years. Three League Cups, two FA Cups, one European Cup. And I have one small, obscure stat I can call my own: I scored goals in fourteen consecutive seasons. I'm told that only the great Billy Liddell beats that, having scored in fifteen consecutive seasons. Overall, I don't think I could have done much more.

Starting out, I could have ended up at another club, but I was blessed to end up at Liverpool. One of the themes running right through my story is good people. I had good people looking after me since I was knee high; people who taught me well and who cared about my progress. That continued at Liverpool. I was taught superbly well by people who took care of my talent and who looked after me as a person. And I got to play with some of the greatest players the game in England has ever seen, and with two of the greatest teams it has ever seen.

And I did my bit, also, to make that childhood dream come true. I'm proud of that, if I'm proud of anything. That I had the discipline and belief and work ethic to make it happen. That I started out, from the age of five really, and that I stuck with it and saw it through to the bitter end some thirty years later. And the end, when it did come, was bitter. But not for long. The parting of the ways was only a blip in the grander scheme. I look back on it all now with pure affection and a million brilliant memories. It was great. It was marvellous. I had the time of my life in Liverpool red.

21

Epilogue

It was a few hours before kick-off in the 1989 FA Cup final. As usual, my parents had flown over for the occasion. Da loved his football, of course, but Ma loved it too and they made many a trip over the years to the big Liverpool and Ireland games. They were in Rome for the European Cup final in 1984, Germany for Euro 88 and Italy for Italia 90. They came to Anfield loads of times and had come over for League Cup finals and Charity Shield games too.

Wembley stadium had these enormous wooden gates they used to open to let the team buses through, bringing us right up outside the dressing rooms. Da would usually arrive at these gates a couple of hours early to collect his match tickets from me. Someone would come down to the dressing room with a message for me that my father was waiting outside. But the stewards had got to know him over the years and on this occasion they told him to go through, no problem. I went out to meet him and there we were, the two of us, standing in the famous Wembley tunnel. The Liverpool and Everton teams would be making the traditional walk down there a few hours later. And I saw him gazing down the tunnel, looking out on to the pitch. So I said to him, 'D'you fancy walking out?' He turned to me, eyes lit up with excitement. 'Jeez, I'd love to.' So we did. He'd been a footballer himself, he knew what a special moment this was for any player who got to experience it. We walked down the tunnel and out on to the edge of the grass. The stadium was filling up. He stood there and looked around and took it all in. He didn't say a word. We turned and went back into the tunnel. I gave him his tickets and told him I'd see him after the game. He said, 'Good luck today.'

It only dawned on me many years later, when I put two and two together, that it was like one of those moments when the wheel comes full circle. Twenty-one years earlier I was the one who was awestruck when he snuck me into the Manchester United dressing room that evening at Dalymount Park. I suppose I was just returning the compliment that day at Wembley.

Four years later, in August 1993, I finally held my testimonial. Newcastle United would provide the opposition on the night and John Anderson was in their line-up. Ando was a Dub, a mate of mine, and he knew my folks. An hour or so before the game I was up in the trophy room at Anfield making final arrangements for a big family celebration afterwards. I was coming down the stairs with my ma when we bumped into John coming up the stairs. Ando stopped for a chat and then he said to me, 'Where's your da?' That was enough to set Ma off again; she ran to the bathroom in floods of tears. It nearly set me off too. Poor old Ando hadn't heard the news. Da had passed away three weeks earlier.

He'd been battling stomach cancer for a couple of years. At one stage it looked like he had beaten it too. In June I was over with the Irish squad in Dublin. We had two World Cup qualifiers coming up, away to Latvia and Lithuania. I took my parents out to dinner one night and very suddenly Da started to feel really unwell. We took him straight to hospital. When I visited the next day Ma was absolutely distraught. The doctors told her the cancer had returned, worse than ever; his time was short. I wanted to pull out of the games straightaway. She felt I should go ahead with them. If I pulled out, Da would probably realise how bad his condition really was. And he was looking forward to seeing me play in them. I had booked a family holiday in Florida and I wanted to cancel it but when I phoned home from Vilnius, my sisters told me that he had rallied and was feeling a lot stronger.

I was in Florida when the call came from Ann. He was in and out of consciousness now. I told her I was cutting short the holiday and getting the next flight to Dublin. Ann told me later that she went back into the hospital ward all excited with the news. She was shouting into his ear, 'Da, Ronnie's coming home! Da, Ronnie's coming home!' And he opened his eyes and he looked at Ma and said, 'Marie, does she think I'm feckin' deaf?!' They all cracked up. He died on 16 July, aged fifty-six. It saddens me still that he wasn't there to see my testimonial. He'd been there at the beginning, I'd have liked for him to be there at the end too. But he'd been there for all the good times. He loved watching me play, in red and in green. I think I made him proud, I hope I made him proud. He'd been a good father to me when I was young and a good friend to me in later years.

Our ma lived for another fifteen years; she died in July 2008. She was a huge loss to us all because all along our mother had been the strong one in our house. Ma never pushed herself forward but in her own way she had a deep influence on us all. She was the backbone of the family, she'd kept it all together. We remember them both fondly and we miss them a lot.

A crowd of 22,000 turned up for my testimonial. I felt honoured and moved that so many of those legendary Liverpool fans came to sing my name, twelve years after they'd sung it on my debut. I guess they wanted to say, 'Well done and thanks for playing your part.' It's my turn to thank them here, not just for that night but for all the days and nights when they made Anfield feel so special for those of us lucky enough to be out on the field.

These days I'm still asked to sign a few autographs and it's nice to be recognised, after all these years. Even kids come up to me here and there looking for me to sign something. Maybe their dads were in the crowd that night and maybe they showed them old pictures from a book or magazine or something. And sometimes the youngsters will get it a little wrong. They'll come up to me and say, 'Didn't you used to be Ronnie Whelan?' And I usually say, 'Yeah, I used to be Ronnie Whelan.'

And I think I still am, to be fair.

Index